Throughout **THE USES OF MUSIC** Dr.
Mussulman reminds us of the ways in which
a recorded performance and a live performance differ in terms of the listener's experience.

Written with both the music student and the
general reader in mind, and recognizing the
great variety of types and styles of music
we encounter daily, the book aims to suggest specific, simple criteria by which *any*
listener might make his own private judgment about *any* piece of music.

Joseph Agee Mussulman, Ph.D., is Professor of Music at the University of Montana, Missoula. A member of the American
Studies Association, the Popular Culture
Association, and the Music Educators National Conference, he is also author of *Music
in the Cultured Generation: A Social History
of Music in America, 1870-1900* (Northwestern University Press, 1971).

the uses of music

an introduction to music in contemporary american life

JOSEPH AGEE MUSSULMAN

Department of Music
University of Montana

Prentice-Hall, Inc., Englewood Cliffs, New Jersey

Library of Congress Cataloging in Publication Data

MUSSULMAN, JOSEPH A
  The uses of music

  "Bibliography of recorded examples": p.
  "Bibliography of books and articles": p.
  1. Music—Analysis, appreciation. 2. Music and society. 3. Music—United States.
MT6.M968U8   780'.15   73-21801
ISBN 0-13-939421-4
ISBN 0-13-939413-3 (pbk.)

© 1974 by PRENTICE-HALL, INC
Englewood Cliffs, New Jersey

Printed in the United States of America

10 9 8 7 6 5 4 3 2 1

PRENTICE-HALL INTERNATIONAL, INC., London
PRENTICE-HALL OF AUSTRALIA, PTY., LTD., Sydney
PRENTICE-HALL OF CANADA, LTD., Toronto
PRENTICE-HALL OF INDIA PRIVATE LIMITED, New Delhi
PRENTICE-HALL OF JAPAN, INC., Tokyo

contents

XV

international trends
in contemporary art music 175

LIST OF ILLUSTRATIONS

preface

This book is based on two premises: that music is sonorous design, and that every single piece of music reflects a general aspect of the society in which it exists.

The first premise enables us to describe any composition in terms of the composer's or performer's manipulations of its essential materials, sound and time. The second recognizes that different kinds of music—such as popular music, film and television background music, mood music, and art music—serve different functions. Further, it permits the discussion of a given composition in the context of its intended use, and requires the evaluation of it only according to the criteria arising from such a use.

The objectives of this book are consistent with the implications of its premises: 1) to bring to your attention various aspects of contemporary musical life you might previously have overlooked; 2) to lead you to a more vivid awareness and a rational understanding of the kinds of music you may already know; and 3) to supply a basic fund of concepts which can serve as foundations for some of the private acts of musical conduct and judgment that may be expected of you in the future. At the same time, the main topic is art music, the kind that is used for the purpose of pure, profound contemplation, that often challenges the listener more than any of the rest. The other kinds are continually compared and contrasted with it, regarding style, function, and creative process.

A textbook does not require an excuse for being, of course, for the accepted way of studying any subject is through the printed word. Nevertheless, in the case of music a book is of secondary importance at best. Since the substance of music is sound, one must seek one's satisfaction and comprehension through the ears rather than the eyes. Therefore you should frequently refer to the recorded examples that have been specially prepared to accompany this book,* striving to perceive as strictly musical experiences the principles that are described in print. References to the examples are placed in the margins as well as the body of the text to facilitate review. Each example is identified in full in the Bibliography of Recorded Examples.

For emphasis, important terms are italicized only the first time they appear. Page numbers on which they occur are italicized in the index, which may thus be used as a study guide.

Certain legal and technical limitations have prohibited the inclusion of several important musical examples. They are not absolutely indispensable, but you will get more out of the general discussion if you can have them at your disposal, either by borrowing them from a lending library or by purchasing them. They may be found in the following albums:

Chapter II (p. 24): Charles Ives, Quartet No. 2. Columbia MS 7027.

Chapter III (p. 31): John Coltrane, "Chasin' the Trane." Impulse A-10.

Chapter IV (p. 34): Benjamin Britten, *Young Person's Guide to the Orchestra,* Opus 34. Columbia M 31808.

Chapter VI (p. 49): Benjamin Britten, *Peter Grimes.* London OSA 1305.

Chapter IX (p. 84): John Philip Sousa, "Stars and Stripes Forever," in *Marches by John Philip Sousa.* Nonesuch H 71266.

Chapter XIII (pp. 149-50): Paul Simon, "Bridge Over Troubled Waters," Columbia KCS 9914. Maynard Ferguson's version, Columbia C 31117; Roberta Flack's version, Atlantic SD 1594.

If, for classroom purposes, the instructor desires to rent a copy of the film *Louisiana Story,* which is mentioned in Chapter XI, he may write for particulars to Contemporary/McGraw-Hill Films, Princeton Road, Hightstown, New Jersey 08520.

After Chapters I-VII have been studied, the remaining chapters may be taken up in any order, since this book is not organized according to historical chronology. A possible sequence might be I-VII, XIV, XV, VIII-XIII.

A piece of music that takes but a few minutes to perform may require many weeks or months of meticulous labor on the part of the composer,

* Available from Prentice-Hall on three LP records.

who must continually bear in mind his potential listeners' immediate impressions. Writing a textbook is somewhat like that, except that an author has the exhilaration of sharing the gestation of his brain child with his willing colleagues and students. To all those who have helped me try to maintain the reader's point of view—including Jeanne, Larry, Lou, and especially Janet—I wish to express my profound gratitude.

Joseph Agee Mussulman
University of Montana
Missoula

I

"the medium is the message"

Before we begin the study of music itself we must try to understand the essential characteristics and qualities of the media through which most of us have the majority of our day-to-day musical encounters as listeners, especially the phonograph and the tape recorder. Also, we need to examine some of the ways in which those media have affected music as a type of human experience and a mode of human creativity. As a preliminary to both, however, it is necessary to consider some of the basic facts about the essential substance of music—sound. The science of sound is called *acoustics.*

SOUND

If we set aside the factor of time for the moment, any sound can be described in terms of three variable characteristics or *parameters: pitch, loudness,* and *timbre.*

Sound is produced when a vibrating body sets in motion the molecules of air around it, causing them to collide with one another. The energy impulse moves through the air with a velocity that decreases in proportion to the amount of friction among the molecules, or until it meets another body by which it is either reflected or absorbed. Sound may be visualized as a series of waves in water, the peaks and troughs representing the extremes of compression and rarefaction in the fluid above and below an imaginary plane which would be the surface of the water in a quiet state.

1

The number of "sound waves" or *cycles* that appear on a segment of that plane representing a second of time is referred to as the *frequency* of the sound. The lower the frequency, the lower the pitch, and conversely the higher the frequency the higher the pitch. The human ear can normally detect frequencies as low as 20 and as high as about 20,000 cycles per second (*cps*).

The distance between the highest and lowest points of a sound wave is termed its *amplitude,* and the aural phenomenon this represents is *loudness,* sometimes called *intensity.* The sound represented in Figure 1-a would be

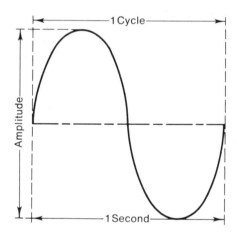

FIGURE 1-a.

louder than that shown in 1-b. The loudness characteristics of a piece of music are referred to individually and collectively as *dynamics.* Technically speaking, loudness is measured by the unit called the *decibel (db),* which is the smallest amount of increase or decrease the average human ear can detect. The threshold of hearing is defined as zero decibels; the threshold of pain is about 120 decibels. The dynamic range covered by a symphony orchestra in a live performance extends from about 40 decibels to approximately 100 decibels. Musical terminology employs a group of Italian words to describe those extremes and various levels between them, such as *pianissimo* (very soft), *piano* (soft), *forte* (loud), and *fortissimo* (very loud).

Towards both ends of the audible frequency range the threshold of

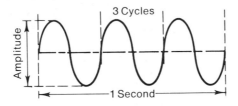

FIGURE 1-b.

Graphic representations of sine waves.

hearing rises. The ear's maximum sensitivity is to frequencies of from 3,000 to 4,000 cps, or roughly within the last six notes on the piano keyboard. That is why some record players have a special means of permitting the listener to "boost" the bass frequencies when playing records at a low level of loudness.

The simplest, purest sound of all, which resembles a human whistle, is called a *sine tone* because it consists of a single *fundamental* frequency that shows up as a sine curve on an oscilloscope (an electronic device that transforms sounds into visual patterns on a screen). Nearly all of the sounds we hear, however, both musical and otherwise, are more complex. The sound produced by a piano string, for instance, consists of a fundamental frequency which, because of its dominating amplitude we readily recognize as the *pitch* of the string, plus a series of higher, weaker frequencies or *harmonics,* sometimes termed *overtones.* Harmonics are also called *partials,* in reference to the fact that a vibrating body such as a string or a column of air moves not only as a whole, but in several proportional segments or parts, each producing a different pitch.

Thus when the piano key is struck which produces the pitch called c_2 having a fundamental frequency of 65.406 cps, we actually hear as many as fifteen or more additional pitches, depending on the quality of the piano, extending as high as 1046.5 cps.

The *timbre* or *color* of a sound is determined by the number, frequencies, and amplitudes of the harmonics it contains. It is partly by means of this parameter that we distinguish a given tone from others of the same basic frequency and loudness; in other words, it is the principal basis for the aural identification of any musical instrument.

The timbre of any acoustical (as opposed to electronic) instrument is

1 2 3 4 5 6 7 8 9 10 11 12 13 14 15

FIGURE 2 Harmonic series.

dependent on its design as well as the material of which it is made. Since the partials present in each tone also change along with the frequency and amplitude of the fundamental, no two pitches of the same instrument will have precisely the same timbre, even at an equal dynamic level. Clearly, the homogeneous combination or *blend* of several identical pitches from as many different instruments of the same type would require that their respective timbres and amplitudes be as nearly alike as possible. The ability to control these parameters is the mark of a well-trained and skillful performer, and good blend is the mark of an outstanding vocal or instrumental ensemble.

Every musical instrument possesses certain inherent characteristics with regard to the beginning, the continuation, and the ending—sometimes called the *envelope*—of any single sound that can be produced with it. The piano, for instance, can produce only sounds that begin with a percussive, instantaneous *attack* or *growth,* and although the sound may either be quickly silenced or allowed to die away slowly, it is impossible to make a single piano note grow louder once the key has been struck. On stringed instruments like the violin, however, and on wind instruments, one can also produce sounds that gradually increase in volume and then either die away or suddenly stop.

It is through the subconscious recognition of envelopes, as well as through timbre, that we identify the sources of sounds. Proof of this may be found in the fact that if we record a piano note on a tape recorder and then cut off or erase its attack and its ending, the remaining sound bears a remarkable resemblance to the corresponding portion of the same pitch played on a flute. We frequently judge a performer on the basis of his command over the envelopes available on his instrument.

Ever since the eighteenth century composers have given performers of their works more or less detailed instructions concerning envelope, and some of the most important words in the musician's vocabulary serve to denote their varieties. *Staccato* means short and detached: each note is to be played with instant growth and instant decay. *Sforzando* means marked or stressed: each tone is to be shaped with instant growth and gradual decay. *Crescendo* denotes a gradual increase in volume, while *decrescendo* and *diminuendo* signify a gradual decrease in volume; both effects may be applied to successions of sounds as well as individual notes. Directions such as *leggiero* (lightly), *marcato* (stressed), *con brio* (with spirit), and *maestoso* (majestically) also call for specific if subtle handling of envelope by the performer.

The overall characteristics of a single tone, which may be represented visually by a line showing the composite pattern of the fundamental and its harmonics, is called its *wave form*. The wave forms of the sounds produced by most musical instruments are generally stable or *periodic*. Some percussion instruments, however, such as drums, cymbals, and gongs, have non-periodic wave forms in which the vibrations of the surfaces produce frequencies and amplitudes that change continuously in relation to one another, thus suppressing the emergence of a definite pitch and leaving only the impression of comparative highness or lowness. Many of the machines we hear around us every day may seem to produce non-periodic or pitchless sounds, but if listened to very closely some of them will prove to emit one or more different pitches.

THE ACOUSTICAL ENVIRONMENT

The room in which music is performed is almost as important as the qualities of the instruments and the skills of the performers. Even the materials of which it is constructed constitute a crucial factor. Various surface materials exhibit different capacities for the reflection or absorption of sound. In a room in which the surfaces are highly reflective the sound will often "bounce" or *reverberate* so long that the result is a lack of clarity and precision. A gymnasium, for instance, in which the cheers of the crowd at a basketball game resound thrillingly may be much too "live" for a musical performance. On the other hand a room that is too "dead" may produce a muffled effect and cause a performance to seem dull and lifeless in spite of the best efforts of the performers. Moreover, most rooms favor certain frequency ranges, which may affect the listener's impression of the sound of an instrument or ensemble either adversely or favorably.

The acoustical features of an auditorium are of prime concern to every musician. The very finest performers can sound shabby in a poor room, while performers of merely average ability may find their efforts enhanced by a flattering acoustical environment. Many listeners tend to ignore the idiosyncrasies of the auditoriums they visit, however. They are apt to be far more sensitive to the qualities of the various electronic media through which they gain most of their musical experiences, forgetting that nearly all music is made by people playing instruments in rooms, and overlooking the effects that such devices as the phonograph and the tape recorder may have upon live sound as well as upon our subjective responses to it.

THE ELECTRONIC MEDIA

The central components of the phonograph and the tape recorder are those on which sound is stored. The phonograph record stores sound in the form of uneven grooves cut in its surface with a stylus that moves back and forth as well as up and down in response to fluctuations in an electric current that correspond to variations in wave forms. On a stereophonic disc the two surfaces of the groove have different contours, as shown in Figure 3,

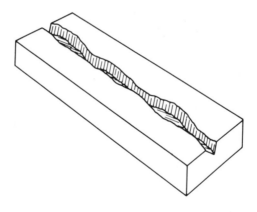

FIGURE 3   Groove in a stereophonic disc.

representing the left and right aural perspectives or *channels* of the medium. Quadraphonic discs operate on a similar principle in a somewhat more complicated way. When the record is played back the pickup stylus is made to vibrate by the variations in the surfaces of the groove, and its mechanical action is turned back into electric current. A tape recording stores sound in the form of magnetism. Electricity is applied to the coil of a small electro-magnet called a *recording head*. As the tape travels past the head, iron oxide

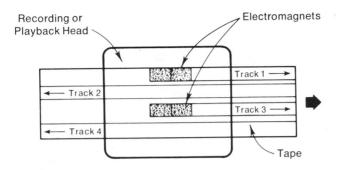

FIGURE 4   Tape recording or playback head.

particles in its surface are rearranged by the alternating current of the magnetic field. In playback the process is reversed.

Sound waves are initially transformed into current through a *microphone;* current is turned back into sound by means of a *loudspeaker.* Microphones emit extremely small amounts of electrical power, while loudspeakers require relatively large amounts in order to make the cone of the speaker vibrate and induce sound waves in the air. Therefore a device for increasing the input signal, called an *amplifier,* must be placed between them. If a microphone puts out .03 milliwatts (thousandths of a watt) of power, and a speaker requires 30 watts, the amplifier must be capable of increasing the power of the input signal 15,000 times. Often a two-step system is used, with a *preamplifier* providing the initial step-up of power.

An amplifier must actually do much more than merely increase the power of a signal. One of its most important functions is to compensate for certain shortcomings of the overall system—including recording and manufacture —which arise from the nature of electricity, the materials of which the components are made, and the principles upon which their operation is based.

For example, since music potentially may use nearly all audible frequencies, either as fundamentals or as harmonics, it is obvious that the components intended to receive, store, and retrieve information representing sound should be capable of handling data for all audible frequencies. More importantly, the system should be able to emit all frequencies at the same level of amplitude as they were received. Unfortunately, this is not normally so. Within a given range of frequencies, say from 30 to 18,000 *Hz* (the abbreviation for *Hertz,* synonymous with cps), the higher and lower frequencies will be received at the amplifier at somewhat lower levels of volume than were present at the microphone.

There are several reasons for this. In the manufacture of a phonograph record it is necessary to reduce the amplitude of the lowest frequencies, for otherwise the wide lateral movement of the recording stylus would sometimes overcut into the adjoining groove, producing distortion at two separate points in the recording. On the other hand, the higher the frequency the greater the amount of contact the recording stylus must have with the disc over a given distance, and the greater the amount of friction or surface noise that will be picked up along with the desired signal. Therefore, during the recording process the volume of the treble frequencies must be increased in order to assure that the desired signal will duly exceed the mechanical noise. Similar phenomena, arising from different causes, are also typical of tape recordings.

In playback, the amplifier must adjust these discrepancies. It must amplify, or "boost," some of the bass frequencies and decrease the volume of the exaggerated trebles so that both "highs" and "lows" will be conveyed to the speakers with a degree of fidelity equal to that of its *midrange* response (from about 250 to 10,500 Hz). A good tape recorder boasts a *frequency response* ranging from 40 to 18,000 Hz at $7\frac{1}{2}$ *ips* (inches per second), with a variation in amplitude of not more than two decibels above or below an optimum level throughout the entire range of response. The efficiency of this so-called *equalization* process is one of the criteria by which we assess the quality of a playback system.

The *signal-to-noise ratio* (*snr*) referred to in connection with the recording of high frequencies is also a characteristic by which the general quality of a system is usually judged, for each part in each component unavoidably contributes a certain amount of operational noise to the sound the speaker ultimately transmits to the listener. At the present time it is the consensus that the total noise level of a system should remain at least 50 db below the loudest undistorted signal the system can reproduce.

No single component of an audio system is much more important than another, but it is at the loudspeaker that the listener can most easily judge the quality of the system, and loudspeakers are susceptible to certain weaknesses all their own which can only partially be compensated for in advance by the amplifier. For instance, it is difficult to build a single loudspeaker that will reproduce all frequencies equally well. It is therefore customary in high quality systems to separate the lows from the highs and to feed the two ranges to separate speakers called *woofers* and *tweeters.*

Another difficulty that must be overcome is the tendency of the material of which a speaker is made to sympathetically resonate, and thus exaggerate, certain frequencies. In addition there is the problem of inertia, which often causes the surface of the speaker cone to be slow in responding to an electrical impulse and reluctant to stop vibrating when the current stops. This characteristic is termed *transient response*.

Finally, there is the matter of focus. Conventional musical instruments radiate their sounds in various ways; some, like the piano and the violin, disperse their sounds widely throughout a room, while others, like trumpets and French horns, focus their sounds more or less definitely. This is an important part of the acoustical identity of each instrument, and is one of the factors any two or more performers must consider when trying to balance their parts with one another. The loudspeaker, however, lends to all instruments the same acoustical characteristics, for it concentrates the sounds it emits upon the axis of the cone, as shown in Figure 5. Stereo-

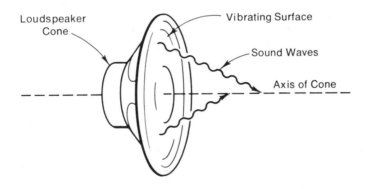

Loudspeaker Cone

Vibrating Surface

Sound Waves

Axis of Cone

FIGURE 5   A loudspeaker.

phonic and quadraphonic systems, using two or more separate channels from recording through playback produce an illusion of the multidimensional aspect of a live performance, but only from the perspective of the microphones with which the recording was made, and only within a comparatively small area directly in front of the speakers.

All of the characteristics of the phonograph and the tape recorder are present in radio and television broadcasting—inasmuch as they involve the use of the other two media—plus certain additional factors peculiar to the means of transmission or storage used. Sound film employs microphones and loudspeakers as well as amplifiers, but uses a storage and retrieval system based on the photoelectric cell, which possesses its own unique limitations and capabilities.

"FIDELITY"

One conclusion to be drawn is that each of the electronic media stands between the performer (*and* the composer) and the listener, and can introduce elements into the listening experience that were not present in the live performance. For instance, a recording may be modified by the electronic addition of a slight amount of reverberation that was not characteristic of the acoustical quality of the room in which it was made.

The listener is seldom if ever privileged to hear the original performance, so he possesses no valid basis for determining the faithfulness of a "high fidelity" recording. He has no way of knowing how closely the sound conveyed to him by the loudspeakers corresponds to that which was present before the microphones, especially with regard to volume and timbre. Only pitch and tempo remain relatively unaffected. One thing he can be sure of, however, is that even though one may try to design an electronic or electromechanical system according to subjective, human, "musical" criteria, the system inevitably operates according to the impersonal and non-musical laws of electricity and mechanics, and necessarily alters the original performance to some degree somewhere along the line. Thus what the listener hears is not just the recording of a performance but simply a recording, period. Clearly, as Marshall McLuhan has said, "the medium is the message." And the message of any medium or technology, McLuhan has noted in *Understanding Media,* "is the change of scale or pace or pattern that it introduces into human affairs." [1]

The foregoing discussion is by no means meant to imply that a performance experienced through an electronic medium is better or worse than a live performance, for such a judgment is a matter of individual taste, and musical taste is an extremely complex aesthetic and cultural phenomenon. Instead, let us now look into some of the ways in which the media have altered the "scale or pace or pattern" of our musical lives.

---

[1] Marshall McLuhan, *Understanding Media* (New York: McGraw-Hill Book Company, 1964), p. 8. Copyright © 1964 by Marshall McLuhan. Used by permission of McGraw-Hill Book Company.

THE CENTURY OF THE PHONOGRAPH

Even though radio broadcasting on a regular schedule did not begin until 1920, electrical recording techniques were not standard until after 1925, and television assumed a major place among the mass media only after 1946, the history of the electronic era in music actually may be traced to 1877, when Thomas A. Edison invented the phonograph.

Edison himself listed "the reproduction of music" among the ten uses he conceived for the phonograph, but he considered his invention to be primarily just what its name denoted—a "sound-writer"—an instrument for office dictation and not a toy to be used for such "trivial" purposes as entertainment. Nevertheless the commercial recording of music got under way in 1890. The technology of the industry remained in an extremely confused and unstable condition for about a decade, however, and the market was consequently limited. It was not until 1901, when the Victor Talking Machine Company was established, that the phonograph began to attract a significantly large audience. Meanwhile, forward-looking individuals had for years been eagerly anticipating the benefits to music which they were certain would result from its perfection and popularity.

"There is a good time coming for the poor man of good taste," wrote one prophet in 1893. He predicted that "besides giving musical pleasure past computation to the million, it will do wonders for the musician. First, it will offer the composer a means of indicating his wishes concerning time and expression. . . . His work, if it has value, will be known to millions where now it is known to thousands, and it will not take a generation for its worth to be recognized." Secondly, "it will become a great teacher of music, as even the phonographic echo of the piano, of singing, or of orchestral work, will be sufficient to furnish pupils with precise models. In the third place, it offers a means for solving tone problems too delicate for the powers of the human ear, and heretofore beyond solution." In other words, comparisons could be made among various performances of a given work in order to determine the precise characteristics of "correct" interpretations.

To be sure, the possibilities were numerous, and not everyone agreed upon the practicality or desirability of them all. One hope, however, was unanimously expressed again and again over a period of perhaps half a century: that the phonograph would everywhere, and among all classes of people, awaken an interest in good music. Whether that or any of the other possibilities have yet been fully realized is a question of almost minor importance. From the clearer perspective of nearly a century of development, we can easily see that the impact of Edison's brain child upon musical life in the United States and elsewhere has been far more complex than was once anticipated.

THE COMPOSER AND THE PERFORMER

The phonograph has indeed given musical pleasure past computation to millions of people, serving as an extension of public concert * life to a great many, and a substitute for it to countless others. But the contemporary composer has not reaped as great a benefit as the early enthusiasts for the new medium may have hoped he would.

To begin with, the momentum of nineteenth-century concert traditions, combined with the historically oriented approaches of those who have sought to systematically awaken interest in good music, has focused wide attention on a relatively few masterworks of the past at the expense of "modern" music of the sort we shall be discussing in Chapters XIV and XV. The eagerness for the new and up-to-date that is characteristic of American culture in general and that is clearly evident in all the other arts has not been conspicuous in music. In effect, the contemporary composer must compete on the record market with Bach, Beethoven, and Brahms.

Although some composers have been able to use the record to establish "official" interpretations of their works, others have somehow been denied that advantage. Igor Stravinsky, perhaps the greatest and certainly the best known twentieth-century composer, was among the first to prepare authoritative recordings of his own works, so that by the forties he had a considerable following. Meanwhile many of the most important compositions of Arnold Schoenberg, his equally significant contemporary, remained comparatively unknown because they were not recorded until the fifties.

The conservative nature of the record industry also limits the contemporary composer's access to the medium. The initial expense of making and distributing a recording is such that a fairly large sale—5,000 to 10,000 albums—must be counted on to make the undertaking economically feasible. This places a great deal of responsibility on the performer who agrees to record a new work, as well as on the producer or musical director who is responsible for the record company's catalog. Understand-

---

* Here the term *concert* is used in a general sense to denote any live public performance. It is more precisely applied to a performance by a group of musicians. A concert given by a soloist is usually called a *recital*.

ably, there is a tendency to favor compositions the appeal of which has been previously established in the concert hall. There are only a few organizations devoted specifically to the underwriting of recordings of new works, such as the Louisville Philharmonic Society, Inc., which received its initial impetus through a grant from The Rockefeller Foundation in 1954 to issue an annual series of "First Edition Records."

A few compositions have been written expressly for the medium of the phonograph, but the temporal dimensions of the record impose limitations within which the composer may not be eager to work. Each side of a twelve-inch long-playing record has a maximum capacity of something over twenty minutes' worth of music, and it is uneconomical to use much less than that.

The tape recording, including the reel-to-reel type as well as the cassette and the eight-track cartridge, is somewhat more convenient to use than the record, but it is even less flexible as a commercial medium. Conventional stereophonic tapes are divided into four parallel channels or *tracks*. Tracks one and three are used as the tape proceeds forward; when the tape is reversed tracks two and four are used, as shown in Figure 4. It is a simple matter to cut the tape to the exact length of the material recorded on tracks one and three, but filling the opposite tracks from a live performance can be somewhat problematical, and blank tape is much more conspicuous than unused record surface. Pure electronic music (see Chapter XV), in which the composer himself creates the sound of his composition and can therefore control its duration down to a fraction of a second, is somewhat more adaptable to these media.

The record also influences the performer's attitudes and ways of working. As the pianist Glenn Gould has pointed out, "the only excuse for recording is to do it differently." [2] Within the older tradition of the live concert, the performer must try to be more or less consistent from one performance to the next. In recording, he is able to devote his entire physical and emotional energies to the task of preparing one consummate performance, to record and rerecord until he is satisfied he has done it as nearly as possible to his complete and permanent satisfaction, and then fix it once and for all. At the same time, the flexibility of magnetic tape, on which all recorded performances are initially stored, facilitates editing or "cutting and splicing," so that the record finally released is apt to represent not just one continuous performance but a composite of several successive "takes."

Still, the performer is placed under considerable pressure, for recordings can be placed side by side, so to speak, and be scrutinized and compared

[2] From the record *Glenn Gould: Concert Dropout, in Conversation with John McClure.* Columbia BS 15.

as if under a microscope. Consequently, in the case of masterworks from the past, all stylistic details must be treated with precise historical accuracy, and innovations in interpretation must withstand the test of objective scholarly criteria as well as subjective taste.

SPACE, TIME, AND THE LISTENER

The phonograph has also modified the listener's experience in several ways. First, it has compressed physical space, bringing the music of all cultures together in a single world of music. For less than the cost of a concert ticket a person can hear a performance that has taken place as much as half a globe away only a few weeks or months before. Thus in the 1930s Japan grew to be one of the world's leading markets for classical records some years before creditable live performances of Western music could be heard there. The same phenomenon has also occurred in many other non-Western nations.

Second, the phonograph has telescoped historical time, diminishing the chronological distance between the past and the present. Under the conditions of musical life prior to the electronic era it was not practical to keep very much old music in the active repertoire from year to year. People attended concerts as much in the expectation of hearing new works as in rehearing proven favorites. But the phonograph has made the entire known history of music equally accessible to everyone. This has led, for instance, to the presence of a piece by the fourteenth-century Italian composer Francesco Landini on the same record with songs by a currently popular folk singer. It has also aided the preprofessional student of music, who once had to study the music of the past mainly by the laborious process of reading scores and imagining their sounds, or by transcribing them on a keyboard instrument.

Third, the phonograph has individualized musical taste. Until the beginning of the electronic age a concert was a comparatively infrequent event, and it was well to postpone final judgment on a new work if it contained elements that stimulated interest yet defied immediate rational analysis. The responsibility to evaluate a new composition could be left to posterity on the assumption that if the work endured repeated interpretations, that in itself was sufficient to recommend it to new listeners in succeeding generations. Now, however, the very presence of a work on a record more or less implies its worth, and its availability to posterity is virtually assured.

The sheer bulk of music available on records not only discourages exhaustive analysis of each new composition or performance by professional critics, but also makes it unlikely the consumer can effectively assimilate and compare several critics' opinions in order to arrive at a consensus. Consequently, it has become imperative for the individual to develop an ability to make judgments on his own.

Fourth, the record has minimized the differences among social values that were once attached to specific styles. Until the middle of the present century, the various levels of aesthetic quality in music were clearly the property of diverse and separate classes, sometimes corresponding to educational or social factors. What is more, those levels were physically separated from one another. One went to a vaudeville theater or a nightclub to hear one kind of music and to a formal concert hall to hear another.

Nowadays, however, the greater one's acquaintance with music of all times and places, the more difficult it is to enumerate the distinctions among various kinds of music, for the medium conveys the music of all the old aesthetic levels without implicit discriminations of any kind. Old and new, sacred and secular, highbrow and lowbrow, easy and difficult, improvised and composed, popular and classical—all can be freely juxtaposed, and we seldom question the propriety of the result.

Fifth, the record and tape have induced among us a widespread tendency to judge the medium rather than the music. It is easier to compute the purely quantitative value of a hi-fi component—the frequency range, SNR, or transient response, not to mention the list price—than to discern the qualitative value of a piece of music it brings to us. One can be an impressively knowledgeable audiophile and still be a musical ignoramus.

Above all, the phonograph changes the listener's encounter from a partly tactile to a wholly auditory one. "To be in the presence of performing musicians is to experience their touch and handling of instruments as tactile and kinetic, not just resonant," Marshall McLuhan reminds us.[3] On the other hand, the record eliminates the visual process by which we can be assured that real people, with whom we are at liberty to identify ourselves, are actually making the sounds. Watching a live performance we can at least tell by the performers' motions when the music is about to begin; a recording gives us no such clues.

McLuhan calls the record a "hot" medium, which "extends one single sense in high definition," which in turn is "the state of being well filled with data."[4] As we have already seen, technologically speaking the record and the tape are indeed "well filled with data." They combine a multitude

---

[3] *Understanding Media,* p. 282.
[4] *Understanding Media,* p. 22.

of musical details into a single experience; they concentrate the full sensibility of the listener upon the axis of the loudspeaker.

As we examine the uses to which music has been put in Western culture we shall observe even more instances in which the record and the other electronic media have had direct effects on the ways music is written, performed, and heard. Yet we should bear in mind that the fundamental principles of sonorous design remain essentially unaltered. Let us now consider those principles briefly and introduce some of the vocabulary that is customarily used to describe their operations.

II

music is sonorous design: scales

The essential materials of all music, no matter what era, culture, use, or function it may represent, are *sound* and *time*. Of course, most of us decline to accept as music just any combination of sounds. Otherwise city traffic, wind in the trees, or rushing water would be called music—which they seldom are except in a figurative or poetical sense. We all recognize "real music" when we hear it—or at least we believe we do—and those "noises" do not qualify for such a lofty designation.

If we as listeners are selective about what we are willing to call music, then the composer, the conscious creator of designs in sound, must also be selective, or else he would create non-music—just "noise." Moreover, as anyone may conclude from the obvious existence of many different kinds of music, there are various ways of putting sounds together to make designs. Thus the creative process in music begins with the selection of some sounds from among an infinite number of possibilities. It further involves the assumption of a set of procedures having to do with the possible relationships among them—*texture, timbre, rhythm,* and *form*—the subjects of the next five chapters. The chosen materials and the particular set of principles governing their manipulation we may refer to as a *musical system*.

Actually, a composer is never faced with the necessity of constructing an entire system by himself. Some of the choices may be determined by the processes of cultural development. For example, although all audible pitches are hypothetically available, from the lowest to the highest, no musical system in the world has drawn upon that entire range of possibilities until

17

the middle of the present century. Instead, every culture has selected certain pitches from the full audible range and its musicians have limited themselves to those alone for the construction of sonorous designs. The pitches used in the music of Western civilization for the past several hundred years have been literally embodied in the instruments we have used. All the remaining pitches in the spectrum have been considered to be outside the system, and have been judged to be "wrong" when introduced either accidentally or intentionally.

From culture to culture pitch choices appear to have been partly natural. Consider, for example, the *interval* of the *octave,* two pitches which seem to blend with one another so perfectly that in some cultures either one is

*II-1 *   regarded as the duplicate of the other (II-1). It can be described in technical terms as the interval of which the upper pitch is produced by vibrations that are precisely twice as fast as those of the lower one. But that does not explain its presence in all musical systems. There must be other reasons that are hidden from our understanding. Its use, in other words, appears to be an a priori fact of human nature.

The elements of a given musical system may also be partly explained as the result of certain technological features of the culture that uses the system. A particular technology, for instance, might determine the kinds of musical instruments that are available, and in turn limit the choice of usable pitches within the octave for all music employing those instruments. One of the earliest ancestors of the clarinet was made of the shinbone of a sheep, with part of a cow's horn attached as a bell or funnel to diffuse the sound. Lacking the kind of technology that would permit the addition of metal keys to extend the reach of the fingers, the instrument could have no more than ten finger-holes, and a correspondingly limited number of pitches could be produced with it. Owing to the benefits of modern materials and to methods of precision manufacturing, the clarinet now has a range of more than forty pitches extending beyond three octaves.

Furthermore, philosophical or religious beliefs about the nature of sound and time might determine the musical system that is favored among a variety of theoretical or technological possibilities. In ancient Greek music, as well as in the music of the medieval Roman Catholic church, one scale was believed to be suitable for music of a masculine character, another was deemed ecstatic and passionate, still another was regarded as feminine and lascivious, and so on.

* See Preface.

THE CHURCH MODES

A systematic arrangement, in consecutive ascending or descending order, of the most important pitches used in the music of a given culture is called a *scale*. All of the pitches used in the music of Western civilization for many centuries past are contained in the *chromatic* scale, which consists of twelve different pitches plus the pitch an octave above the first. All the pitches are equidistant from one another, and that distance, or *interval,* is called a *half step*. In Example II-2 you will hear the chromatic scale played   *II-2* on the flute. Try to sing or whistle along with the flute in order to obtain a subjective, physical sense of the "distance" between pitches that are a half step apart.

Until the latter part of the nineteenth century, scales of only seven different pitches, in various arrangements of half steps and *whole steps* (the interval encompassing two half steps) supplied all the materials necessary for the building of the tremendous body of music which is our present heritage.

From the early part of the ninth century to the end of the Renaissance (about 1600) a system of twelve scales formed the basis of most of the official music of the Roman Catholic church. They are referred to as the *church modes,* even though the same scales may also have been used in the secular music of the times. Six of the church modes are illustrated in Figure 6-*b* through *g,* and the first four are played for you in Example II-3. During   *II-3* the Renaissance all of them were given the names of ancient Greek modes that originally had denoted the nation with which each was supposedly associated. Gradually all of the modes were dropped from common usage except two, the *Aeolian* and the *Ionian*. During the seventeenth century the Aeolian mode became known as the *minor scale,* and the Ionian the *major scale*. From then until the end of the nineteenth century virtually all the music of Western civilization was based on those two scales, although the Dorian, Phrygian, Lydian, and Mixolydian modes continued to occur in European and American folk music, and they still are used occasionally in rock and jazz. Example II-4 is an early American folk song in the Dorian   *II-4* mode.

THE MAJOR/MINOR SYSTEM

Any of the above scales may begin on any of the twelve pitches of the chromatic scale, but the first pitch (and its octave "duplicate") is always

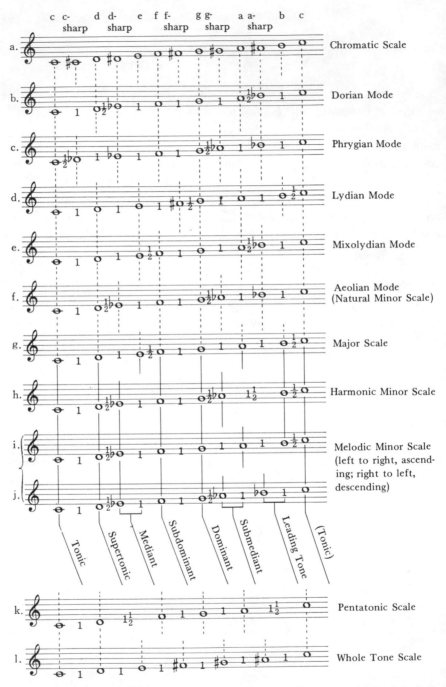

FIGURE 6 The most common scales in Western music. Observe that only seven letter-names are used. The remaining pitches of the chromatic scale are designated by the symbols ♯ (called a *sharp*) and ♭ (called a *flat*). The sharped versions of *c, d, f, g,* and *a* sound the same as the flatted versions of the next pitches above.

20

regarded as the *tonal center*. In the major/minor system the term *key* is used to designate the tonal center of a composition. The expression "key of *C*," for instance, means that *C* is the first degree of the scale used in a given piece. A scale in a major key contains the interval of a *major third* (two consecutive whole steps) between its first and third degrees; a minor scale uses the interval of a *minor third* (a whole step plus a half step) between the same two degrees. Listen carefully, several times, to Examples II-5 and II-6 and try to recognize the differences between the two scales at those points.   *II-5*

While there is but one major scale pattern, there are three distinct varieties of minor scales (Figure 4-*f, h, i, j*). The third and sixth degrees of the *harmonic minor* scale are a half step lower than those of the major scale, as you may hear in Example II-6. The harmonic minor scale is heard in   *II-6* the line played by the cellos and basses in Example II-7, an excerpt from   *II-7* the *Finale* to the Symphony No. 2 in D Major, opus 43 by the Finnish composer Jean Sibelius.* The melody in the treble register, played first by the solo trumpet, then by English horn, and finally by various other woodwinds, is in the *natural minor* scale (the Aeolian mode).

The *melodic minor* scale in its ascending order is the same as the major scale except that the third degree is lowered a half step; in the descending order the seventh, sixth, and third degrees are lowered (II-8).   *II-8*

Each of the seven different pitches in the major and minor scales has a name denoting its relative position in a functional hierarchy of importance (see legend below Figure 6-j). The lowest, like its octave duplicate, is termed the *tonic* note; all the others, owing to the ways in which they have been used in constructing melodies and harmonies, have acquired implicit tendencies toward the tonic as a tonal center. Next in importance is the fifth, or *dominant* degree, and immediately below it is the *subdominant* degree. The third step is called the *mediant* since it lies midway between the lower tonic and the dominant, while the sixth, the *submediant,* is midway between the subdominant and the upper tonic. Logically, the second note of the scale is called the *supertonic,* while the seventh, or *leading tone,* is the one that "leads" via the interval of a half step to the upper tonic.

The most familiar closing patterns or *cadences* in the melodies of Western music are the rise from the leading tone to the tonic and the fall from the supertonic to the tonic. (In Example III-6 the former may be heard as

* The word *finale* (fee-náh-lay) is applied to the final composition in a larger work comprising three or four separate compositions, each more generally referred to as *movements*. Various multi-movement types will be discussed in Chapter VII. The word *opus* (abbr. *op.*) followed by a number indicates the chronological position of that work in the composer's total output.

the last two notes of the alto part, played by the oboe; the latter is illustrated in the last two notes of the soprano part, played by the flute.)

EQUAL TEMPERAMENT

Ever since the early part of the eighteenth century the pitches of the chromatic scale have been *tuned* so that all the half steps are equal. This manner of tuning, called *equal temperament,* makes it possible to begin a major or minor scale on any one of the twelve pitches with the assurance that all its intervals will be *in tune.* Thus equal temperament enables the musician to *modulate,* or move from key to key, freely while remaining within the same basic pitch system.

Actually, equal temperament is reliably available only on fixed-pitch instruments such as the piano, the organ, the harp, and *fretted* instruments.* On most wind instruments there are at least a few pitches that are slightly "out of tune" owing to the effects of certain acoustical problems and constructional idiosyncrasies. Therefore, performers on wind and fretless stringed instruments, as well as singers, must develop the ability—often through the most rigorous practice—to hear and correct differences in tuning, or *intonation,* that are all but unnoticeable to the untrained ear.

Most experienced listeners with consciously developed or educated musical tastes, and even many of those who have no rational understanding of music at all, can sense whether or not a performance is "in tune." It may be said, in fact, that the majority of listeners in our culture are rather obsessed with the expectation of equal temperament in most of the music they listen to. People of other cultures are often found to be much more tolerant in this regard, even though they may reveal similarly rigid concerns with respect to the treatment of other parameters—rhythm and tempo in the case of certain African tribes, for example.

ATONALITY

Throughout the nineteenth century the ever-increasing frequency with which composers in Western culture modulated or otherwise introduced pitches foreign to the central key of a given work (*chromaticisms*), increasingly weakened the major/minor system in the classical tradition and established the preconditions for a new system. By the middle of the present century the major/minor system had ceased to serve as the basis for much

---

* A *fret* is a thin strip of material attached to the neck of a guitar, mandolin, or lute against which the player's finger is pressed to shorten and thereby raise the pitch of a string.

of the new art music composed in Europe or the United States, even though the serious music embodying it still constitutes the bulk of our classical concert and recorded musical repertoire, popular musicians still use it, and it is still taught as a required course in every music school.

Around 1910 Arnold Schoenberg began to employ all twelve tones of the chromatic scale as the pitch material of a procedure in which the concept of *tonality* or tonal center was avoided. The result is termed *atonality*. Since all the intervals in the chromatic scale are equal, there can be no hierarchy within the octave, and even the octave loses its polarizing power. The old aural signposts, the melodic cadences which are essential to the major/minor system, are now eliminated. The word atonality carries a negative connotation—"non-tonality"—but the principle it implies was conceptualized in a positive manner in 1923 by Schoenberg himself in what is called the *twelve-tone* or *dodecaphonic system,* which will be explained in Chapter XV.

THE PENTATONIC SCALE

Although patterns corresponding to our Church modes and major/minor scales are found in several cultures, a specific kind of five-tone or *pentatonic* scale is also common throughout the world. The usual pentatonic scale consists of five pitches within the octave arranged in intervals of whole steps and minor thirds (II-9). It may be thought of by persons who are   *II-9* familiar with the piano keyboard as being represented by the five black keys.

Pentatonic melodies are sometimes found in the traditional music of the American Indians, like the Flathead (II-10), as well as in the music of   *II-10* most civilizations in the Eastern hemisphere. They also appear frequently in the folk music of Western civilization.

If, as in Figure 6-*k, c* is used as the lowest pitch, it will be seen that the fourth and fifth degrees of the major and minor scales (the subdominant and dominant pitches) are also present in the pentatonic system, but the third and seventh degrees are missing. Therefore it is easy to combine pentatonic melodies with accompaniments in the major/minor system, as in the *arrangement* of the Negro spiritual, "Ain'a that Good News," which will be discussed in Chapter VIII.

OTHER SCALE SYSTEMS

A six-note scale consisting of six pitches a whole step apart, and thus known as the *whole-tone* scale, has occasionally been used in Western art music since the end of the nineteenth century. In the whole-tone scale (Fig.

6-*l*), the fourth, fifth, and seventh degrees of the diatonic scale are missing, so it is impossible to establish a tonal center by means of the usual cadential patterns of the major/minor system. An example of it may be found near the end of the finale to Charles Ives's *Quartet No. 2* (see Preface).

Any arrangement of any number of different pitches is conceivable as a scale. Within the chromatic scale alone there are some 479,001,600 possible combinations. Some civilized cultures use many more scales than we. The classical music of South India alone draws upon seventy-two scales or *melas* of five, six, and seven notes, and in the Hindustani music of North India there are ten different scales known as *thātas*.

Within the past several decades composers in Europe and the United States have begun experimenting with the use of pitches hitherto excluded from our standard theoretical system. The American composer, Harry Partch, for instance, works in scale systems consisting of as many as 43 pitches per octave; they are playable, incidentally, only on instruments designed especially by Partch himself (II-11). Now the synthesizer, the basic instrument of electronic music which will be described in Chapter XV, makes available to composers any pitch within the limits of audibility, and even employs frequencies beyond the audible range at both extremes for control purposes. Finally, *chance* music (see pp. 50 ff., 188 ff.) often dispenses entirely with scale systems.

II-11

III

texture

Some cultures seem to have no need for a vocabulary with which to describe or discuss music or a musical experience. In Western culture, however, we sometimes find it necessary to conceptualize about music in order to make rational judgments concerning specific experiences, and to share our tastes with others. Paradoxically, all music by its very nature defies complete and satisfactory translation into words. Language is fundamentally so different from pure sound that we are often compelled to resort to analogies in order to elucidate our understanding.

One of the most important analogies is that of *texture,* though it is also one of the most confusing. As defined in the dictionary the word refers to the appearance of a fabric resulting from the woven arrangement of yarns or fibers. But music is obviously not palpable stuff—it cannot be handled like yarn or woven, since sounds do not really move up and down or back and forth. Yet we have become accustomed to the notion of pitches with relatively rapid rates of vibration as being "high" and those with comparatively slow vibrations as being "low." Furthermore, even though time does not really proceed in a linear fashion, we have come to think of music in general as a more or less intricate "fabric" of sound flowing from left to right in space. We refer to these vertical/ horizontal characteristics as its texture.

MELODY

The strongest horizontal thread of the musical fabric is usually called *melody.* In a sense the word melody is synonymous with *tune,* but the musician uses the first term generically in reference to any coherent succession of pitches and specifically to denote a relatively elaborate type, and reserves the word tune to designate a simple and easily remembered melody.

Some melodies are long and continuously unfolding, like the ones with which J. S. Bach's Brandenburg Concerto No. 5 (Example VII-2) begins. Others consist of short, clearly separated sections called *phrases,* as in the theme of Brahms's *Variations on a Theme by Haydn* (Example VI-4). Some melodies are constructed mostly of pitches that are relatively close together, like the theme of Brahms's *Variations,* and we describe them as being *conjunct.* Others consist mainly of pitches that are spread wide apart, as in the excerpt from Anton Webern's Cantata No. 1, Opus 29 (Example XV-2), and we say such lines are *disjunct.* (Try to hum or sing along with any of the more conspicuous lines and you will get the point.) Most, however, are partly conjunct and partly disjunct. One melody may span a wide, another a narrow, *range;* either may possess a *tessitura,* or average range, which lies in the high, middle, or low *register* of a given instrument or voice.

A melody that is easy to sing will be relatively conjunct, in a fairly narrow range, with its tessitura in the middle register of the human voice. The melody of the "Star-Spangled Banner" defies all three of these conditions. It is inspiring, indeed, but it is somewhat easier to play on an instrument such as the piano or the trumpet than it is for the average person to sing.

MONOPHONY

Music which consists of a single melodic line performed by a *soloist,* or by a group of performers in unison or in octaves, without accompaniment, is said to be in *monophonic* texture. (You will notice that our analogy with fabric breaks down immediately—one cannot weave cloth with only one thread—but we shall have to use the conventional musical terminology for lack of anything more precise.) Monophonic music is pure melody; it can be either instrumental or vocal, or both.

Monophonic texture is found in the folk music of the West and the classical and folk musics of all non-Western cultures, and is used exclusively among many preliterate peoples. The music of the medieval Roman Catholic church, called *plainchant, plainsong,* or *Gregorian chant,* which
III-1 is sung by male voices in unison (III-1), is the largest body of strictly

monophonic music remaining in the Western classical tradition. A recent example of monophonic music is "The Lord's Prayer" from Leonard Bernstein's *Mass* (Example XII-2).

HETEROPHONY

When several performers execute essentially the same melody at the same time but with occasional and slight melodic or rhythmic differences, the result is called *heterophony*. To Western ears a heterophonic performance usually implies that the participants do not all know the tune very well, or else they are unskilled, or just careless; in any case it is interpreted as a sign of informality, and is therefore excusable.

On the other hand, in preliterate and non-Western musics heterophonic techniques may not only be deliberate but very intricate. The intermittent melodic disparities in the chant sung by a group of Buddhist monks in Example III-2 may seem to us to be merely accidental, but they are in fact the intentional results of the skillful manipulation of a single melodic formula. Similarly, Example III-3 is from a performance by a Balinese *gamelan,* or orchestra, in which all the players are simultaneously devising subtle variations on a simple melody.

III-2

III-3

POLYPHONY

Music in which two or more independent and unique melodies are presented simultaneously is said to be *polyphonic* or *contrapuntal* in texture. It is recognizable to the ear from the fact that the melodies are individually coherent yet distinct from one another in one or more parameters—pitch, rhythm, register, envelope, or timbre.

Polyphonic texture, which is found in the musics of many cultures, has long been prevalent in the music of the West. In fact, it dominated the tradition of serious sacred and secular music during the five centuries prior to about 1600 A.D., and music historians have come to refer to that period as the "polyphonic era." In Chapter VIII we shall have occasion to examine typical examples of Renaissance polyphony, such as the *madrigal* and the *motet.* A great deal of music written since the end of the Renaissance is partly or entirely polyphonic also, including especially the *fugue,* which we shall discuss in Chapter VII.

Example III-4 is a passage in two-part polyphony from the symphony, *Mathis der Maler* (Mathias [Grünewald] the Painter) by Paul Hindemith.

III-4

The independence of the melodic lines is established not only by the differences in the order of pitches used in each, and by the obvious contrast between the tone colors of the instruments playing them, but also by rhythmic factors. The trombone melody contains relatively long note values, giving the impression of a slow pace in that part, in comparison with the string melody which moves in shorter notes, suggesting a faster rate of motion. Polyphonic texture in which the rhythmic patterns of the respective lines are different from one another is said to be *polyrhythmic*.

III-5   African drum music is polyrhythmic without being polyphonic insofar as there may be no melodic lines in the usual sense. The use of instruments of contrasting character helps to set the various lines of rhythmic activity apart from one another (III-5). Owing partly to the African influences present in them, rock and jazz often exhibit polyrhythmic characterics at least in the percussion section, if not also in the melodic parameter.

If you have not had much experience in concentrated listening, you may have difficulty recognizing polyphonic texture. With a little practice, however, you will soon learn to shift your attention quickly from one line to another and back again; you will thus develop your ability to remember bits of melodic design long enough to keep track of the several strata of the musical design.

HOMOPHONY

In *homophonic* music one melodic line dominates the texture throughout, supported by one or more lines of lesser melodic import whose main function is to supply the notes of successive vertical structures called *chords*.

III-6   Example III-6 presents in succession the *alto, tenor,* and *bass parts* of the first eight measures of a tune by Stephen Foster, "Ring, ring the banjo." (The parts are played by oboe, clarinet, and bassoon, respectively.) Next the three parts are heard together; then the *soprano* part, which in this case is the tune, is played by the flute. Finally the tune is heard above the three lower parts. The accompanimental character of the lower parts, both individually and collectively, is evident in their relatively static natures, compared with the tune. Since all the parts employ the same note values at the same time, the texture is not only homophonic but *homorhythmic*.

III-7   Example III-7 illustrates the same tune with an accompaniment that uses exactly the same chords, but asserts the meter of the tune rather than its rhythmic details. This familiar type of accompaniment is called a *vamp*.

CHORDS

In order to more fully understand homophony and the differences between it and polyphony, we must clarify the term *chord*. Usually it is applied only to vertical structures consisting of three or more different pitches sounded simultaneously. In the major/minor system chords are built only of intervals of a major or minor third. A chord consisting of two superimposed thirds (three pitches) is called a *triad*. Three thirds produce what is called a *seventh chord* because the uppermost pitch is the seventh step above the lowest (III-8). Similarly, a chord consisting of four thirds is called a *ninth chord*.   *III-8*

Within a given key chords have the same relationships with one another as their lowest pitches, or *roots*. The triad built on the fifth degree of the scale is called the *dominant triad;* the seventh chord built on the same degree is called the *dominant seventh chord,* and so on. In nearly all the classical and popular music written between 1600 and 1900, and all popular music since then, most of the notes of the bass line function as roots of triads or other chords built of superimposed thirds.

For nearly three hundred years, from shortly after 1600 to nearly 1900, the progression from the subdominant triad to the dominant triad (or dominant seventh chord to the tonic triad (IV-V-I) was the most important cadential chord pattern in Western music, and it still is the most common one in the popular idioms (III-9). In fact, a great many popular songs are   *III-9*
built mainly on these three chords.

Triads, seventh chords, and ninth chords are not the only kinds of vertical structures that have been used, even in Western music. The Russian composer Alexander Scriabin selected six of the pitches found in the overtone series—the eighth through the fourteenth (see Figure 2)—and arranged them so as to produce five consecutive fourths—*c, f-sharp, b-flat, e, a, d.* He used this *quartal* structure, which he called the "mystic chord," as the basis for the harmonies and melodies of his symphony entitled *Prometheus, Poem of Fire.*

CONSONANCE AND DISSONANCE

Theoretically, the *consonant* intervals in the major/minor system are the unison, octave, third, sixth, fourth, and fifth; the *dissonant* intervals are the second, seventh, and ninth. Thus a triad is a consonant chord; seventh and ninth chords are dissonant. Compositions consisting mostly of simple triads, like Examples II-4 and VI-3, are apt to sound more consonant to the average listener than those using many elaborate chords. More dissonant still may be music that belongs essentially within the major/minor system but contains numerous chromaticisms as in Example V-8. Most dissonant of all would be music consisting of chords built mainly of dissonant intervals, as in Examples III-12 or XV-2.

However, consonance and dissonance are also related to factors other than intervals and chords. One *voicing* of a chord that places several dissonant intervals close together in the same register may sound extremely harsh, while in another voicing the same pitches removed from one another by an octave or two and placed in widely separated registers may result in a relatively consonant sound. The instruments used, the tempo, and the dynamic level also help to determine the ultimate effect of a theoretically dissonant sonority. The third movement of Anton Webern's Cantata, for instance, uses chords built almost exclusively of dissonant intervals, but the overall context makes the effect more consonant than if shriller timbres were played faster or louder, as in Example XI-2.

Dissonance is usually associated with unpleasantness and tension and consonance with satisfaction and repose, but these are arbitrary, subjective responses. Experience, psychological makeup, and even physiological conditions may cause one man's consonance to be another man's dissonance. As you study the recorded examples in this book you should keep this in mind. Do not dismiss a sound as being unpleasant until you have listened to it repeatedly and analyzed your initial response to it.

OTHER TYPES OF TEXTURE

The majority of compositions in both the classical and popular traditions in Western music from the late eighteenth through the twentieth centuries are neither exclusively polyphonic nor homophonic, but rather combine the two in some way. In some pieces the textures alternate, or else one may be modified so as to resemble the other. In Example III-10 from the first movement of Mozart's Symphony No. 41 in C Major, fragments of melodic material called *motifs* are distributed among various instruments, lending the effect of polyphonic texture even though only one melodic idea is present at any time.

III-10

Three or more polyphonic lines will, of course, produce vertical structures as by-products, so when a polyphonic texture is made homorhythmic, it will sound as if it were actually homophonic. On the other hand, one or more of the accompanying parts in a homophonic texture may assume a degree of independence that challenges the main melodic line for the listener's attention. That is, a subordinate part may assume the importance of what is called a *countermelody,* serving to complement or embellish the main melody.

The *art song,* a vocal solo genre that was cultivated chiefly in the nineteenth century, also was homophonic in principle. However, in its noblest manifestations, such as the songs of Franz Schubert, Robert Schumann, Johannes Brahms, Henri Duparc, and Gabriel Fauré, the accompaniments were often polyphonic in effect. For instance, the selection from the *song cycle* (a group of songs dealing with a single theme), *Dichterliebe* (Poet's Love) by Robert Schumann, heard in Example III-11, is essentially a   *III-11* melody accompanied by a fairly simple sequence of chords. However, the pitches of the chords are played not simultaneously but consecutively as *arpeggios.* Moreover, throughout the first two phrases of each verse one note in each chord is emphasized so as to produce a countermelody. The resultant texture has a decidedly horizontal, polyphonic thrust.

DENSITY

The types of texture we have examined so far represent simplified concepts of linear relationships among separate pitches. Monophony and polyphony emphasize the horizontal dimension; homophony combines a horizontal melody with vertical chord structures. But there are still other ways of conceiving musical texture.

When the consecutive pitches in a horizontal line occur at a rate faster than about 1/20 of a second each, we tend to perceive them as one continuous sound. Thus a *glissando* on a harp or piano is heard not as a series of discrete pitches—as a rapid scale or arpeggio, which it actually may be —but as one rising or falling sound. Serious composers, especially during the nineteenth century, often relied upon this phenomenon for the production of special effects. A harp glissando may be heard at about 20 seconds from the beginning of Claude Debussy's *Afternoon of a Faun* (Example V-8). In the jazz idiom, the extremely rapid playing of scales and arpeggios by the saxophonist John Coltrane produces what have appropriately been termed "sheets of sound" as in his "Chasin' the Trane," (see Preface).

The blending of separate pitches so as to obliterate their individual identities has been extended from the horizontal dimension to embrace the entire texture. Beginning before the turn of the present century serious composers like Debussy and Richard Strauss introduced into their works passages in which the sounds of separate instruments are so thoroughly fused that melodies and harmonies as such tend to disappear, and the result can best be described not in terms of lines at all, but of *densities,* which may be considered thick or thin, opaque or transparent.

III-12   In *Atmospheres* (III-12), by the contemporary Rumanian composer György Ligeti, this principle has been exploited to the extent that some of the parameters normally considered essential are entirely absent. As the composer himself has pointed out, "the sonorous texture is so dense that the individual interwoven instrumental voices are absorbed into the general texture and completely lose their individuality." There are, he says, "no 'events,' but only 'states,' no contours or forms, but instead an uninhabited, imaginary musical space. Tone color, usually a vehicle of musical form, is liberated from form to become an independent musical entity." [1]

[1] Quoted by John Briggs, in the Philadelphia Orchestra program notes, 1965–66.

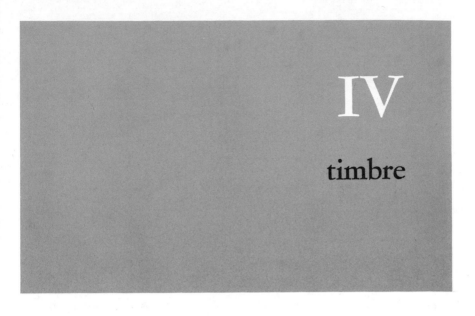

IV

timbre

As we have noted in Chapter I, the principal characteristic by which we distinguish a given sound from others of the same pitch and volume, and by which we identify its source or cause, is called *timbre*. The term is synonymous with *tone color*, which in turn suggests once again our normal tendency to describe sound in terms of visual and tactile experiences. Since there is no general agreement concerning the analogous hue of any particular pitch in the chromatic scale, we usually speak of tone colors as bright, or dark, or mellow, and so on.

In fact, the association of pitches with specific colors, known as synesthesia, seems to have no more than the slightest physiological basis, and the names of the hues of the spectrum have been applied to sounds only in an arbitrary, figurative sense. Nevertheless Alexander Scriabin scored his *Prometheus* for a full orchestra plus a mechanical device of his own invention called a "color keyboard," used to project light tinted according to his theory of pitch-to-color relationships upon a backdrop above the orchestra. Not surprisingly the work, which was first performed in 1911, has been the object of renewed interest following recent developments in the area of *multimedia* (aural-plus-visual) presentation.

There are, of course, an infinite number of ways to make sound, and therefore an infinite variety of timbres is available. Only within the last half century or so have composers in Western civilization seriously begun to explore the full range of possibilities. Since the early 1950s the electronic synthesizer has revealed timbres hitherto unimagined by either the serious composer or the performer of popular music.

THE ORCHESTRA

The *orchestra* as a standardized group of stringed, wind, and percussion instruments began to evolve early in the seventeenth century. Until the end of the eighteenth century most orchestras consisted of no more than 25 players. Today an orchestra of this size is termed a *chamber orchestra.* In the nineteenth century the orchestra grew to include up to 100 instruments and came to be known as the *symphony orchestra,* which remains the principal concert medium in Western musical life.

A typical large symphony orchestra contains the following distribution of instruments, classified for practical purposes into four families: *strings* (18 first violins, 16 second violins, 12 violas, 10 cellos, 8 double basses *), *woodwinds* (1 piccolo, 3 flutes, 3 oboes, 1 English horn, 3 clarinets, 1 bass clarinet, 3 bassoons, 1 double bassoon), *brasses* (4 trumpets, 6 French horns, 4 trombones, 1 tuba), and *percussion* (4 timpani, plus other instruments as needed, such as glockenspiel, bass drum, tenor drum, chimes, xylophone, cymbals, celesta, and harp). The sounds of many of these are systematically illustrated in an interesting composition by Benjamin Britten entitled *The Young Person's Guide to the Orchestra,* Op. 34 (See Preface).

The orchestra is capable of producing a great many different timbres. Each instrument possesses its own distinctive color, and the combined sounds of any two of them will produce another color, three will produce a fourth, and so on. If there were only twenty different instruments in an orchestra, not counting those of the percussion section, it would theoretically be possible to create more than 1.5 million separate colors on any one pitch. Considering in addition the slight differences in timbre among the registers of each instrument, and the minute discrepancies that often exist between the timbres of two instruments of the same kind, the total sum obtainable from a full symphony orchestra is probably incalculable.

Fortunately the composer is not intimidated by this staggering potential. On the contrary, beyond the challenge to expand the melodic and harmonic possibilities of specific scale systems, the exploitation of the coloristic capacities of the orchestral palette has been one of the main interests of nearly every great composer for at least a hundred and fifty years. The art of distributing notes, melodies, or rhythms among various instruments so as to achieve a desired expressive effect is called *orchestration.*

* The word "double" indicates that the instrument sounds an octave lower than the next highest instrument in the same family.

FIGURE 7-a The New York Philharmonic in rehearsal under the direction of Pierre Boulez, as seen from the rear of the violin section. The conductor's task is to mold the separate sounds of the numerous instruments into a total sonority that represents his understanding of the composer's intentions. He is both a director and an interpreter. (The word *philharmonic* means, literally, "love of music.") Courtesy, New York Philharmonic.

The respective timbres of the various pitches in a given texture may be blended into an opaque, *homogeneous* sonority in which the tone colors of the individual instruments are virtually obscured by the total effect. The ultimate realization of homogeneity using conventional instruments is to be found in the works of composers like Ligeti, whose *Atmospheres* (review Ex. III-12) is scored for an eighty-seven-piece orchestra. Instead of assigning all the first violins to one part, all the second violins to another, and so on, every instrument in the entire orchestra has a separate part to play, though it is impossible to perceive this by ear.

On the other hand, timbres may be chosen so as to contrast strongly

FIGURE 7-b   View from a balcony at a performance by the orchestra in Phil-harmonic Hall, Lincoln Center for the Performing Arts. The interesting shapes on the walls and ceiling are "baffles" that help to diffuse the sound evenly throughout the auditorium and minimize the distortion that would result from excessive echoing. Courtesy, New York Philharmonic.

with one another, producing a comparatively transparent, *heterogeneous* sonority in which the individual instruments are more or less clearly dis-tinguishable. In Igor Stravinsky's *L'Histoire du Soldat* (The Soldier's Tale) the seven solo instruments that make up the ensemble have timbres that contrast with one another rather stridently at times. Consequently the at-tentive listener is almost always able to follow their respective lines with *IV-1*   ease (IV-1; also listen to Ex. XV-1).

NON-ORCHESTRAL INSTRUMENTS

Many important instruments that have not been permanently admitted to the standard orchestral families are in widespread use. The cornet, the baritone horn, and the euphonium, for instance, are brass instruments often found in the marching band and the concert band, but are not usually present in the symphony orchestra. Some instruments, such as those that have belonged mainly to the realm of popular music, have been prohibited from inclusion by social or cultural determinants.

The saxophone, invented by Adolphe Sax in 1846, has long been included in the marching and concert bands, and is one of the most eloquent members of the jazz ensemble, but it is rarely heard in symphonic music, partly because a great deal of the traditional concert repertoire performed nowadays was composed before the saxophone became widely known, but also because most composers of classical music have considered it to belong properly to the other two idioms.

Technological factors also have entered in. The harpsichord, a keyboard instrument in which the strings are plucked, instead of being struck with felt hammers as in the piano, was once the mainstay of every instrumental ensemble. As the modern symphony orchestra began to evolve, however, the harpsichord lost all chance of retaining its place in the ensemble because of its delicate sonority. Moreover, the envelope peculiar to the sound of the harpsichord prohibits the execution of slow, sustained *(legato)* melodies: as soon as the string is plucked the sound begins to die away. This is one reason why solo music for the harpsichord typically contains ornate embellishments and many rapidly repeated notes.

Similarly, during the seventeenth century the violin began to replace older instruments of similar design but of considerably softer sound known as *viols,* because the violin's sonority could more satisfactorily fill large auditoriums such as opera houses. Also, being designed somewhat differently than the viol, the violin was more suitable for the development of virtuoso performance techniques. Nevertheless, the process of the change from viols to violins took about a hundred years and required the skills of some great instrument makers like Antonio Stradivari, Niccolò Amati, and Giuseppe Guarneri.

THE ORGAN

No single instrument can create a more varied array of timbres than the pipe organ, on which sound is produced by air forced from a bellows through pipes resembling whistles. A pipe organ consists of from two to five keyboards or *manuals* placed one above another, plus a keyboard for the player's feet called a *pedalboard.* The keyboards are connected, most often electrically, with a number of complete sets or *ranks* of pipes, each rank having its own timbre. A small, two-manual organ may consist of only ten ranks in all, while a large one may have as many as one hundred. The rank with the sound traditionally associated with the pipe organ is called the *diapason.* Among the rest are usually some whose sounds approximate those of various instruments of the orchestra.

The pipe organ has one technical characteristic that is readily apparent to the attentive listener: a pipe can produce only one envelope—instant growth and instant decay—at one steady-state dynamic level. Most modern organs do include a *swell box,* which is a cabinet enclosing several ranks and having louvres that can be opened and closed, to give an illusion of crescendo and decrescendo. However, the most effective means of increasing or decreasing volume is by adding or subtracting ranks through the manipulation of switches or *stops,* and *couplers.* Thus changes in volume will inevitably result in changes in timbre.

Unlike the more familiar *electronic organ,* which is mass produced and often portable, every pipe organ is the individual product of a highly skilled artisan, and is designed with careful attention to the relations between the instrument and its acoustical environment. Thus no two pipe organs, even of similar size, will sound exactly alike in all respects.

THE VOICE

The human voice in general is perhaps the most remarkable of all musical instruments, since it is capable of such a wide variety of timbres and expressive effects. Yet this fact may be somewhat difficult to appreciate, for while our own voices are important parts of our individual identities, and we control our relationships with others not so much by what we say as by the "tone of voice" with which we say it, most of us normally use our voices in a comparatively restrained and consistent manner. We even tend to react in amusement or suspicion toward anyone who speaks with a dialect or inflection markedly different from our own, or who uses his voice in an extravagant manner. Correspondingly, our appreciation of various kinds of singing is apt to be obstructed by our hesitancy to be objective about unfamiliar vocal sounds.

The timbre of a given voice is determined first by physiological factors— the size and shape of the skull and resonating areas such as the pharynx and the sinuses, as well as the capacity of the lungs and the general physical stamina of the individual. These characteristics are largely inherited, and thus may often be traced to racial or national origins, but they may also be affected by climate, diet, and other cultural circumstances.

Of course, the singer's language is a major determinant of vocal timbre, but articulation, inflection, volume, and accent or stress are also influenced by one's social position, occupation, neighborhood, home environment, and peer group, and there are vocal styles among singers to correspond to each of these variables. Even the technology of a culture can have far-reaching effects on the vocal styles of its singers. The American Indian singer, for example, was once judged on the carrying power of his voice; nowadays he is able to develop slightly different vocal characteristics because he has the benefit of electronic amplification.

Finally, the timbre of a singer's voice is affected by strictly musical traditions. The rock singer cultivates a certain timbre which is noticeably different from that of the folk singer, the blues singer, the country/western singer, the musical comedy star, and the evangelist, not to mention the opera singer and the classical concert artist. Notice the sometimes striking differences among the vocal timbres heard in the examples accompanying this book. To begin with you might compare II-4, III-2, III-11, V-1, V-7, VI-3, XIV-1, and XV-2.

In the art music of Western civilization since about 1800, musicians have classified singers' voices into six compasses or ranges, three female (from highest to lowest, *soprano, mezzo-soprano,* and *contralto*) and three male (*tenor, baritone,* and *bass*). In choral compositions the middle voice of each group is often ignored. Among opera singers, on the other hand, the coloristic peculiarities of some voices have led to further classifications. There are the *dramatic* soprano, *lyric* (light) soprano, and *coloratura* (agile) soprano; the *lyric* tenor, the *Heldentenor* (heroic), and the *tenore robusto* (robust); the *basso profundo* (very low) and the *basso cantante* (light).

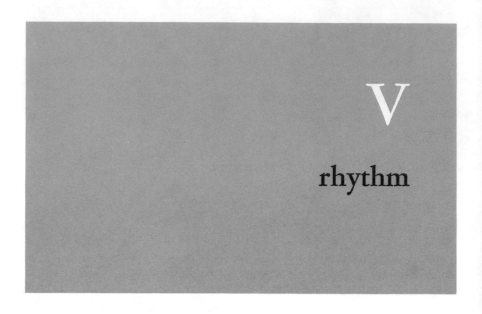

V

rhythm

The word *rhythm* has many different shades of meaning in the English language, but the Indo-European root of the word means simply *to flow*. In most of the arts rhythm is essentially the flow of time. Since we live *in* time its flow is unnoticeable to us unless we can distinguish one instant from another. In the language arts, time is marked by words; in dance it is marked by movement as well as music; in film its flow is marked by moving visual images as well as literary or linguistic events; in painting, sculpture, and architecture the time one occupies with the observation of the object is marked by consecutive perceptions of details. One may also recognize intimations of physical gestures in the relationships of lines and masses, thereby bestowing temporal qualities on those spatial dimensions.

The rhythmic life of almost any piece of music is a more or less complex matter, for every sonorous event serves more or less to divide time into segments. The fundamental temporal parameter of most musical designs, however, is the arbitrary unit of time called the *beat*. The beat is so named because it is often indicated visually by the up-and-down movements of a conductor's hand or the stroke of a drum. Thus a beat is not merely the sound that marks time but the entire interval of time spanned by a figurative gesture, whether is is occupied by sound or by silence. A beat may be divided into halves, fourths, thirds *(triplets)*, and so on, like any interval of time.

METER

The overall timespan of nearly every piece of music can be calculated in terms of groups of beats called *measures* or *bars.* The basic scheme of accented or unaccented beats is called the *meter.* The groups are set off from one another by the presence of a primary accent, or *downbeat,* which defines the first beat of each measure. An accent may be present qualitatively as the loudest sound in the group, it may be evidenced by a special timbre, or it may be longer than the rest.

Meters are indicated in conventional Western musical notation by means of symbols called *time signatures* which resemble fractions, such as 2/4, 3/8, or 4/2. The upper figure denotes the number of beats per measure, while the lower figure indicates to the performer the kind of note the composer has used to represent each beat. In the three time signatures just mentioned the lower figures specify the quarter note (♩), eighth note (♪), and half note (♩), respectively.

Most Western music employs meters that are either *simple* or *compound.* Simple meters may be basically *duple,* consisting of two beats, the first of which is accented (1-2); *triple* or *ternary,* with an accented beat followed by two relatively unaccented beats of equal duration (1-2-3); or *quadruple,* comprising an accented beat followed by three relatively unaccented beats, though sometimes the third beat bears a secondary accent (1-2-3-4). Example III-6 is in simple duple meter; Example II-7 is in simple triple meter.

In compound meters, two, three, or four ternary patterns are grouped into one measure with a primary accent falling on the first beat, or downbeat, of the first group, and secondary accents on the first beat of each remaining pattern. Two triple patterns may be juxtaposed to produce a six-beat measure (1-2-3-4-5-6); three triple patterns can be combined to produce a nine-beat measure (1-2-3-4-5-6-7-8-9), which may sound like a slow simple triple meter with each beat divided into triplets.

Finally, duple and ternary patterns may be combined into measures of five, seven, or more beats, with secondary accents occurring on various beats within each measure. A five-beat measure might consist of a duple pattern followed by a ternary pattern, or vice versa; a seven-beat measure may sound like 3 + 4, 4 + 3, 2 + 3 + 2, or 2 + 2 + 3. The "Gloria tibi" from Leonard Bernstein's *Mass* is in 5/8 meter in the combination 3 + 2: 1-2-3-4-5 (Example V-1).

V-1

ISOMETRIC RHYTHM; MULTIMETRIC RHYTHM

When the temporal flow of a given composition is based on a single meter continually reiterated we say the rhythm is *isometric*. By definition all of the beats are of equal duration, and all the downbeats are equidistant. A great deal of Western classical, as well as most popular, music is isometric. Indeed, to the layman the very word rhythm probably denotes only this kind of metrical organization. However, the word still basically means *flow,* and the rhythmic parameter of a piece may consist of measures among which the primary accents are not equidistant, or the beats are not equal in duration. The effect, in either case, is termed *multimetric* or *additive.*

Multimetric rhythm is found in the musics of many cultures, including the art music of Western civilization written since the latter part of the nineteenth century. The "Promenade" from *Pictures at an Exhibition,* by the Russian composer Modest Mussorgsky, begins with a phrase in which the meter consists of one measure of 5/4 followed by one measure
V-2   of 6/4 (**V-2**).

A more complex example of multimetric rhythm is found in the music to the ballet *Appalachian Spring,* by the contemporary American com-
V-3   poser Aaron Copland (V-3). To begin with, the notation is clearly multimetric, the passage—measures 69-84 in the printed music—bearing the consecutive time signatures 4/4, 4/4, 6/8, 6/8, 4/4, 4/4, 5/4, 4/4, 4/4, 4/4, 4/4, 4/4, 2/4, 4/4, 7/8, 4/4. It should be noted that the duration of the eighth note remains constant throughout the passage, and that all beats are therefore proportional to one another. Of course, even an experienced listener is unlikely to be able to distinguish the exact sequence of meters, either as written or as heard, for the tempo is rapid. The actual tendency will be for the listener temporarily to suspend his inclination to "feel" or anticipate the metrical patterns.

The use of *syncopation* makes the passage from Copland's work sound even more intricate metrically than it appears on paper. Syncopation is the prominent displacement of an accent from its anticipated or written position, either by means of sudden loudness or a striking change in timbre, or both. That is, a strong qualitative accent with virtually the force of a primary accent is placed at a point that is not normally stressed, such as the second or third beat of a ternary measure or an instant either before or after the precise beginning of any beat. Syncopation is an essential element in ragtime and jazz. There its presence in a melodic line is made all the more obvious by contrast with an isometric pattern played by other instruments, especially the drums.

The horn theme from *Till Eulenspiegel's Merry Pranks* by Richard Strauss is another example of deliberate metrical ambiguity (V-4). Listening to a recording of it, one might assume it is notated multimetrically beginning on the first beat of a measure, and would little suspect that it is notated in 6/8, and that it begins on the second beat of the measure. Here, as in the Copland work, the importance of the live concert experience is illustrated. If you could see the conductor giving the downbeat just before the first note of the melody and see him beat the time for the rest of the phrase, the rhythmic character of the music would be strikingly different than the purely aural experience allows. A new element of tension between seen and heard meters would be introduced.

V-4

Closely related to rhythm and meter is *tempo,* which is the speed or pace of the metrical beats. Traditionally a number of Italian words are employed by composers to indicate tempos in a relative sense within fairly broad limits, including: *largo* (very slowly), *lento* or *adagio* (slowly), *andante* (walking), *moderato* (moderately), *allegretto* and *allegro* (fast, cheerfully), *vivace* (quick, lively), *presto* (very fast), and *prestissimo* (as fast as possible). These terms, occasionally modified by words like *molto* (very) and *non troppo* (not too . . .), are often used to designate entire compositions, or movements of larger works, in lieu of more descriptive titles. Furthermore, tempos can be specified quite precisely by the composer with regard to the number of beats per minute. Example V-3, above, is from a section of *Appalachian Spring* which the composer has marked "Allegro ($\quad$ = 160)," meaning "Fast—specifically, at a tempo of 160 quarter-note beats per minute." The conductor may use a mechanical or electrical device called a *metronome* to determine exactly how fast a specified tempo should be.

FREE RHYTHM

The rhythmic characteristics of some music cannot be described in terms of meter. A piece in which strong accents are virtually absent, and in which the durations of the sonorous events are not exactly proportional to one another but indefinite and continually changing, is said to be in *free* rhythm. Music in free rhythm gives the impression it is being thought up on the spur of the moment, or that it is merely a prelude to another piece in stricter, metrical rhythm. In certain types of traditional music of India the opening section, called the *alāp,* is a rhapsodic, free-rhythmed improvisation in which the notes of the *raga* are gradually revealed; this is followed by the *pallavi* section, which is set in the steady, metrical *V-5* rhythm called the *tāla* (V-5).

Modern Western notation is not really adequate for the indication of free rhythm, since all its symbols represent proportional time values. Therefore terms are often used to indicate that the music is to be played in a *rubato* manner, which means a constantly fluctuating tempo, an alternation of *accelerando* (speeding up) and *rallentando* (slowing down).

The Toccata in D Minor by J. S. Bach, for example, is notated in 4/4, *V-6* but properly performed in free rhythm (V-6). The narrative episodes called *recitatives* used in operas and oratorios are also often notated isometrically, although in performance the singer is expected to follow the natural rhythm of the words with respect to accents and temporal values. *V-7* The effect may be heard in Example V-7, an excerpt from Handel's *Messiah*. Gregorian chant is frequently performed in free rhythm, though it may also be interpreted as if it were multimetric, consisting of successive duple and ternary groupings (review Ex. III-1).

Similarly, much modern Western classical music, such as Debussy's *Afternoon of a Faun*, gives the impression of being in free meter, whereas it is actually written and performed in a strictly metrical manner. Debussy's work is notated multimetrically in measures marked 6/8, 9/8, 12/8, and 3/4. The eighth note, which represents the basic pulse common to every measure, remains more or less constant in value throughout the piece. Owing to the very slow tempo, the accentless *tremolos* in the stringed instruments and the wave-like glissandos in the harp, the intricate polyrhythms, the homogeneity of the timbres, the gradualness with which dynamic changes take place, and the relatively subdued character of such accents as do occur, the essentially metrical nature of the music is largely obscured. By these means Debussy has made the sonorous experience of this composition correspond to, and perhaps arouse, not the usual physical, motor responses often associated with metrical music, but the dreamlike, disembodied flow of time and feeling of an idyllic reverie *V-8* (V-8).

Free rhythm rarely appears in popular music. "Selim," from the album *V-9* *Live/Evil* by the jazz trumpeter Miles Davis, is a notable exception (V-9).

THE TOTAL RHYTHMIC LIFE OF A COMPOSITION

As we noted at the beginning of this chapter, the flow of time in music is marked not only by beats but by all sonorous events. A brief analysis of the opening portion of the second movement of Beethoven's Symphony No. 8 in F Major will show the ways in which each of the parameters of a composition can contribute to its total rhythmic life. Listen to the entire movement, observing all the ways in which time is marked in the music. Try to get a feeling for the varied temporal dimensions the music embodies in terms of beats, tempos, durations, melodic shapes, timbres, and dynamics (V-10).

V-10

First, the woodwinds and French horns play a staccato line of seven notes, equal to one another in duration, weight, timbre, and pitch. There is no audible clue as to whether the meter is duple or triple. When the violins enter with a melody, however, their meter is obviously duple, judging from the motion of the line and the proportionate durations of the successive pitches. The second violins and violas reinforce the duple pattern, while the cellos and basses echo the rhythmic pattern of the violin line twice.

Changes of color have marked time in somewhat broader spans: A space of woodwind color, a space of new color dominated by violins and violas, and another of cello and double bass timbres. So far the dynamic level has been stable. Colors, durations, and pitches have changed, but no one beat has been perceptibly louder than any other. Suddenly three notes played *fortissimo* (very loudly) serve to mark off yet one more span of time. Thus the movement unfolds.

Still another aspect of the rhythmic life of this movement would be revealed in a live performance. A surprisingly slow 2/4 meter, with the fifth note of the opening phrase falling on the second beat of the first measure, could be seen in the time-beating of the conductor as well as in the gestures of the players. Then we would more fully appreciate the kinetic quality that a musical experience can have through the correlation and contrast of the various visible and audible events which mark time.

THE AURAL EXPERIENCE OF RHYTHM AND METER

Since we undergo the majority of our musical experiences via the radio, the phonograph, and the film, it is necessary to point out that it is not so much how a work is notated but how it strikes the listener that is important. If the rhythmic life of a composition *sounds* regular, it *is* isometric; if the accented beats *seem* to be irregularly spaced, the piece *is* multimetric; and if it gives the *impression* that it is in free rhythm, it *is*, regardless of the way in which it was written down by the composer or thought of by the performer.

In much Western music, including some current popular music, the details of the rhythmic parameters—pulse, accent, meter, tempo, and so on—are much more difficult to perceive than the melodic, textural, or timbral ones, and the ultimate comprehension of a complex work may be indefinitely postponed by persistent aural illusions deliberately built into it by the composer. This is one criterion by which some people assess the worth of a piece of music.

VI

form: superposition

Form is the broadest overall temporal dimension of a sonorous design. It is the end result of the combination of all the other parameters.

Let us assume you wish to compose a piece of monophonic music, and that you choose not to imitate some existing composition in any way, but to be entirely original. First you must select a pitch system, a rhythmic system, and a means of producing sound. Then you may conceive a pattern of several consecutive pitches in a given timbre and rhythmic scheme. You begin from a state of repose, or silence, and proceed through an area of melodic and rhythmic activity until you choose to return to a state of relative inactivity—to a tonic note, to a relatively long temporal value, or to silence. You have invented one complete musical idea, or *theme*. The challenge you face next is how to extend your design in time.

Fundamentally, you have two alternatives: you may repeat the same idea literally or you may proceed to a different idea. The first alternative, which we may call the principle of *sameness,* would assure *unity* and would imply a satisfying predictability up to a point, but would have a boring effect if continued indefinitely. The alternative, *differentness,* would assure *variety* and would consequently arouse interest or curiosity for a while, but would ultimately result in a feeling of utter unpredictability and unrest in the listener. In effect an excess of either will require that the imbalance be reversed or else that the design be brought to a close.

What any composer must try to do, therefore, is achieve a delicate

47

balance between sameness (unity, predictability) and differentness (variety, unpredictability). He will aim to minimize the possibility of tedium and stimulate the greatest possible interest and satisfaction in a willing listener, not just from moment to moment, but from the beginning to the end of his composition. Two procedures in which the normal demand for optimum balance between these polarities has been defied are the *strophic* song and the *round.*

STROPHIC SONG

A strophic song is one in which the melody and the accompaniment, if any, are repeated literally for each of the several stanzas or *strophes* of a poem. Not only is sameness paramount in the music alone, but the poem and the music are related in ways that further emphasize unity. The rhythmic characteristics of each strophe will usually coincide more or less precisely with those of the music in terms of meter, accents, and lengths of notes. Moreover, there will sometimes be noticeable similarities among the endings of the melodic phrases corresponding to the rhyme scheme of the poem. Although some of the words may be repeated along with their melodic phrases as a *refrain* or *chorus,* the only element of variety will lie in the text, which is often narrative. Indeed, the monotony of strict strophic form compels the listener to devote most of his attention to the story, for which the music serves merely as a vehicle.

Outside of Christian hymnody, strict strophic form is seldom extended very far in the music of Western civilization. The song from Schumann's *Dichterliebe* (Example III-11) is strophic, but only two short stanzas are sung, and variety is introduced in the *coda,* or concluding section. Even preliterate peoples unselfconsciously introduce variations in extensively repetitive music.

THE ROUND

The round is perhaps most readily exemplified in the familiar seventeenth-century song, "Three Blind Mice," consisting of a melody only eight measures long which may be sung by as many as four groups of singers, with each group beginning the melody on the same pitch, but two measures later than the preceding group. Since the parts are identical they are equal in importance, so the resulting texture is polyphonic, or contrapuntal. Since they imitate one another it is called *imitative counterpoint.*

A diagram in which every two-measure phrase of the familiar round is designated by a different letter will look like this:

A B C D A B C D A B C D etc.

A B C D A B C D A B C etc.

A B C D A B C D A B etc.

A B C D A B C D A etc.

Once all four voices have entered, every phrase of the melody will be heard in one voice or another at all times. According to the usual method of performance all the singers repeat the melody until someone signals a halt, or until the participants begin to tire of the monotony. Clearly, the overall duration of the performance of a round will be limited to no more than a minute or two, owing to the inability of adult Western listeners to tolerate much more of an extension of unrelieved unity.

The round was especially popular in Europe during the seventeenth and eighteenth centuries, and numerous ones—some of exquisite beauty— were composed by men like Hadyn, Mozart, and Beethoven. During the notorious reign of Charles II (1660-1685) a less sedate type of round known as a *catch* was cultivated in England. Not only was the text of the catch usually humorous, but the melody was often contrived so as to enhance the humor. Many catches were said to consist of "three parts obscenity and one part music."

As simple as the procedure appears to be, the round rarely occurs in the music of preliterate cultures or non-Western civilizations. Moreover, because of the absence of any possibility of variety if one adheres strictly to the definition of the round, it is seldom employed in Western music. A unique exception is found in Act I, scene *ii* of the opera *Peter Grimes* by the contemporary British composer Benjamin Britten (see Preface).

At the point in the opera where a fight is about to break out in a pub in the English fishing village that is the setting for the story, one of the fishermen cries out, "For peace sake, someone start a song!"—and the rest begin a round: [1]

> Old Joe has gone fishing and
> Young Joe has gone fishing and
> You know has gone fishing and found them a shoal.
> (Repeat)
> Pull them in in han'fuls and in canfuls and in panfuls.

[1] *Peter Grimes:* Music by Benjamin Britten. Text by Montague Slater. Copyright 1945 by Boosey & Hawkes, Ltd.; Renewed 1972. Used by permission of Boosey & Hawkes, Inc.

(Repeat)
Bring them in sweetly,
Gut them completely,
Pack them up neatly,
Sell them discreetly.
(Repeat)
O haul away! O haul away!
(Repeat)

Britten's round transcends the ordinary limitations of the genre in several ways. For one thing, the orchestra does not merely duplicate the singers' parts, but plays a separate accompaniment. The full orchestra plays one loud chord, staccato, on the first beat of every fourth measure while various instruments, beginning with the timpani or kettle-drum play a simple rhythmic idea on one pitch throughout, which is identical with the rhythm of the first phrase of the melody. Since they are different from the voice parts, one would expect these devices to contribute variety, but in effect they reinforce the unity of the song.

The principal element of variety lies in the rhythm of the whole melody, which at first seems to the ear to be multimetric. It must be heard several times before the isometric pattern of 7/4 (2 + 2 + 3) becomes apparent to the listener. Meanwhile the initial impression of complexity heightens the feeling of tense excitement at that particular moment in the opera.

Musically, the powerful unifying elements of the round serve to sustain the mood just long enough for the dramatic purpose. After only a minute and twenty seconds the momentum of the round is allowed to falter, the mood changes slightly, and an episode ensues which is much more varied in all respects, though it is based on the melody of the round.

Another contrapuntal procedure in which one voice or part imitates another strictly, from beginning to end, is the *canon*. The canon is not as compactly unified as the round, however, since its melodic material changes continuously throughout, and a strong element of variety is thereby maintained in that parameter while unity prevails in timbre and meter.

CHANCE

Music that emphasizes variety to the virtual exclusion of any unity is even rarer than that in which unity dominates. Of course, many art songs are *through-composed* rather than strophic; that is, new music is introduced for each stanza of the poem, often pointing up the progress of the dramatic or lyrical contents of the text. But even in this procedure in which variety is ostensibly the objective, some unifying factors are usually introduced, such as repetitions of melodic or rhythmic motives.

During the past few decades, however, a number of composers of serious music in the West have experimented with the application of the laws of chance to the processes of composition, or performance, or both. The composer may employ dice, a mathematical formula as Yannis Xenakis does, or some other arbitrary scheme, to establish the precise details of rhythm, pitch, density, volume, and timbre, or else he may specify certain parameters and instruct the performers to use their own judgment in executing the composition. In either case, if some sort of unifying factor is not deliberately introduced by the composer, the odds that one will occur by chance may be slight. *Chance* music is also known as *aleatory* or *indeterminate* music, though there are differences among the connotations of the three terms on which there does not yet seem to be general agreement.

A classic example of chance music is *Imaginary Landscape No. IV* (1951) by John Cage, one of the foremost innovators in twentieth-century music. One remarkable feature of this work is that it uses as its sonorous medium twelve ordinary radios instead of conventional musical instruments. The composer himself has explained his unorthodox compositional procedure: "What brings about . . . unpredictability is the use of the method established in the *I-Ching* (Book of Changes) for the obtaining of oracles, that of tossing three coins six times." By this means numbers are arrived at representing frequencies in kilocycles, durations, and amplitudes. The result is "a musical composition the continuity of which is free of individual taste and memory (psychology) and also of the literature and 'traditions' of the art." [2]

It will be seen that the laws of chance have been allowed to determine the characteristics of each parameter. If a performance were to take place at a given time, date, and place, with equipment of a given quality, the composition would sound one way. But if any of those conditions were altered in the slightest degree, the sound would be quite different. At a given instant a specific broadcast frequency may produce any one or more of an infinite variety of pitches and timbres, or it may carry no sound at all other than that of the transmission or receiving system itself. What is

[2] John Cage, *Silence* (Cambridge, Mass.: The M.I.T. Press, 1966), pp. 57, 59. Copyright 1961 by John Cage.

more, radio broadcasting as a medium tends to favor variety rather than repetition, so it is more than likely that any performance of *Imaginary Landscape No. IV* will reflect that emphasis under any conditions.

Since we normally desire and expect a balance between unity and variety in all our experiences, this kind of music is apt to be enjoyed most by the rare listener who finds chance inherently exciting—the "born gambler." In any case, nearly all music is consciously designed to satisfy normal human expectations within the context of a particular cultural milieu and its adopted musical system, and it therefore exhibits some sort of balance between sameness and differentness, whether an unfamiliar listener is able to perceive it or not.

There are two fundamental ways of achieving balance: by *superposition* or by *juxtaposition*. That is, *sameness and differentness may be presented simultaneously (superposed) in different parameters, or alternately (justaposed) in a single parameter*. Both solutions may actually appear in the same composition, but often one or the other clearly dominates the structure.

SUPERPOSITION: OSTINATO PROCEDURES

In the hypothetical composition proposed at the beginning of this chapter, the composer might choose to reiterate the rhythmic pattern and the timbre of his initial idea, but continually change the pattern of pitches. Given a polyphonic or a homophonic texture, additional possibilities are available for the simultaneous combination of unity with variety in different parameters. In some of the classical music of India unity is most obviously supplied in a lengthy composition by the continuous playing of a single pitch, or *drone*—also called a *pedal point* or *bourdon*—on the *tambura* (a stringed instrument which is plucked).

In Miles Davis's "What I Say," unity is provided throughout more than half of the long performance (21 minutes, 11 seconds) by the incessant repetition of a simple motif in the bass register called an *ostinato,* while variety is maintained in melody and timbre by the remaining instruments *VI-1*   (VI-1).

The ostinato procedure was frequently employed during the baroque era. In J. S. Bach's Passacaglia in C Minor an eight-measure ostinato (also called a *ground*) in ternary meter is stated first in the bass register of the organ. Subsequently, while this melodic idea is repeated over and over, contrasting melodic and rhythmic material is introduced in the remaining lines of the polyphonic texture. The excerpt from this work heard in Example VI-2 might be illustrated graphically as follows, with *VI-2* a solid line standing for the presence of unifying material and the symbol *x* for variety:

Ostinato	———————————————————
Meter	———————————————————
Tempo	———————————————————
Texture	———————————————————
Tonality	———————————————————
Timbre	x x x x x x x x x x x x x x x x x x x
Other melodic and rhythmic material	x x x x x x x x x x x x x x x x x x x

The *chaconne,* also a common baroque structural procedure, relies for unity upon a reiterated idea that is merely an eight-measure pattern of chords in ternary meter. Lacking a specific and readily recognizable melodic theme, the chaconne offers the composer more of an opportunity to exploit melodic variety than the passacaglia. Consequently it is often more difficult to follow the design of a chaconne aurally. Unfortunately the term chaconne has so often been used interchangeably with passacaglia that the listener is apt to be misled. For instance, we shall encounter a so-called chaconne in Chapter IX that actually fits the definition of the other term.

In principle, every popular song in *blues* style is a chaconne, in that it is usually built upon numerous repetitions of a simple chord pattern. The main differences are that blues frequently employs a twelve-measure chord scheme in quadruple meter (4/4), consisting of four measures of the tonic chord (I), two measures of the subdominant (IV), two measures of tonic (I), one measure of dominant (V), one measure of subdominant (IV), and two measures of tonic (I). The harmonic scheme can easily be followed by listening carefully to the bass line. Another difference between the blues pattern and the chaconne is that the chords of the blues typically are in a major key, while the melody has the characteristics of a minor scale. Additional distinctions between classical and popular styles will be discussed in Chapter XIII. In Example VI-3 "The Celebrated *VI-3* Walkin' Blues," you can hear two statements of a twelve-measure blues pattern out of the total of eight repetitions that comprise the entire performance. (The tempo is very slow; each beat is divided into three parts.

Incidentally, the instruments heard in this performance by Taj Mahal are electric guitar, mandolin, harmonica, bass, and drums.)

Ostinato, passacaglia, and chaconnne techniques serve to provide unity in a composition not merely through the repetition of a melodic idea with its inherent rhythm, meter, and tempo, but also by establishing and reinforcing the identity of a tonal center. Therefore the composer who uses them must try to offset potential monotony with respect to that parameter.

THEME-AND-VARIATIONS

We have been describing ways of maintaining unity or sameness in one parameter while simultaneously introducing variety in another. The unifying factor in each case has remained clearly recognizable throughout each example. A similar but far more subtle technique is called *theme-and-variations*. This requires a delicate balance of sameness and differentness within the same parameter—melody—throughout an extended composition.

A theme sixteen to thirty-two measures in length, often a symmetrical melody consisting of four sections arranged in the order *a-a-b-a,* is stated clearly at the outset. It is then repeated a number of times, each repetition being altered by more or less complex variations in melodic detail, timbre, rhythm, meter, tempo, key, or even chord progression. It has usually been the composer's intention that the presence of the theme be at least vaguely recognizable throughout the composition, but that sufficient variety be evident to encourage continued interest.

One recognizable instance of theme-and-variations procedure will be heard in Example XIV-5. Britten's *Young Person's Guide to the Orchestra* (see p. 34) is a set of variations on a theme written by an earlier English composer, Henry Purcell. Another example, in which variation occurs in timbre alone, is Ravel's well-known *Bolero.* Johannes Brahms's *Variations on a Theme by Haydn* is even more difficult to follow (VI-4). The example contains the first four measures of the theme followed by the first four measures of two of the ensuing variations. Listen to the theme again and again, until its contour is firmly fixed in your memory. Then listen to the variations of the same phrases and whistle or hum the theme along with the orchestra. You will find the tune still fits even though the orchestra isn't playing it. In other words, a significant part of the composition is in your own mind!

VI-4

VII

form: juxtaposition

The other solution to the fundamental problem of balancing sameness (unity) with differentness (variety) is to place them side by side, or juxtapose them. That is, a unifying idea or section of music may be alternated with one or more contrasting ideas. The principle of juxtaposition (or *repetition-after-contrast*) may be applied to any one or more parameters, but throughout the history of Western music, as well as in the music of Eastern and preliterate cultures, it has most often been applied to melody. In Debussy's *Afternoon of a Faun* (V-8), for example, the distinctive flute melody heard at the beginning reappears near the end, resulting in a large *ternary* or *three-part* form which may be represented graphically by the formula *A-B-A*.

The principle of juxtaposition may be readily discerned in short compositions like hymn tunes, folk songs, and current popular songs. The Stephen Foster tune, "Ring, ring the banjo" (III-6), for instance, may be graphed *a-b-c-b,* because the second and fourth lines of the tune are identical, and are alternated with contrasting material.

During certain eras, and in certain types of music, the principle of juxtaposition has been used more frequently than in others. In twentieth-century classical music the unifying material is sometimes difficult to remember and recognize upon its return. Composers of the eighteenth and nineteenth centuries, on the other hand, preferred symmetrical structures with obvious attributes of clarity and balance, and their listeners grew to expect the repetition of the opening melodic material after a section of contrasting character, and to enjoy the feelings of anticipation and satisfaction which such designs aroused.

THE MINUET-AND-TRIO

Music for the *minuet,* a dance said to have been popularized by Louis XIV, was typically in ternary *(A-B-A)* form. The center section, called the *trio* from the fact that originally it was written in three-voice texture, was contrasted with the first and third sections in terms of melodic material, tonality, and instrumentation, as well as texture.

Both the minuet and the trio were cast in *binary (A-B)* form. Each consisted of a pair of complementary melodic ideas embodying a compromise between sameness and differentness: the end of the second melody bore some resemblance to the first, thereby implying ternary structure even though the section as a whole was clearly articulated into two separate segments. The repetition of both the minuet and the trio is an important aspect of the overall design. The minuet-and-trio may be diagrammed as a three-part grouping of binary sections as follows:

A(minuet)   B (trio)   A (minuet)

‖: a :‖: b :‖   ‖: c :‖: d :‖   a–b (no repeats)

VII-1   Example VII-1 is a minuet-and-trio by Franz Joseph Haydn. A *scherzo* is structurally identical with the minuet but suggests a more jocular and energetic mood.

THE CONCERTO

Another structure in which sameness and differentness are juxtaposed is found in the first movement of the baroque *concerto grosso* ("large concerto"; the noun *concerto* derives from the Italian verb *concertare,* which once meant "to co-ordinate" or "to unite"). In the first movement the texture, timbre, and melodic material of a string orchestra called the *ripieno* ("full") are alternated and contrasted with those of a small group of soloists called the *concertino.*

Throughout the first movement of J. S. Bach's Brandenburg Concerto
VII-2   No. 5 (VII-2) the ripieno repeats its melodic material—not always literally, but always recognizably—several times among sections of contrasting material in contrapuntal texture played by the concertino of violin,

flute, and harpsichord. The scheme of the melody, texture, density, and timbre of this movement may be diagrammed as follows:

	A	B	A	C	A	D
Melody	——— x x x x ——— x x x x ——— x x x x *etc.*

	A	B	A	B	A	B
Texture	——— x x x x ——— x x x x ——— x x x x *etc.*

	A	B	A	B	A	B
Density	——— x x x x ——— x x x x ——— x x x x *etc.*

	A	B	A	B	A	B
Timbre	——— x x x x ——— x x x x ——— x x x x *etc.*

In general, the principle of juxtaposition is also fundamental to the structure of the *solo concerto,* which has had a much longer and more interesting history than the concerto grosso. Many of its earliest and greatest examples were conceived by the leading performer-composers of the eighteenth century such as Antonio Vivaldi and Giuseppe Torelli. During the classical era the evolution of the solo concerto was advanced by the compositions of Mozart, and in the nineteenth century by those of Chopin, Liszt, Paganini, and similar figures who were not only composers but also brilliant performers. An important feature of the solo concerto was the *cadenza,* a short unaccompanied episode in which the soloist, as if improvising, displayed the full extent of his technical facility in rapid scale passages, arpeggios, and other elaborate melodic embellishments. Moreover, in the solo concerto the structural procedure associated with the first movement of the concerto grosso was replaced by what has come to be known as *sonata form.*

SONATA FORM

Sonata form was one of the most common structures in late eighteenth- and nineteenth-century instrumental music. During the baroque era the term *sonata* had been used to denote any composition intended to be played on an instrument or by a group of instruments, but it gradually came to be applied to a specific formal plan. Sonata form consists of an *exposition* in which two melodic themes of contrasting character and key are presented (if the first were in the key of c, the second might be in the key of g). In the solo concerto the orchestra usually plays one theme, the soloist the other. After a literal repetition of the entire exposition for the purpose of fixing the themes in the listener's mind, comes a section called the *develop-*

ment, followed by the repetition or *recapitulation* of the exposition. This return of the original material differs from the initial statement, in that both themes are now in the first key. The recapitulation ends with a coda. Sometimes, as in many of the works of Haydn, the whole structure was preceded by a short *adagio* introduction.

The development section is the most important of all, for it is here that the composer displays his insight into the expressive potential of his themes. To *develop* a theme means to separate it into its most interesting motifs and subject them to modulation, rhythmic and intervallic expansion and contraction, imitation, and changes in register, timbre, or type of line (staccato, legato). The result is a passage of extreme contrast and tension that stands out from the exposition and recapitulation despite its organic relationships with one or more of their melodies. Example III-10 contains the closing theme of the exposition, followed by the beginning of the development section, in which several of the above devices may be heard, from the first movement of Symphony No. 41 in C Major by Mozart.

RONDO FORM

Superficially, the scheme of the melodic parameter of the concerto grosso happens to coincide in general outline with what is called *rondo* form. However, in the rondo the *A* section (sometimes itself called the rondo) was often a complete, symmetrical song-form, while the intervening sections might consist of contrasting melodic material in rather free form, or even developmental episodes in various keys, timbres, and textures. In its simplest form, it could best be represented by the letter scheme *A-B-A-C-A-D-* etc.

Rondo form is implicit in the *A-B,* verse-refrain pattern of much Western folk music when two or more verses are sung, but it also occurs in the music of other cultures. It is to be found, in principle at least, in a certain type of the classical music of India, although its outlines are extremely difficult for the inexperienced Western listener to perceive, owing to the complexity of the *ragas* and the intricacy of the variational procedures to which they are subjected.

THE FUGUE

Another structural plan in which repetition and contrast appear successively in the same parameter is the *fugue.* A fugue is a monothematic contrapuntal composition consisting of an *exposition* in which the *subject* is stated in each of the (usually) four parts or voices, followed by a series of alternations between *episodes* consisting of new material and restatements of the subject. As diagrammed—*Exposition-B-A-C-A*-etc.—it appears to resemble rondo form, but the distinctions are that the subject of a fugue is less often song-like than that of the rondo, and it is treated consistently in contrapuntal fashion.

Fugal procedure evolved during the baroque era, and the course of its evolution is reflected in the organ fugues of J. S. Bach, such as the Fugue in G Minor illustrated in Example VII-3. Composers in succeeding cen- *VII-3* turies have been attracted by it too, however: Britten's *Young Person's Guide to the Orchestra* (see p. 34) concludes with a fugue. Those who have sought to fuse the historically separate traditions of jazz and serious music have found it readily adaptable to their aims. Example VII-4 is the *VII-4* fugal conclusion of the Jazz Suite for Brass by J. J. Johnson.

PROGRAM MUSIC

A composition with a title denoting a structural scheme like sonata or fugue is referred to as *absolute music;* one bearing a title with literary or pictorial connotations that the listener is to keep in mind is called *program music.* A single-movement orchestral work of the latter type is called a *symphonic poem* or *tone poem.* In most instances the composer's aim is not to imitate the structure of the poem or story, or the details of a scene, but merely to evoke a corresponding mood. Therefore he observes the inherent demands of sonorous design with respect to the balancing of unity and variety, often resorting to simple three-part structure as Debussy did in *Afternoon of a Faun,* which was inspired by Stéphane Mallarmé's poem of the same name.

COMPOUND INSTRUMENTAL FORMS

The procedures discussed so far represent only a few of the possible solutions to the composer's basic problem of balancing unity and variety. Nevertheless, with the exception of chance, they have all been used so often in Western music that they are conventionally referred to as "the forms of music." Most of them are commonly grouped together as independent movements of *compound forms.*

In its older and larger sense, for instance, the term sonata denotes a three- or four-movement work for solo piano, or for a solo wind or stringed instrument, usually with piano accompaniment. The movements may differ in key and occasionally in texture, but they differ most conspicuously with respect to melodic material, mood, tempo, and structure. In a typical sonata from the classic or romantic eras the tempos of the movements are likely to be: I. *Allegro;* II. *Adagio;* and III. *Allegro* or perhaps *Presto.* With regard to structure they are sometimes: I. sonata form; II. three-part form; and III. rondo. Overall, the sonata is unified mainly by the consistency of the instrumentation, as well as by its general style—a concept we shall discuss presently.

Compound forms for ensembles of solo instruments, referred to categorically as *chamber music,* include the *string quartet,* which in terms of tempos and structures, at least, is simply a sonata for two violins, viola, and cello; and the *piano trio,* a sonata for piano, violin, and cello. There are also sonatas for five or more solo wind or stringed instruments which are called, logically, *quintets, sextets, septets,* or *octets.*

The *trio sonata* is a type peculiar to the baroque era, written in three-part texture for two melody instruments (usually violins) and a bass instrument, with an accompaniment improvised on a harpsichord or organ. The individual movements were sometimes cast in various dance forms, as in the *suite.*

The *suite* is a collection of dance pieces intended for listening rather than dancing. During the baroque era it included the French minuet as well as dances from other European countries, mostly in binary *(A-B)* form with distinctive tempos and moods. Among the most important of these were the *allemande* (a German dance in duple meter at a moderate tempo), the *courante* (a lively French or Italian dance), the *saraband* (a dignified dance in slow triple meter, probably of Mexican origin), and the *gigue* (a vivacious dance in 6/8 meter which evolved from the Irish "jig"). See also p. 119.

A *symphony* is, in a broad sense, a four-movement sonata for full orchestra, with a minuet-and-trio after the second movement. A *concerto* is a sonata for a soloist (or a group of soloists) and orchestra; the minuet (or scherzo) is usually omitted.

The fugue has often been paired with an introductory *prelude* or *fantasia* (titles having no specific structural connotations), a *toccata* (Example V-6), or a *passacaglia* (Example VI-2).

COMPOUND VOCAL FORMS

The largest compound form in the vocal medium is the *opera,* a drama for singers with orchestral accompaniment that is performed on a stage with action, costumes, scenery, and lighting effects.* Generally, an opera is divided into *acts* containing several *scenes*. The first act is preceded by an orchestral *overture*. In most eighteenth- and nineteenth-century operas the scenes are made up of dramatic or lyrical songs called *arias,* often in three-part form, which are separated by short solo recitatives. Some scenes may also contain pieces in various forms for chorus or ensembles of solo voices, and some may include dances or ballets. Following the precedent established by Richard Wagner in his so-called *music dramas* such as *Tristan und Isolde* (1865), opera composers have sometimes conceived each act as a continuous whole, producing expansive structures of interlocking musical and dramatic episodes like those in Britten's *Peter Grimes.*

Another large form for voices and orchestra is the *oratorio,* which is religious or contemplative in character, rather than dramatic, and is performed in a church or concert hall without scenery, costumes, action, or special lighting. Like the opera, the oratorio contains solo arias and recitatives (Example V-7), but the chorus usually occupies a much more prominent position. The choral movements are often in elaborate contrapuntal textures resembling fugues. A *Passion oratorio* is based on the story of the trial, crucifixion, and resurrection of Christ.

The *cantata* is similar to the oratorio with respect to the structures of its individual movements, but it is considerably shorter, and usually is devoid of dramatic content. In Chapter XII an example of an eighteenth-century Lutheran church cantata will be discussed, as will the *mass,* another important compound vocal form.

In the popular idiom there is the musico-dramatic *operetta,* along with its uniquely American derivative *musical comedy.* Both are theatrical in character but are not coherent compound musical forms like the opera. They consist of overtures, lyrical or humorous songs and choral numbers, and dances, but the narrative of the simple plot is presented in the form of spoken dialogue rather than in musical recitative. An indication of the basic structural difference between opera and musical comedy is the fact that a recording of, say, *Peter Grimes* will contain the complete work, whereas a recording of a musical comedy like *Man of La Mancha* will include only the songs and some of the dance music. The standard forms used in musical comedy songs will be discussed in Chapter XIII.

---

* Obviously the phonograph record, through which many persons have their main exposure to opera, focuses the listener's attention on the music and the voices at the expense of the equally important visual parameters. Dedicated opera lovers do not mind this of course, but the fact remains that opera must be seen to be fully appreciated.

STRUCTURE AS EXPERIENCE

It would be naive to regard the forms of music, either simple or compound, merely as molds into which a composer pours his ideas, for form is not an independent musical parameter but a result of the working-together of all parameters. At most, these formulas are only arbitrary, hypothetical limitations a composer might use as guidelines.

The more music one listens to the more exceptions to these generalizations one will encounter. It has already been pointed out that the principles of superposition and juxtaposition often appear in the same composition, although one may be more conspicuous than the other. In Example VII-2 unity is present throughout in meter and tempo, but the structure obviously is based on the juxtaposition of unity and variety in melody.

Of course, perceptions of unity and variety are partly subjective. Atonal and twelve-tone music, with its apparent emphasis on variety in most parameters, may sound "all the same" to the unaccustomed listener, while one who senses the logic in the same work may regard a performance of a popular tune as unbearably repetitious. In either case, one who strives consciously to locate the elements of unity in a work that at first seems to him cacophonous or disorganized, or the elements of variety in one that initially strikes him as monotonous, will learn to understand not only the music but himself, since the appreciation of any piece of music is a reflection of his own capacity to comprehend structures in sound and time. The aim of intelligent listening should be not just sensuous pleasure but the pleasure of discovery.

Actually, the comprehension of the structure of any piece of music is one of the most difficult aural feats of all. It is relatively easy to learn to identify textures, meters, or the instruments of the orchestra. But the perception of form requires the ability to *remember* specific patterns of pitches and rhythms, as well as timbres and textures, and to recognize them if they return, or realize that they do not. The trouble most of us have in acquiring this ability arises from the fact that in normal day-to-day living we need only remember things that can be named or described with words, while the sounds of music have no specific meanings that can be put into words. To listen to music intelligently is to learn to think in terms of abstract sound rather than concrete objects or actions.

STYLE

For the average person wishing to become a more intelligent listener the most readily attainable objective is simply an understanding of the varieties of *style* that exist in the music of contemporary Western culture. The *style* of any composition is the specific result of the composer's manipulations of all the parameters—melody, texture, timbre, rhythm, and form—of the system within which he elects to work. The details of his design are determined not only by his personal proclivities but also by his cultural background, his orientation with respect to traditions, the tendencies of his historical era, the technology of his culture, his nationality, or the genre to which his composition belongs.

Nearly anyone can recognize some of the more obvious differences among styles even though he may not be able to describe their causes. By this time, for instance, you surely can tell Ligeti (Example III-12) from Beethoven (V-10), or Oriental music (III-2, 3) from that of the American Indian (II-10). And who cannot distinguish popular from classical style, in general? Even if you cannot guess the name of the composer of a given piece you may suspect that it belongs to a particular style-period—Renaissance, Baroque, Classic, Romantic, or Impressionist, and so on. (For the chronological scope of these eras, see pp. 226-29.) Within each era there may be more or less clear distinctions among the styles of separate nations, or even of cities. The music of Haydn and Mozart, for example, is typical of the style of late-eighteenth-century Viennese classicism. The work in question may be in the style of the opera, the symphony, or the string quartet, etc.

THE PRACTICAL DETERMINANTS OF STYLE

Above all, the ways in which a composer handles his materials are governed by the use his composition is intended to serve and the function it is to fulfill. (When we speak of the uses of music we mean the objective situations in which musical performances may occur; when we speak of functions we refer to aspects of subjective human responses to music.) Every use implies a fairly definite set of stylistic requirements, limitations, and possibilities for innovation with which the composer must reckon if his music is to function properly. Consequently, no single style is apt to function equally well in all possible usages, much less for all possible listeners.

Consider a composition intended to be used as art—that is, for the purpose of pure, profound contemplation. If the composer elects to address himself to a specific type of audience, then the scale system he employs and the way he treats this and all the other parameters must be related somehow to the stylistic traditions to which his audience is accustomed. Otherwise his audience might not recognize his intention, and his music will fail to function as art.

The remainder of this book is about the basic uses and functions of music in contemporary Western culture. Our objectives will be to learn to distinguish among the styles associated with them, to seek to understand the limitations as well as the possibilities inherent in them, and to discover some ways of using that understanding as a basis for valuative judgments. It is extremely important to remember that no hierarchy of values *among* the several uses of music is to be inferred from the ensuing discussions. Of course, if the reader wishes, he is free to arrange such a hierarchy for himself, and he might even find herein ample arguments to justify his personal prejudices. *In any case, the music belonging within each usage may only be judged fairly according to the criteria implicit in that particular style.*

VIII

music as accomplishment:
vocal music in
the secondary schools

One of the most vigorous areas of musical activity in Western culture, but especially in the United States, from the standpoint of the numbers of participants, the overall size of the audience, and the total monetary investment, is that which takes place in the public and private secondary schools principally through the means of choruses, bands, and orchestras. Broadly speaking, a systematic exposure to music, whether as listeners or as performers, is considered essential to the adequate preparation of young men and women for a full and meaningful adult life. Education in music is designed primarily to awaken an appreciation of the aesthetic qualities of music used as art, and to stimulate active patronage of that aspect of our general musical life which is conducted chiefly by professional musicians in concerts, opera, and on records.

Their hypothetical relationships notwithstanding, professional art music differs substantially from secondary-school music because of the contrasting details of their respective usages. To be sure, both the participants and the listeners in school musical activity may secure a considerable degree of the purely aesthetic satisfaction one expects to derive from an artistic experience, but in the majority of secondary schools music functions principally as a skill. It is cultivated chiefly for the rewards which the mastery of its materials and techniques can provide the performers, as well as for the satisfaction and pride of parents, teachers, and the community at large. Thus school music and the art music of adult professional concert life differ not only in terms of the motivations and the abilities of most of the performers, in their financial foundations and in the makeup of their audiences, but also to a considerable extent in repertoire.

THE CULTURAL DETERMINANTS

To begin with, the association of music with the process of education means that the music should be for the most part "serious" in character, although popular music is also important. Further, it means that a wide variety of historical, national, and ethnic styles ideally should be included in the repertoire. Finally, an upper limit on musical capability and maturity is established by the fact that the participants in school music programs are limited to bona fide students who are usually excluded from the program automatically upon graduation.

Second, the school music program must satisfy the aesthetic, social, and psychological needs of the teen-age participant. Among these are the need for early, if not immediate, satisfaction of his aesthetic appetite once work on a piece of music is begun; a sense of identity and individuality in comparison with his musical peers; and evidence of achievement for the benefit of his adult relatives and friends. In other words, the music must be easy enough that most participants can master it in relatively few hours of rehearsal with limited training and talent, but difficult enough that a certain degree of achievement will be clearly evident to all parties concerned.

Third, because music in the schools is almost wholly supported by taxes, nearly every adult in the community has a vested interest in the music programs of the schools he supports. More importantly, all taxpayers are considered to be potential members of the audience for school music activities, especially as long as their sons and daughters are involved.

Fourth, at least a part of the school music program is usually designed to be of a particular service to the community, and thus ultimately to function as an object of overall civic pride. The maintenance of a marching band, a pep band, a jazz group or "stage band," and a "swing choir," and the presentation of entertainment for service clubs, church groups, civic occasions, and the like, are obligations for which the energies and talents of the students are sometimes extensively exploited.

On the other hand, adult professional concert life—as represented, say, by live or recorded performances by the New York Philharmonic symphony orchestra or the Metropolitan Opera Company—reflects an entirely different set of cultural circumstances. To begin with it is strictly commercial, relying for its existence upon private support, including sales of subscriptions and individual tickets as well as outright donations or endowments from wealthy individuals or foundations. Tax monies are drawn upon only in isolated instances, and then are normally granted and administered either directly by the federal government or through local or state arts councils.

More importantly, adult concert life is carried on by professionals who earn part or all of their livelihood as performers. Mere learners are not welcome among them. Finally, their performances are presented exclusively for the serious contemplation of more or less knowledgeable devotees of the art, who are motivated by aesthetic rather than personal considerations.

NON-PROFESSIONAL ACTIVITY AFTER HIGH SCHOOL

Musical life in the secondary schools is not entirely a closed circle, to be sure. For one thing, it supplies the initial impetus and background for the thousands of teen-agers who each year enter college and university music schools to begin studies aimed toward professional careers as teachers or performers. Thus practically all of the most talented, serious young musicians in the United States are concentrated on college campuses where they devote their full time for at least four academic seasons to the study and practice of the art of music under teachers, many of whom are or have been professional performers in their own right.

Although some of the music that collegiate musicians study is similar in style to the kind they previously performed in high school, the majority of it is identical with that which properly belongs to the repertoire of professional concert life. In addition, the presence of competent young performers under expert coaching, the availability of cost-free rehearsal time and facilities, and the handling of ticket sales, publicity, and concert management by the institution encourage the production of original compositions by both students and faculty. As a result, the college campus is not only the center of musical activity in its own locale and a conservator of time-honored musical traditions, but a potentially significant arena of creative inquiry and innovation from which the future of art music in this country may derive needed nourishment.

Indeed, it is debatable whether collegiate performances should be considered professional or amateur. Pre-professional musicians naturally strive to attain the highest possible degree of excellence, and this tendency often produces results of truly professional caliber. The Oberlin College Choir, for instance, is but one of many such organizations in this country whose skill and polish are of consummate quality, and who are frequently featured in presentations of major works for chorus and orchestra by professional orchestras. Likewise, the Eastman Wind Ensemble is among the most notable of the numerous college bands whose work is unsurpassed by the very best of the few professional bands in existence.

ADULT AMATEUR MUSICAL LIFE

Music education in the secondary schools also provides a foundation in music for the thousands of persons who each year join adult amateur groups. Such groups continue to flourish despite the attractions of the tremendous variety of other pastimes. The number of adults involved is small, of course, compared with the total number who have participated in school bands, choirs, or orchestras, for it consists mainly of those who as school musicians developed the most technical skill, reading ability, and appreciation of the pleasures of musical accomplishment.

In amateur civic musical organizations emphasis frequently is placed on the continued musical education of the performer, and professionals are usually engaged as conductors to ensure that musical goals will be consistently high. In nearly every instance, however, adult amateur musical activity is regarded primarily as a means of self-expression, as in the secondary schools. With respect to the types and styles of music performed, therefore, it is essentially conservative, and in this way is chiefly to be distinguished from wholly professional concert life.

Perhaps the greatest degree of carry-over from school to adult amateur musical activity, proportionately, is in the field of orchestral music. There are nearly 1,500 community orchestras in the United States at the present time, not to mention some 300 youth symphonies which are partly or entirely independent of schools, and more than 88 percent of their members play strictly for pleasure, without remuneration. Amateur chamber music societies also attract large numbers of string and wind players, as well as pianists.

The number of high school band musicians who continue to play after graduation is comparatively small. There are fewer than one-third as many adult amateur bands as orchestras, despite a three-to-one ratio of bands over orchestras in the schools, and many of these are active only during the summer months when some high school and college bandsmen are free to fill vacancies for which no adults are available. Adult amateur band repertoire is generally identical with that of the schools.

Adult amateur choral activity undoubtedly exceeds that of bands and orchestras combined, although there evidently are no reliable statistics available. In the direct line of the adult choral tradition of the nineteenth century are the "choral art" societies devoted to oratorios and the shorter choral classics of the past five centuries, excluding the music written expressly to satisfy the special psychological and aesthetic tendencies of teenagers. Even older but still very much alive is the tradition of barbershop music, stylized into a unique male quartet genre in the early twentieth century, and institutionalized in 1938 in the Society for the Preservation and Encouragement of Barber Shop Quartet Singing in America, Inc.

Then there are groups that concentrate on popular vocal music, and still others that devote a part or all of their energies to amateur music theatricals. Finally, and most numerous, there are countless volunteer church choirs whose motivation is Christian service rather than personal gratification, though the latter benefit is often present.

Except for the last-named, many of the foregoing are civic organizations which depend for their financial support upon membership fees, ticket sales for their few (from one to five) concerts each season, and nominal contributions from patrons; others are sponsored by industries as part of company recreation programs.

Opportunities for solo performances by adult amateurs are quite limited. Outside of incidental occasions for members of choirs, bands, or orchestras, they are provided by community or neighborhood music clubs in which the members perform for selective audiences.

Finally, music education in the secondary schools fulfills to a significant degree its primary aim of cultivating a potential audience for live, recorded, and televised performances of music of various kinds. Until the end of the eighteenth century the support of music was traditionally in the hands of an aristocracy; it was a matter of *noblesse oblige*. But that tradition has long since been supplanted, and what was once the obligation of a select few is now the privilege of all who choose to exercise it. To be sure, exposure alone, made possible by the convenience of the electronic media, may help to arouse serious interest in music among some, but the potency of formal education in music is undoubtedly the most effective agency for the propagation of musical patronage in contemporary American culture.

When patronage was the responsibility of an elite class, criticism was unnecessary and taste was largely a matter of fashion. But now that it is every citizen's prerogative, each listener must accept responsibility for making independent judgments, perhaps referring to professional critics and program annotators for information, but ultimately relying on his own knowledge and experience. And since musical activities in the secondary schools and among adult amateurs are so large a part of American culture, it is especially important that they be judged intelligently, too. Let us then briefly explore the backgrounds of the school music tradition and examine some examples of its typical repertoire.

VOCAL MUSIC IN THE SCHOOLS

Vocal music antedated instrumental music in the secondary schools, and it still involves by far the greatest number of participants in choirs, madrigal groups, glee clubs, and various other types of ensembles, yet it remains the remotest of all school musics from that of adult professional concert life.

To begin with, there exist only a few American professional choruses comparable to the great symphony orchestras in ability, technique, and polish, to which the high school graduate's musical allegiances might be shifted. Furthermore, with but one or two exceptions, even the choirs that have been widely acknowledged to be among the greatest in the world, led by such eminent conductors as Robert Shaw and Roger Wagner, have not been permanent organizations of long standing like the major orchestras. Only one or two professional choirs currently maintain regular seasons in residence in any city. Still, since their personnel are all highly skilled, the repertoire they present is often considerably more demanding both of the performer's abilities and the listener's capacities than is school choral music. We shall hear an example of this type of choral repertoire in Example XV-2.

From the colonial era until the end of the nineteenth century choral activity in America was carried on principally outside the public schools. Meanwhile, the aim of both public and private music education was the development of musical literacy, meaning the ability to sing at sight. Later, as choral activities were gradually expanded in the secondary schools, school choirs tended to follow the precedents established by the older tradition, singing part songs, anthems, and choruses from oratorios.

Part songs are characteristically homophonic in texture and strophic in structure. The melody is located in the uppermost voice, and there is a minimum of melodic or contrapuntal interest among the lower voices to distract attention from it. The soprano section of the chorus reaps all the laurels; the altos, tenors, and basses have to secure their rewards from the pleasure of serving in supporting or "harmonizing" roles. The Stephen Foster tune in Example III-6 is set in part-song style. A part song for male voices is called a *glee.*

Anthems (generally, choral songs of praise) and choruses from oratorios may be either homophonic or polyphonic in texture, and are usually through-composed—that is, different melodic material is used for each line or stanza of the text. In any case they are nearly always accompanied, with the voices *doubled* (duplicated) by the accompanying orchestra or keyboard instrument. Little skill is required of the singers other than the ability to sing in tune with the instruments.

Beginning shortly before 1910 a few college choirs began to cultivate what soon came to be known as the *a cappella* tradition—choral singing without the accompaniment of instruments. Among the founders of the new trend were F. Melius Christiansen of St. Olaf College in Northfield, Minnesota, and Peter Christian Lutkin, Dean of the Northwestern University School of Music in Evanston, Illinois. For a variety of reasons—some academic, some practical, but all ultimately aesthetic—they drew heavily upon the sacred and secular choral repertoire of the Renaissance, the music of the Russian Orthodox church, and the religious folk songs of the American Negro.

THE MOTET

The most important sacred vocal form during the Renaissance was the *motet,* a polyphonic composition for voices which originally was used in the worship services of the Roman Catholic church. The text of the motet usually is a portion of a passage of Scripture, the remainder of which was once sung to Gregorian chant, and consists of but a few phrases, or at most a few sentences, of Latin prose. Therefore the motet is free of the regularity of phrase-lengths and the symmetry that would be imposed by rhymed metrical poetry. Each line of the text is set to new melodic material.

Unity is contributed by the homogeneous vocal sonority which maintains a mood of restrained expressiveness throughout. Rhythmically, the motet proceeds with a steady underlying pulse which is manifested by accented syllables and occasionally by delicate dissonances called *suspensions.* The polyphonic texture of three, four, or five voices, as the case may be, also unifies the structure. Usually the polyphony is imitative, and the independence of the respective voices is clearly apparent, as in the motet *Vineam meam* by Giovanni Pierluigi da Palestrina (VIII-1). The imitative texture *VIII-1* also permits the successive sections of the piece to be interlocked, thus adding to the coherence of the design. When every syllable of the text is sung simultaneously in all voices the homorhythmic result may resemble homophonic texture, as in a hymn, but even then all voices usually are equal in melodic interest. Sometimes variety will be introduced by alternating imitative and homorhythmic sections.

```
S                        Vi------- ne-- am   me-----am non cu--sto-- di----------------------
A        Vi ------ne-am me-------am non cu-sto-di---------vi, non cu------------sto-di--
T₁                                          Vi--------ne- am   me-am non cu--sto-
T₂  Vi-ne-am me-----am non cu-- sto-- di------vi,
B
```

```
S    -vi, . . . . . vi-ne-am me---am,              vi-----ne---- am me-am non cu-
A    --------------------------vi                      vi-- ne--am  me-
T₁   -di-vi, . . . . . . . . . . .  non . . . . . . . . . . . . . cu-------sto-di---vi.
T₂                        vi-ne--am  me-----am non cu-sto-di---vi,
B              Vi----ne-am me---am non cu-sto-di---------vi,          vi---ne-
```

```
S    -sto- di-------------------- vi. . . . . . . . . .         In----- di-ca mi-hi   quem
A    ------am non cu- sto---di-------------vi.   In-----di-ca mi---------hi,      quem
T₁                          In--- di--ca   mi------------------hi,      quem
T₂   non cu-------------------sto-di-------- vi.   In-----di-ca  mi---------hi,
B    -am me-------am non cu-sto-di-----vi.   In----- di-ca  mi---------hi,
```

```
S    di-li-git a-ni-ma me----------------------a
A    di-li-git a-ni-ma . . . . . me-a, . . . .        in-----di-ca mi-hi, quem di- . . .
T₁   di-li-git a-ni-ma me--a, . . . . .              in-----di-ca mi-hi, quem di- . . .
T₂                  in----di--ca  mi-----------hi . . . . . . quem . . . . di- . . .
B                  in-------di--ca mi---------hi,quem . . . . di- . . .
```

FIGURE 8   The beginning of the Latin text to Palestrina's motet, *Vineam meam non custodivi* (Example VIII-1), presented so as to help the listener follow the independent voices of the polyphonic texture. The initials at left stand for Soprano, Alto, First Tenor, Second Tenor, and Bass. In translation the entire text, which is from the biblical *Song of Solomon* (1:6-7), is as follows: "Mine own vineyards have I not kept. Tell me, O thou whom my soul loveth, where thou feedest, where thou resteth at noon: for why should I be as one that turneth aside by the flocks of thy companions."

In the modal polyphony of the Renaissance, chords were merely the coincidental by-products of simultaneous events in the horizontal fabric, and they did not function independently so as to lead away from a tonal center and back again, or to modulate to a different tonal center, as in the major/minor system. The absence of variety in this respect, together with the emphasis on unity in texture, timbre, meter, tempo, and dynamics, with variety present chiefly in text and melodic material, tilts the balance of the two forces in the direction of unity, and has the effect of limiting the duration of most motets to no more than three or four minutes.

The twentieth-century college choral conductors who first explored the resources of the Renaissance motet assumed on the strength of spurious nineteenth-century authority that the motet had always been performed by voices alone. It has since been determined that if conditions demanded it the voices were doubled by instruments to assure accuracy of intonation, but historical truths have scarcely influenced the subsequent cultivation of the new tradition in the schools. Motets by Jacob Arcadelt, Orlando di Lasso, Tomás Luis da Victoria, Heinrich Isaac, Cristóbal de Morales, Thomas Tallis, William Byrd, and above all Giovanni Pierluigi da Palestrina—men whose very names had been all but forgotten outside the church for more than two hundred years—have been edited and published in modern notation with instructions that they are to be performed a cappella.

MADRIGALS

It is more difficult to make brief generalizations about Renaissance secular music than about the motet, for without the conservative influence of the church, the secular genres tended to develop from decade to decade and from country to country according to strictly musical and literary impulses. The nomenclature was as varied as the styles—*canzonetta, balletto, villanella,* and *madrigal*—though the term *madrigal* is now commonly applied to all of them indiscriminately.

The leaders of the early twentieth-century college choral tradition drew upon such examples of the madrigal as exhibited characteristics comparable to those of the motet: polyphonic texture, different music for each line of text, brevity, and a cappella performance. They also found an attractive feature in the *word painting* employed in many such works, a technique whereby natural sounds, physical movements, or specific sentiments were represented either literally or analogously in the music. In addition they revived some of the types containing dance-like rhythms, and some with refrains. Above all, the fragile sensuous beauty of the music itself, for which each performer—ideally only one or two to a part—felt himself to share an equal responsibility, was sufficient to assure lasting interest in madrigals among both college and high school musicians.

A typical example is "Hark, all ye lovely saints above," by Thomas

Weelkes (VIII-2). This is properly called a balletto because of the strophic structure, the division of the five-line stanza into two repeated sections, and the *fa-la* refrains:

> Hark, all ye lovely saints above,
> Diana hath agreed with Love
> His fiery weapon to remove.
>   Fa, la, la, ...
> Do you not see how they agree?
> Then cease, fair ladies; why weep ye?
>   Fa, la, la, ...
>
> See, see, your mistress bids you cease,
> And welcome Love, with love's increase;
> Diana hath procured your peace.
>   Fa, la, la, ...
> Cupid hath sworn his bow forlorn
> To break and burn, ere ladies mourn.
>   Fa, la, la, ...

Consistent with the Renaissance composers' tendency to permit the natural accentuation of the words to determine the flow of the music, the piece is strongly syncopated over a steady pulse, producing a more lively effect than the limping iambic tetrameter of the poem would suggest. The rather intricate polyrhythmic counterpoint of the *fa-la* refrains balances the homorhythmic, almost homophonic, texture of the verses with which they are juxtaposed, resulting in a highly unified symmetrical structure that might be graphed *A-B-C-B,* or *a-b-c-R-d-e-R.* Notice, in the last line of each stanza, the appropriately plaintive mood of the music, created by the use of relatively longer note values in poignant suspensions.

RUSSIAN CHURCH MUSIC

The music of the Russian Orthodox church appealed to the founders of the modern a cappella tradition largely because of the massiveness of its sonorities. The use of musical instruments had always been absolutely prohibited in the Russian church, and so a genuine and vigorous a cappella music had been developed. During the nineteenth century some of the best Russian composers—including Sergey (Sir-gáy) Rachmaninoff, Alexander Gretchaninov, and Peter Tchaikovsky—contributed to the liturgical repertoire. They composed quasi-polyphonic pieces which featured *voicings,* or spacings of notes, of crucial chords in order to take advantage of the depth and fullness produced by the overtone series in a spacious cathedral. The results were dense, towering, resonant sonorities quite in contrast with the restrained and transparent style of the Renaissance motet and madrigal.

Moreover, Russian church music, which had been infused with some of the elements of contemporary folk music and which still remained slightly influenced by ancient ecclesiastical chant styles, represented a mysterious culture at the periphery of Western civilization, whose very exoticism was an important aspect of its appeal to American musicians and students.

A favorite among American school and church choirs for many years has been a beautiful short anthem by the Russian composer Paul Tschesno- *VIII-3* koff (VIII-3). In the first half the text—"Salvation is created in [the] midst of the earth, O our God"—is set to a flowing hymn-like melody in a homophonic texture of rich sonorities (notice the resonance of the basses), which begins at a low register and low dynamic level, rises to a high register at a fortissimo, and returns again to the lower register (and to the opening tonal center), pianissimo. For the second half of the piece the same music is repeated to the word "Alleluia," which is Latin for *Hallelujah,* a contraction of the Hebrew expression meaning "Praise ye the Lord." Viewing the work as a whole, it is easy to recognize the powerful unifying effect of the two identical, symmetrical arches of sound, balanced by variety in the text.

NEGRO "SPIRITUALS"

At the turn of this century, the traditional religious music of the American Negro was fully as exotic an idiom to American musicians and laymen alike as the music of the Russian church, or even of the Renaissance. Beginning as early as 1872, however, when the Jubilee Singers of Fisk University were catapulted into fame at the World Peace Jubilee in Boston, and continuing with the establishment of choirs at other Negro colleges like Tuskegee and Hampton, white Americans gradually became acquainted with the so-called "spiritual."

The songs the Negro choirs sang had originated as collective, unwritten expressions of the religious fervor of their people and not as products of individual composers. They were a singer's music more than a listener's. Unrehearsed and heard in the context of the worship service, a given spiritual was apt to sound different each time it was sung; only the qualities of spontaneity and rhythmic vitality were immutable. Therefore the black college groups had to devise performances which would meet some of the standards that musically educated white listeners might be expected to apply: "correct" harmonizations; balanced and blended choral sonori-

FIGURE 9 The Advanced A Cappella Choir, Kenwood High School, Chicago, conducted by Lena McLin. The principal aim of the choral program at Kenwood is to develop participants into musically intelligent, inquisitive, and self-confident individuals. Members are also encouraged to explore their own potentials for musical creativity. Courtesy, Kenwood High School.

ties in at least four parts; uniform attacks and releases; clear dynamic contrasts; and uniformity of rhythmic interpretation. Among the most important musicians who eventually supplied them with written arrangements of the genre were John W. Work, Sr. and John W. Work, Jr., Harry T. Burleigh, Clarence Cameron White, and R. Nathaniel Dett. These men, all Negroes, succeeded in capturing the essential stylistic elements of the most memorable songs of their race.

VIII-4   All of the classic examples of arranged spirituals—such as Burleigh's "Were You There," Dett's "Listen to the Lambs," and William L. Dawson's "Ain'a that Good News" (VIII-4)—display one or more of several typical characteristics: interesting melodies, sometimes containing inflections later to be identified with the blues; exciting rhythms, including simple but insistent syncopations; rousing refrains alternating with narrative or homiletic verses, often of but one line, suggesting the ancient call-

and-response pattern. Study the recorded example carefully and try to distinguish the unifying factors from those that contribute variety.

Since the melodic and rhythmic qualities of the spirituals arose partly from the close relationships of words and music, the arrangers invariably indicated that a somewhat stylized Negro dialect should be used by the singers. When white choirs began to assimilate the published arrangements of the spirituals into their own repertoires, their enthusiasm for the purely aesthetic appeal of the music was doubtless enhanced by the function of the spirituals as a means of identifying with the black race. The performance of Negro music by whites did not necessarily lead to racial tolerance and it was no substitute at all for civil rights, but it was a potential path to a unique area of understanding that was open only to singers.

CHORAL MUSIC FOR THE SCHOOLS

Steadily over the past fifty years or so, owing partly to the emphasis on the study of music history in the training of musicians and music teachers, more and more long-forgotten choral works—especially from the great eras of polyphony, the Renaissance and the baroque—have been unearthed and republished in more or less authoritative editions. Also, an increasingly widespread interest in folklore and ethnomusicology has brought to light a rich store of the indigenous musics of virtually all Western cultures, and thousands of such songs have been arranged for choral performance. In turn, the a cappella tradition has assumed a general educational value which, in theory at least, sometimes supersedes purely aesthetic values: as a historical document, a motet or a folk song can serve as an introduction of the singer to other times, places, and peoples.

Beginning late in the 1920s the a cappella choral tradition began to be cultivated in the secondary schools as well as in the colleges. At the same time the repertoire borrowed from other traditions was being supplemented by composers who devoted themselves mainly to the tailoring of compositions especially for school choirs. These men have met the growing demand for music that would not only embody the same strengths as the choral classics but also employ texts meaningful to modern youth. Because they must be both willing and able to subordinate their purely creative impulses to the exigencies of the school situation, their names will seldom be found in the programs of professional adult choirs, much less on symphony orchestra or opera programs.

The least of these journeymen have merely parodied the best features of the classic models, but the best have produced real masterpieces—works that satisfy all the basic requirements of the genre but are original as well as practical: they are genuine works of art, worthy of pure contemplation, even though they are rarely heard outside the high school auditorium.

VIII-5   A classic of the genre is Randall Thompson's "Alleluia" (VIII-5), written in 1940 for the opening of the Berkshire Music Center, an important summer school of music near Lenox, Massachusetts. The sensuous beauty of the homogeneous vocal sonority, the fluency of the Renaissance-like polyphony, and the simplicity of the basic melodic material belie the intricacy and ingenuity of the work's structural cohesiveness.

The piece obviously is unified by its one-word text, though at the same time variety is introduced through the treatment of the word: the diminutive motif to which it is set at the opening is subjected to permutations and extensions of pitch and rhythm which reveal it in various accentual patterns—Ál-le-lú-ia, Al-lé-lu-iá, Al-le-lú-ia, and Al-le-lu-ía. The music is also propelled forward by means of simple repetitions as well as by the use of *sequences* (repetitions of melodic motifs at successively higher or lower pitch levels) which bring about modulations to new tonal centers.

As an aid to the aural comprehension of the ways in which unity and variety are balanced, you may study the following diagram while listening to the recording. A clock or watch with a sweep-second hand will facilitate location of the features shown. The letters below the line indicate similarities and contrasts among the sections of the piece with respect to melodic and rhythmic material. You will notice that unity and variety are juxtaposed for somewhat more than half the work, and that the piece ends with new material except for the repeated-note statement of the word by the altos just before the "Amen," which serves as a significant unifier since the same monotonic pattern has been heard frequently from the very first.

The straight lines identify the passages in which a tonal center is clearly established; the wavy lines represent passages of relative instability. Major keys are indicated by capital letters above the line, minor keys by small letters. The gradual increase in tension, which is heightened by an acceleration in tempo and an overall rise in tessitura, culminates in a climax which strongly emphasizes the tonal center of the piece, and makes it symmetrical in this parameter.

In general, all choral works of whatever era or style which are most suitable for use by school choirs share four fundamental characteristics:

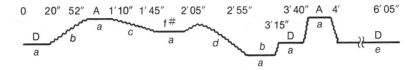

FIGURE 10   Diagram of Randall Thompson's "Alleluia."

1) Technically, they are well within the capacities of young singers. The parts move mostly in conjunct lines of limited range in the most comfortable registers of the respective voices. Phrases are usually short, with more or less symmetrical contours; they are seldom very chromatic and almost never atonal, for atonal music naturally contains many consecutive dissonant intervals in disjunct lines that are too difficult for the inexperienced or incompetent singer to recognize aurally, and thus to sing. Rhythmic features are comparatively simple and often stress recurrent rhythmic motifs. Such works contain some challenges in one or more respects, to be sure, but their severest difficulties can be overcome by an expert conductor with a patient choir in but a few hours of rehearsal.

2) At the same time, the best choral music for school use contains a maximum of interest for each singer; no section is relegated permanently to a subordinate position in the total scheme. Every part contains some memorable melodic or rhythmic moments or contributes pitches that are essential to the harmonic or contrapuntal fabric. The emphasis is upon sonorous effects rather than musical invention or development. The most satisfying sonorous and rhythmic devices encourage feelings of unity and cooperation among the performers.

3) School choral works are short, averaging from three to four minutes in overall duration. This is a convenience in that it permits the teacher to introduce sufficient variety into his rehearsal periods—which seldom exceed one hour—to correspond with the relatively short attention span of the ordinary participant. Furthermore, it permits sufficient variety in programming to assure sustained audience interest in a concert of from sixty to ninety minutes in length.

4) The text of a typical example of good school choral music will contain but a few fairly simple ideas which, if their significance is not primarily historical, will appeal to the adolescent's feelings about religion, morality, nature, love, friendship, beauty, and so on.

VOCAL SOLO PERFORMANCE

The technical facility and knowledge that a high school musician relies upon in chorus, band, or orchestra rehearsals and performances is most often acquired through private study which is ancillary to the principal activities of the organization, and which is carried on mainly outside of school hours.

The repertoire of the teen-age student of singing may include some seventeenth- and eighteenth-century songs in Italian, such as "Tu lo sai," by Torelli; some German songs usually referred to by the German word for song, *lied* (plural, *lieder*), from the early romantic era, such as Schubert's "Der Lindenbaum"; one or more of the less demanding operatic arias like "Voi che sapete" from Mozart's *The Marriage of Figaro;* one or two excerpts from an oratorio such as Handel's *Messiah* or Mendelssohn's *Elijah;* and occasionally an easy contemporary art song like Samuel Barber's "Sure on this Shining Night." Any one of these might be found on a professional artist's program in an urban recital hall, as well as in a college campus auditorium.

The rate of progress in voice training depends in large part upon the rate of physiological growth of the individual. Normally one does not commence intensive development of the voice until after puberty. Then, a female voice may mature with respect to range, resonance, and control early in the twenties, while a male voice might not attain an equivalent maturity until several years later. Meanwhile, during the teens, a certain amount of effort may be devoted to the cultivation of the student's personality as it affects his stage presence or ability to "put a song across," and in this connection a certain amount of folk, popular, or semi-classical music may be studied in which purely musical factors are subordinated to considerations of the mood or style or characterization implied in the text.

The differences between spoken diction and sung diction are considerable in English, with its many varieties of vowel sounds, its fluid diphthongs and eloquent consonants. This fact, together with the emotional involvement into which the singer may be drawn by a text in his own language, may interfere with the objective study and practice of tone quality or "voice production" in the abstract. Therefore the Italian and German songs are often sung in their original languages, the word-sounds being learned by rote. Italian is considered good for beginning voice study since the rules for its pronunciation are comparatively few and easy to remember.

The most suitable songs for teen-age voice students are rather tuneful and consequently easy to memorize, a feature which permits the student and the teacher to concentrate on other more important pedagogical matters; the melodic phrases are mostly diatonic, limited in range, and short enough to be sung comfortably by singers whose breath capacity and control may be limited for various reasons. Finally, the accompaniments are simple enough that they can be played by any competent student pianist.

IX

music as accomplishment: instrumental music in the secondary schools

Although the wind-instrument *band** has a long and complicated history reaching back into the fifteenth century and beyond, the most important type in modern times has been the military band. The fundamental aspects of its uses and functions have determined the characteristics of the sound and the repertoire of the contemporary school band.

THE WIND BAND: HISTORICAL DETERMINANTS

The military band developed out of a specific need for music in outdoor settings to give signals, to enhance public ceremonies, and to arouse martial spirits. The most appropriate instruments were naturally those which could be heard most clearly over the other sounds in the immediate environment, such as the noises of crowds, marchers, horses, and so forth. Lyrical violins, eloquent violas and cellos, and mellow flutes were obviously much less effective out-of-doors than trumpets, trombones, clarinets, cymbals, and drums. During the late nineteenth and early twentieth centuries, in fact, numerous instruments were designed expressly for the marching band, such as the saxophone, the baritone horn, and the sousaphone. The basic requirements of outdoor music remain implicit in one function of the school band—performing at civic ceremonies and school events like parades and athletic events.

---

* More loosely, the word *band* is also used to denote any unusual combination of wind and percussion instruments, as in *rock band, jazz band.* In the seventeenth century it was even applied to large ensembles of stringed instruments.

The primary physical characteristic required of band instruments was portability: they had to be playable while the player himself was marching. All the stringed instruments are portable, to be sure, but aside from the fact that their sounds are too subdued for them to work well in the open air, they are extremely sensitive to changes in temperature and humidity. Also, the necessity for continuous, delicate control of the pressure of the bow on the string makes it extremely difficult to play a violin or viola while walking; a cello can be played only while seated; a double bass must be rested on the floor or ground.

The fact that the members of a military band are soldiers first and musicians second has always meant the instrumentation is liable to change from time to time. Thus, while a composer of symphonic or operatic music might safely assume that the conductor of an orchestra would see to it that a basic standard instrumentation was maintained in the organization at all times, or that specific additional instruments might be secured for a given performance, the composer of music for the band has had to make allowances for the vicissitudes of military life.

Since the purpose of military band music was to unify the steps of many marchers, the percussion section had to be at least as prominent in the overall sonority as the wind instruments, and it had to remain consistently so throughout an entire composition. The percussion section of the orchestra is employed mainly for its coloristic qualities, but in the military band the bass drum, snare drum, and cymbals serve an essentially extra-musical purpose.

All the conditions enumerated so far—loudness, portability of instruments, flexibility in instrumentation, and clarity of meter and melody—affected the structure and the melodic style of the music written for, or adaptable to, the band. The most effective, practical melodies would be those consisting of phrases short enough that they could easily be played on one breath while marching. Melodies lying within a limited range in the middle or high register could be clearly heard outdoors over the sound of the percussion instruments, the prominence of which further assured that the tunes would be in duple meter (2/4 or 6/8) in a lively tempo, with little embellishment to obscure their contours and with only simple alternations between staccato and legato to introduce variety in type of line. In fact, all subtle nuances of color and dynamics that would be unnoticeable in the outdoor setting or unappreciated by an undiscriminating audience were avoided. Long, intricate, asymmetrical designs were clearly out of place in military music.

Furthermore, development—the exploration of the organic potential of a given theme, which was the focal point of the sonata—was ill-suited to compositions intended to be heard in passing. One must hear the entire five-to-ten minute movement of a work in sonata form in the sheltered environment of a concert hall in order to follow the developmental process. On the other hand, an entire march must be totally perceivable in the time it might take a marching band to pass into and out of audible range —perhaps three minutes. Therefore, the structure of the march relies almost entirely upon continuous melodic interest with but one or two excursions into closely related keys.

THE BAND'S MUSIC

Throughout the seventeenth and eighteenth centuries many of the major European composers like Lully and Handel wrote marches for the wind band. After the revolutionary era of the late eighteenth century the band gained importance as a popular medium, calling forth a steadily increasing amount of such music. The trend culminated late in the nineteenth century in the works of the "March King," John Philip Sousa. His inimitable pieces still represent the epitome of concise idiomatic writing for the band: memorable tunes set off against interesting countermelodies and catchy embellishments in the other parts. There is no padding; every note counts.*

Sousa's universally popular "Stars and Stripes Forever" displays all the typical features of his marches (see Preface). After a 4-measure introduction (two beats to the measure—*left*-right!) a 16-measure tune is played and repeated once, followed by another repeated 16-measure tune. Next we hear a 32-measure tune called a *trio,* in a three-part texture consisting of a legato line in the middle register accompanied by a staccato bass part emphasizing the downbeat of every measure, and trumpet flourishes above. A 24-measure interlude or *break* follows (known among bandsmen as the "dogfight" of a march), and the melody of the trio reappears with a sprightly countermelody from the piccolos. The interlude and trio are heard once more, with the latter now further decorated by a countermelody from the trombones.

The structure is marked by continuous changes in timbre and dynamics as well as melodic material; it even ends in a different key than the one in which it began. Nevertheless the repetitions of melodies that seem to

---

* Sousa also introduced the *sousaphone,* a portable tuba designed so as to project its sound forward rather than upward, thus substantially reinforcing the bass line of the ensemble.

complement one another in style and spirit do have the effect of suggesting unity in the piece as a whole. Furthermore, the gradual buildup of energy and interest toward the final grand statement of the trio tune makes the cumulative variety and growth seem completely logical.

The military band fulfilled an indispensable function on the American frontier in the nineteenth century, providing music for social dancing and casual listening as well as meeting its official obligations. The band's usual repertoire thus included the *waltz* (a Viennese dance that originated in the Austrian peasant Ländler), the *quadrille* (a type of square dance), and the *polka* (a Bohemian dance in quick duple meter). Bands also played medleys of current popular songs, as well as transcriptions of arias and overtures from familiar operas by Bellini, Rossini, Verdi, and others, all featuring pretty melodies and simple rhythmical accompaniments. In transcribing from the orchestral medium to the band, the violin and viola parts were given to the high woodwinds (clarinets, flutes, alto saxophones), and the cello parts to low woodwinds and the mellower brasses (trombones, baritone horns, euphoniums).

THE CONCERT BAND

Throughout the nineteenth century the wind band and the symphony orchestra remained essentially separate in terms of functions and audiences, and consequently in terms of repertoire. The orchestra developed a relatively elite following while the band played to the masses. Thus while we now look to the symphonic tradition of the romantic era for many of the acknowledged masterpieces of orchestral art music, there is virtually nothing of the kind from that period in the literature for the band. A few works for band were written by several of the leading composers of orchestral music, like Mendelssohn, Weber, and Berlioz, but they were either beyond the capabilities of most military bands, and beyond the tastes of the bands' audiences, or else not as idiomatic and effective as works of lesser pretensions. Therefore they were infrequently played and rarely imitated. However, during the latter part of the century, as men like Sousa and Patrick Gilmore slowly transformed the military marching band into the concert band, a taste began to emerge for original wind music of serious artistic value to supplement the transcriptions from orchestral literature.

The rich twentieth-century tradition of concert band music was initiated by men like the English composer Gustav Holst and continued by other symphonic composers of similar stature including Ralph Vaughan Wil-

liams, Percy Grainger, Paul Hindemith, Darius Milhaud, and Aaron Copland. In his First Suite for Band (IX-1), composed in 1909, Holst showed
that it was possible to give symphonic substance to band music while ex-
ploiting the unique coloristic capacities of the wind ensemble, without
stooping to the mere stringing together of pretty tunes as in the pot-
pourris.

IX-1

The first movement of the Suite is entitled Chaconne, but it has all the
characteristics of the form customarily labeled passacaglia (see above, p.
52). It is a variation form based on an 8-measure theme in triple meter
which is repeated without interruption a total of sixteen times. Variety is
introduced through continual changes in timbre and dynamics and by
using contrapuntal accompaniments of contrasting melodic or rhythmic
identity. The theme itself is also subjected to slight modifications, leading
to a suggestion of *A-B-A* structure in that parameter alone. The sixth
time, for instance, it is played in very short note values. In the tenth and
eleventh statements—just after the alto saxophone plays it—the theme is
heard upside down, with a resulting shift from major to minor. The next
statement is actually in the Phrygian mode, while the thirteenth returns
to the central tonality of E-flat major. Only the rhythm of the theme remains unchanged until the final statement, in which both the pitch and
the rhythm of the theme are altered slightly, though with a highly dramatic effect. Compare this analysis with the diagram on p. 53, and try
to draw your own graph showing how unity and variety are balanced in
Holst's work.

THE SCHOOL BAND

After about 1920 dance bands in night clubs began to displace both
military and professional bands as entertainers, leaving a vacuum in the
bands' traditional roles and contributing to the virtual disappearance of
those organizations from the mainstream of our musical life. Simultaneously the development of bands commenced in the secondary schools,
where educational goals reunited the several functions the band was traditionally fitted to serve—entertainment, marching, and concert performance. Moreover, in the thirties and forties the marching band became a
show-group as well, and the football half time exhibition occasionally
proved to be more interesting than the sporting event it was intended to
enhance.

The repertoire of the school band may include some Sousa marches and

FIGURE 11   The Hersey High School Band in a moving formation during a half time show at a football game. Obviously, the music must have prominent melodic and rhythmic features in order for the performers to stay in step with one another. Careful preliminary planning followed by many hours of rigorous practice is required for the production of such spectacles. Courtesy of Donald Caneva, Director of Bands, John Hersey High School, Arlington Heights, Illinois.

a few other classics from the "golden age" of the military and professional bands, but the bulk of it has been supplied by composers who, like their counterparts in the field of school choral music, are capable of working comfortably and efficiently within the limitations of the genre. The best of the literature, represented by the works of men like Paul Creston, Peter Mennin, H. Owen Reed, William Latham, Norman Dello Joio, Warren Benson, Vincent Persichetti, and Clifton Williams, have drawn upon the models supplied by Holst and the other pioneers in symphonic band music, modified by the peculiar requirements of adolescent performers and their audiences.

Forms are generally clear-cut and often symmetrical with the respective sections of the structure set apart from one another by distinct harmonic cadences. The notes of crucial chords are often distributed among the various choirs of instruments so as to achieve maximum brilliance and variety of color. Extreme chromaticism and atonality are avoided, and tonal centers are stable, unthreatened by frequent or distant modulations. Every part contains the highest possible degree of rhythmic and melodic interest consistent with the capabilities of the player who has perhaps had but a few years' experience. Only moderate demands are made with respect to technical factors such as complicated fingerings, rapid passages or runs, wide skips, or awkward combinations of intervals.

IX-2   A notable example of contemporary school concert band music is the *Incantation and Dance* by John Barnes Chance, written for the Greensboro, North Carolina Senior High School Band (IX-2). The work opens with a slow flowing melody, seemingly in free rhythm, which consists of phrases that gradually grow in range and length. This is heard first in the musky low register of the flutes, and then in the low woodwinds and brass under an ostinato countermelody. The theme is begun again a whole step higher, but is presently interrupted by the sound of *maracas* (dry gourds containing seeds which usually are shaken, but here are swirled to produce a continuous hissing effect).

Immediately the *claves* (pron. kláh-vays; hardwood sticks struck together with a penetrating click) introduce a fast syncopated pattern destined to become the framework of a melodic theme. This is followed by another pattern on the *gourd* or *guiro* (pron. gweé-roh; a notched gourd scraped with a stick) and another on the *tambourine* (a small hand-held drum with metal discs or "jingles" in its frame). Soon the *timbales* (or *tom-toms*) and *timpani* (or *kettledrums*) are added, and still later the *whip* (actually two flat pieces of wood slapped together). All this intricate rhythmic polyphony is carried on over a long sustained chord or pedal point.

Meanwhile a terse melodic figure is heard in the dry, hollow sound of the *temple blocks* (slotted spheres of wood struck with hard mallets). After a forceful pronouncement by the trombones the same figure is taken up and expanded successively by several combinations of instruments over a syncopated accompaniment. A sudden change in density and a gradual dissipation of the momentum of the steady underlying pulse provides a brief contrasting interlude. The percussion episode reappears once more with its temple block figure, which is subsequently developed in a more elaborate manner than before. Notice how energy is intensified and climaxes built by increases in rhythmic activity, density, and volume.

In summary, within the slow *Incantation* unity and variety are super-

FIGURE 12   Percussion instruments heard in *Incantation and Dance* by John Barnes Chance. (Example IX-2): *a.* maracas, *b.* claves, *c.* guiro, *d.* tambourine, *e.* timbales, *f.* timpani, *g.* whip, *h.* temple blocks. Courtesy Ludwig Industries.

posed: The unifying effect of the repeated melody is slightly exceeded by variety in timbre, density, and tonal center. In the fast *Dance* unity and variety are juxtaposed within melody and tempo, and partly in rhythm and timbre, but there are so many exciting contrasts in the latter two parameters that the listener may initially be unaware that the structure is roughly symmetrical, or *A-B-A*.

THE SCHOOL ORCHESTRA

The school orchestra brings its participants as well as its audiences closer to the realm of adult professional musical life than either the chorus or the band. This is because, to begin with, most of its material belongs to the historical mainstream of orchestral art music. A concert by a good high school orchestra might include a symphony by Beethoven (Ex. V-10), Haydn (VII-1), or Mozart (III-10), and a movement or two from Mussorgsky's *Pictures at an Exhibition* (V-2), or Virgil Thomson's suite from *The River,* any of which might also be found in the repertoire of a professional symphony orchestra, and all of which are available in one or more commercial recorded versions.

School orchestral repertoire shares with school choral and band music the requirement that it be easy enough for relatively inexperienced performers to execute, but this is mitigated for the winds by the fact that since no more than two of each of the principal woodwind and brass instruments are usually called for, only the most competent players in the school need be used.

In adult professional concert life there are far more full-time professional opportunities for string players than for wind players or singers, though more high school students take part in the latter activities. Stringed instruments now appear in some of the most insignificant rock recordings, and they are evidently indispensable to background music of almost every kind. Nevertheless, there are only about 7,000 school orchestras in the United States as against 20,000 school marching and concert bands, plus thousands of "stage bands," and perhaps three or four times as many choruses as all bands put together.

INSTRUMENTAL SOLO MUSIC

The music the student pianist plays belongs, like that of the vocalist, to the repertoire that is apt to be found on professional artists' recitals: Bach *inventions* (continuously unfolding contrapuntal pieces in two or three parts), Beethoven and Schubert sonatas, Chopin waltzes, and perhaps pieces by Debussy, Kabalevsky, or Bartók. Since the pianist may, and usually does, begin his study earlier than the singer, at the age of six or eight years, by the end of his high school career he may be able to play music that is comparatively difficult. Much of it may in fact be chosen chiefly for its pedagogical value and may be played and listened to not only for purely musical enjoyment but also to display a certain level of technical achievement. On the other hand, the young pianist sometimes spends a considerable amount of his time learning to sight-read and accompanying singers and instrumentalists, so his total repertoire may be no larger than theirs.

After high school even pianists of superior talent have only limited opportunities for further activity. Professional positions in the fields of performance and accompanying are very few in number, and the competition for them is severe. Amateur pianists may occasionally perform for their families and friends in impromptu situations, and may accompany church choirs or civic choirs, and sometimes amateur soloists. In addition, many amateurs as well as professionals teach piano privately. This is an extremely important occupation and a fairly remunerative one in some places, for beyond the personal pleasure a student may ultimately obtain, some facility on the piano is considered fundamental to almost all other advanced musical studies, and is a prerequisite for graduation from nearly every college and university music school in the United States.

Other student instrumentalists may, like pianists, begin private lessons at an early age, physiological factors permitting, but their repertoires are even more limited since the primary aim of study is to increase basic technical skills as rapidly as possible, making participation in the school band or orchestra commensurately more rewarding. The instrumentalist will normally learn no more than half a dozen important pieces in his entire course of study, and although these may be works of art by major composers they are rarely heard outside of secondary-school music festivals, or recitals by faculty members or students on college campuses.

High school instrumentalists are often able to play music far more difficult than that which singers of comparable talent and training can handle. One reason is that although an instrumentalist definitely must develop a high degree of aural acuity in order to play in tune, the playing of correct notes is partly a matter of manual dexterity. Singers, on the other hand, must strive to think in terms of abstract, non-denotative sounds; thus the high regard among them for the individual with the ability to remember specific pitches, sometimes referred to as "relative pitch."

STANDARDS OF JUDGMENT

The composer of music for use in the secondary schools faces exactly the same fundamental challenge as the composer of art music for the professional concert hall—to extend a sonorous design in time while maintaining a delicate balance between unity and variety. Yet we may conclude from the foregoing discussion that since the details of the other aspects of school musical life are unique and are not found in adult professional concert life, performances in each area must often be judged according to separate criteria for the sake of honesty and fairness.

For instance, the professional should be fully capable of executing acceptably any piece of music, no matter how difficult. Precision of intonation, rhythmic accuracy, maturity and refinement of instrumental or vocal tone, and control in the handling of the most minute nuances of a composition are all to be looked for in a professional performance. Moreover, the individual's personal involvement, while it may indeed be profound and sincere, is of little direct import.

On the other hand, the school or adult amateur performance may be assessed partly in terms of the intensity and enthusiasm displayed, for this may be taken to reflect the extent of the participants' self-satisfaction; the nonprofessional often makes up in spirit for some of his technical inadequacies. Most important of all, performances by nonprofessionals should be judged on the basis of the degree to which the individual or the group exhibits the best features of music offering challenges commensurate with the abilities of the performers.

X

music and the

human environment

One of the most common uses of music in contemporary Western civilization is as background to random human activity in order to qualify space and time and to humanize alien environments. This unique genre, sometimes called *mood music,* differs from art music in that it is intended to be heard but not actively or purposefully listened to.

Much of the time our use of music in this way is circumstantial, owing to the convenience and the impersonality of the electronic media. That is, music is often merely allowed to be present, playing softly in the background without any deliberate relationship to the conditions of the particular environment. Even art music is sometimes caused to function in this way unintentionally. Consider the occasions when you may have tried to play a favorite recording, either classical or popular, for a group of friends, only to have some irrelevant conversation erupt spontaneously—often, to your dismay, just as the music arrived at the passage you especially wanted them to appreciate.

At the same time, the phonograph and the tape recorder allow us to transmit music into any environment at will, and the nature of music, as well as of our basic physiological responses to it, permits us to do so with predictable results. In other words it is possible, and often highly desirable, to deliberately design music that will produce a specific reaction in a specific group of people without their paying much, if any, attention to it.

93

THE PHYSIOLOGICAL EFFECTS OF MUSIC

Ever since the first wordless cry was uttered, no doubt, men have observed and exploited the power of music to affect human conduct and well-being. Its unique capacity was acknowledged by the ancient Egyptians and Greeks, as well as by the Chinese, the Hindus, and the Arabs. Preliterate as well as certain literate cultures have relied upon the supposed supernatural powers of music to assure fertility, to achieve success in hunting or courtship, to arouse the courage of their warriors and intimidate the enemy, and to heal the sick. In the First Book of Samuel (16:14-23) in the Old Testament we are told how David the Psalmist exorcised evil spirits from the sickened Saul.

Late in the nineteenth century scientists began to discover that certain effects of music upon the human organism were not at all imaginary or legendary but very real—that music does indeed alter blood pressure, pulse rate, and respiration, and can even influence the electrical conductivity of the body. Music has been shown to be capable of increasing or decreasing muscular reflexes and energy, and of thus modifying endurance and reducing or delaying fatigue.

Furthermore, music can alter the threshold for certain sensory stimuli and affect mental and emotional suggestibility. J. S. Bach's *Goldberg Variations,* written in 1725, was the composer's fulfillment of a commission from a princely insomniac for some "soothing music for the clavier [harpsichord]" to be played for him in the night by his personal musician, Johann Goldberg. The work comprises a set of thirty variations in passacaglia form on a theme which originally was the bass line of a saraband, a popular dance form of the time. It is now considered a work of art, though for all its technical ingenuity, which continues to astound musicians, it still can have a somewhat soporific effect on the casual listener.

In modern medicine an entire science has arisen which is devoted largely to the therapeutic uses of music in the treatment of mental and emotional illnesses. It is not precisely known to what extent the apparently physiological effects of music are really a result of the individual's previous musical experiences. In any case, it is certain that for one reason or another music can and does have definite effects upon both the conscious and the unconscious modes of experience. Furthermore, owing to a wide variety of both internal and external circumstances, not all individuals respond to music in the same way or to the same extent, and even individual variance is apt to be extreme under different conditions. However, there is enough consistency in the responses to music among contemporary civilized people to allow certain assumptions to be made about its potential effects.

THE FUNCTION OF MUSIC AS BACKGROUND

Because these generalized predictions are possible, certain kinds of music are now being used to offset some of the adverse effects of modern industrial technology on human sensibilities. For example, music may be used to relieve the boredom of simple repetitive tasks. In the mailing room at Prentice-Hall, Inc., where simple manual exercises had to be repeated continuously for hours on end, the introduction of carefully programmed background music into the immediate environment resulted in a net increase of 8.03% in productivity. The music may simply have provided a refreshing element of variety in an otherwise monotonous situation, but it may also have had direct effects on the muscular coordinations of the workers.

As more and more manual operations become automated the need for alertness on the part of employees tending complicated high-speed machines becomes crucial. It appears that efficiency in such so-called "vigilance tasks" can be measurably increased by the playing of appropriate background music.

Music can be used to modify attitudes in less tedious situations as well. In the usual American eight-hour workday routine there is what has been termed an "industrial efficiency curve," according to which fatigue sets in and efficiency declines twice each day, reaching the lowest ebb around mid-morning and again around mid-afternoon. It has been determined that the reduced attentiveness which this condition causes can be mitigated by introducing steadily brighter, more stimulating music as the curve approaches its lowest point, and returning to somewhat less lively fare as the curve climbs again toward the middle and end of the workday.

In some situations neither boredom nor the effects of the "industrial efficiency curve" are involved. Instead the natural sonorous environment may contain sounds that interfere with the workers' powers of concentration. Intermittent noises can be extremely distracting if they contrast sharply and suddenly with the normal sonorous character of an environment, even though they may not be very loud in themselves. As you know, the creaking of a house which may go unnoticed during the day may be quite startling during the relative silence of the night.

In a comparatively quiet office, therefore, background music may be introduced to raise the overall sound level so that infrequent and sudden noises are made less distracting. For similar reasons music is now being used in some intensive coronary care units in hospitals in order to shield the patient from sudden noises that might alarm him and jeopardize his condition.

On the other hand, a given environment may be altogether too quiet for the maximum efficiency and comfort of the persons using it. In a place where confidential conversations are carried on, freedom of communication may be inhibited by the possibility of one's being overheard. But the proper background music can provide an invisible curtain around individuals and small groups. In this case strictly acoustical factors must be considered.

Normal human speech in the English language covers an amplitude range of between 30 and 75 decibels, and a frequency range of from 100 to 7500 Hz. As long as the background music introduced into such an environment remains somewhat above the lower limits of these ranges and does not often approach the upper ones, certain speech sounds will tend to blend in with it, becoming inaudible beyond a distance of a few feet, and a semblance of privacy will be granted to at least some of the people in the room.

At the same time, the intelligibility of speech in the English language depends on the audibility of consonants whose frequencies lie roughly between 500 and 4800 Hz. Therefore any sound, musical or not, that emphasizes those frequencies at a level of, say, 50 decibels, will appreciably interfere with communication. Since Western music contains a great many pitches and timbres that include frequencies within that scope it is essential that a very careful balance between loudness and frequency, as well as timbre, be maintained in background music where spoken communication is essential.

Finally, music is used in public places like restaurants, hotel lobbies, doctors' and dentists' offices, and airline terminals, as well as in conveyances such as buses and planes, in order to humanize the impersonal atmosphere of the environment. It is a truism that a person can feel more isolated in a large crowd than in the seclusion of his own room if the crowded place is unfamiliar, and if the people are strangers to one another. Where is the lone traveler more alone than among two or three hundred passengers cruising at 500 mph, 30,000 feet in the sky, or hanging onto a strap in a bus or commuter train at rush hour? A familiar tune—even a vaguely familiar one—may provide a welcome source of self-identity, thus reducing anxiety and nervous tension.

These functions of background music have the practical economic effect of improving efficiency, morale, and safety, and of increasing productivity among employees or satisfaction among customers. Our technological civilization grows more complicated, more dehumanized, more mobile, and noisier every day. We need music's ministrations not just during our leisure hours as an accomplishment, as entertainment, in ceremonies, or even as art, but sometimes in our workaday lives. Even people who "hate music" need it.

THE SPECIAL CHARACTERISTICS
OF BACKGROUND MUSIC: STYLE

The fundamental criterion that mood music must satisfy is necessity. It is not always beneficial or even desirable. In certain circumstances and for

FIGURE 13 Mood music is customized for situations rather than for listeners, and production efficiency is important. Here, various pieces of mood music are being *dubbed* from fifteen different tapes on the giant eight-track deck at the operator's left into a 14-inch twin-track master tape. Duplicates are made on high-speed copiers and distributed to franchise-holders throughout the world. Courtesy Muzak ® Corporation.

certain people, it can even have regrettably adverse effects. When almost anyone can buy a cheap, convenient playback system for a few dollars, and draw from a virtually unlimited supply of music commercially available on discs, tapes, cartridges, and cassettes in any record shop or supermarket, gross abuses of the craft of background music programming are bound to occur.

The second requirement is stylistic appropriateness. The usual accusations of musical purists notwithstanding, "nondescriptness" is neither a desirable nor a typical attribute of effective mood music. On the contrary, there is a fairly well-defined canon of stylistic characteristics that composers, arrangers, and programmers of mood music must observe. The specific details of the style have been arrived at both scientifically and empirically by specialists in human engineering and communications psychology employed by leaders in the mood-music industry such as the Muzak ® Corporation. Some are positive factors that serve to indicate the areas in which imagination may be exercised.

Tempos may range from about 40 beats up to 130 beats per minute. Slower tempos work best behind vigilance tasks, since research seems to indicate that slower tempos induce slower pulse rates which are often accompanied by increased alertness. On the other hand, one of the elements of "brightness" which is important in combatting the adverse effects of the downslope of the "efficiency curve" is a gradual increase in tempo from one piece of music to the next.

Meters and rhythmic patterns are classified by Muzak's ® experts in an order of increasing brightness and designated according to the names of three old dance types and a march: the *fox trot* (an indigenous American ballroom dance that once was the basis of the bulk of our popular music) is in 4/4 meter at an average tempo of about 70 quarter notes per minute. The *waltz* is in 3/4 meter at a tempo of around 80 quarter notes per minute. The *samba* (a Brazilian popular dance that had a strong influence on the mainstream of American popular music during the 1920s) is in duple meter at a tempo of approximately 90 half notes per minute. The *quick-step* (the standard military march in the United States) is in 6/8 meter at a pace of 100 or more dotted quarter notes per minute.

Timbre also is carefully manipulated by custom designers of background music. The louder and the higher the frequency—say above 4,000 Hz—the more stimulating the sound. Increases in volume at progressively lower frequencies have a somewhat similar effect. Alertness appears to be one of the direct results of the imposition of brighter timbres upon a work situation. Thus the music programmed at the very bottom of the "industrial efficiency curve" in an office or factory will include selections featuring the higher instruments in their upper registers. Where more soothing effects are desired, of course, one would want music using mainly mid-range frequencies and therefore employing chiefly violas and cellos, trombones, or tenor saxophones, and using trumpets and violins mostly with *mutes* which suppress the upper frequencies among their overtones.

Density of sound is another important variable in the designing of background music. Though there is no conclusive data available, research relative to the effects of frequency on alertness clearly suggests that there is a measurable difference between the stimulus value of a full orchestra and that of a chamber ensemble or a small "combo."

One aspect of mood music design is purely technical. In order to secure the greatest possible amount of stimulation in terms of timbre and density it is imperative that the recording and playback equipment be capable of reproducing a frequency range of from about 40 to 15,000 Hz at all optimum levels of loudness. For the purpose of comparison we might note that the practical frequency response of an inexpensive intercom system or an AM radio receiver is apt to be limited to about 5,000 Hz, while a cheap record player might have an effective range extending only from about 70 to 7,000 Hz.

The tunes that work best in most situations are fairly brief; they cannot be extended much beyond three or four minutes even in the most imaginative and interesting arrangements. Moreover, no single composition taken alone can be assigned an absolute mood or "stimulus value." Such values accrue only when a piece is heard in a total musical context consisting of several pieces. Finally, once a value has been established in terms of a melodic type, a tempo, a rhythmic pattern, a timbre, or a density, then any variation has a positive stimulus value and, conversely, postponement of change (up to the point where monotony gives way to annoyance) has a negative value. This means that the programmer of mood music is faced with the problem of controlling the elements of unity and variety, or sameness and differentness, over extended periods of time to produce a controlled effect on the individuals in a given environment. In a remote sense, his task is similar to that of a composer, except that his success may ultimately be measured in terms of productivity, of dollars and cents, rather than the subjective reactions of critics or audiences.

NEGATIVE FACTORS

Another set of determinants serves to define the outer limits of style in mood music. These specifically exclude from consideration all techniques and devices that would interfere with the intended function of a piece.

Anything that might attract someone's attention by the abruptness of its occurrence must be avoided, including sudden and extreme changes in tempo, timbre, density, consonance and dissonance, or volume, and any device that would result in a conspicuous increase in tension. The second movement of Haydn's Symphony No. 94 in G Major would likely make unsuccessful background music in certain situations, as one might judge from its nickname alone—the *Surprise Symphony*. Compositions by Arnold Schoenberg (Example XI-1) or Anton Webern (XV-2) might also have to be rejected on this basis.

Any feature that would lead to a more insidious distraction must also be rejected. Elaborate polyphonic texture, especially employing imitation, may challenge the ear to follow its intricacies—it naturally sounds "busy." Therefore Bach's Fugue in G Minor (Example VII-3) might be less useful than a piece in homophonic texture. Insistent unifiers like ostinatos and pedal points might fix one's attention on the music. Miles Davis's "What I Say" (Example VI-1) demands that the listener deliberately ignore the ostinato figure and seek whatever elements of variety are present in the rest of the texture. Indeed, listening to this piece is a kind of vigilance task in itself. Vocal performances are often unusable as background music, especially if the words are not only understandable but arresting, as in the passage from Leonard Bernstein's *Mass* heard in Example XII-2.

Most of us are conditioned to expect the structures of popular songs and dances to be built of short, symmetrical phrases, as we shall see in Chapter XIII. More complicated structures, and especially those built of extremely long or irregular phrases, are likely to be distracting. Hindemith's *Mathis der Maler* (Example III-4) might be unsatisfactory as background music for this reason.

Evidence of extreme physical exertion in performance, such as extended solos with elaborate embellishments, might be excluded in some instances. Stravinsky's Piano Concerto (Example XV-1) would not work well, therefore, nor would jazzman Maynard Ferguson's version of "Bridge Over Troubled Waters." Uninterrupted music conveys an impression of superhuman exertion. After all, real live musicians do have to rest. Muzak's ® engineers have concluded that fifteen minutes of music alternating with fifteen minutes of silence is the ideal solution to this problem. A symphony by Gustav Mahler, then, which may last as long as an hour and a half overall, would be impractical for that reason alone even if it satisfied all the other requirements of the usage.

Stylistic incongruities of any sort, such as those which produce humorous effects, would be unlikely to help music function well as background.

Heterogeneous or bizarre timbres such as might be heard in some of the music of Partch (Example II-11), Ligeti (III-12), Schoenberg (XI-1), or Webern (XV-2) are clearly inappropriate. Absurd topical associations have to be avoided, such as the playing of seasonal music at the wrong time of the year.

Finally, each selection should correspond with the conditions of the social situation in which it is meant to function. A piece in the style of a work by Haydn or Mozart, for instance, might conceivably help to reinforce an atmosphere of exclusiveness in a showroom of expensive automobiles. The same piece, however, could be entirely out of place on a used-car lot where a popular idiom might establish a more suitable environment.

In the process of delineating the requirements and limitations of mood music we have also pointed out some of the characteristics that might be found in art music, which is intended not to be just passively heard, but actively listened to. That is, functionally, mood music and art music are diametrically opposite. Consequently the criteria appropriate to the evaluation of one are the reverse of those applicable to the other, at least at the present time.

"CLASSIC" MOOD MUSIC

The existence of mood music as a functional category is not peculiar to the twentieth century. In the traditional Roman Catholic Mass, for instance, especially as celebrated in the larger cathedrals where the remoteness of the high altar is a barrier to personal involvement in the act of worship, there are several points at which either there is action instead of speech, or else the words being recited cannot be heard by the congregation. To maintain continuity in the required mood of reverence, therefore, church authorities in the seventeenth century permitted the playing of musical "filler." Compositions designed for this purpose, usually written for organ, or for organ and strings, were often referred to by the term *sonata da chiesa*—church sonata (concerning this use of *sonata,* see above, p. 57).

In eighteenth-century secular life terms like *divertimento, serenade, notturno* or *Nachtmusik* ("night music"), and *cassation* designated music of a light, entertaining character suitable as dinner music, or to enliven the atmosphere in some similar social situation like an official reception or a garden party. Such pieces were no doubt used by many composers as exercises in techniques of composition, for there is evidence of a considerable transference of stylistic detail from their genre into the principal concert music of the time—the symphony, the concerto, and the string quartet.

But while the repertoire of the latter employed standardized structures, textures, and instrumentation, the outstanding characteristic of early-day background music was variety in those respects.

Stylistically, eighteenth-century background music, like modern mood music, constituted what we would call "easy listening," and its melodic and rhythmic characteristics often reflected influences of the music of the people—peasant songs and dances that we might think of as country/western, as well as the urbane march and the minuet.

The quantity of this music was so great, its need and function so taken for granted, and so little musical comment made about it that it is next to impossible to identify it nowadays except by the titles we have mentioned above. Music historians have rarely seen fit to record the fact that a given work was conceived for so lowly a function as to be purposely ignored.

XI

music in films,
theater, and ballet

One of the most important uses of music in Western culture is the enhancement of the emotional qualities of words, actions, or images in film and television dramas. Functionally, this use is related to that of so-called *incidental music* in the legitimate theater, and to the music of the ballet theater, but since the arts of theater and ballet are historically rooted in technological and sociological conditions different from those of the mechanical and electronic media, we must consider them separately. However, since the aesthetics and techniques of film and television drama are almost identical, especially with respect to the use and function of background music, we can discuss them both simply in terms of the film.

THE FUNCTIONS OF MUSIC IN THE FILM

The film is a theater of illusion. The camera readily accomplishes superhuman feats of movement, focus, and perspective, and the results are merely two-dimensional, larger-than-life images accompanied by louder-than-normal voices and sound effects. It is mainly in the imagination of the viewer that these elements are endowed with a semblance of reality, but this process of humanization can be substantially aided by music. Indeed, the effects of music on the viewer of a film are at once so subtle and so necessary that most of us are more apt to notice its absence than its presence.

To be sure, music cannot by itself convey the facts of a story, for it cannot impart information or "say" anything at all in concrete terms. But music does have an intrinsic power of expression insofar as it can be "a tonal analogue of emotive life." As Susanne Langer has put it, music represents essentially "the forms of human feeling—forms of growth and of attenuation, flowing and stowing, conflict and resolution, speed, arrest, terrific excitement, calm, or subtle activation and dreamy lapses—not joy and sorrow perhaps, but the poignancy of either and both—the greatness and brevity and eternal passing of everything vitally felt." [1] This is the basis of music's expressiveness, and this is the power which is called upon to affect the emotional range and force of the visual and literary parameters of the film. The result of the union of these elements depends on the nature of the relationship that the filmmaker decides shall prevail.

In the most general, and least expressive, association of music with a film, music can be used merely to fill silence or mask unwanted sounds and to encourage empathy with the figures on the screen. The importance of music for this purpose was discovered very early in the history of the movies. Without naturalistic sounds emanating as it were from the screen itself the audience would tend to be distracted by human noises—coughing, the rustle of clothing, or talking. Thus during the so-called silent era— up until the late 1920s—music functioned somewhat like the mood music we have already discussed. Even now, in the case of classroom instructional films in which the information is largely visual or narrative rather than dramatic and there is little emotional content, music can help sustain the viewer's attention by offsetting the noise of the projector.

To fulfill this function the music needs only to be more or less consistent with the film in mood and tempo. In any event, since its connection with the film is of a general nature, music intended for this purpose can easily be composed and recorded before dialogue or narration is added to the film. Prerecorded music may even be drawn from a standing library in which compositions are catalogued according to the moods they are supposed to suggest, such as passion, danger, fear, and so on. Such music is apt to be emotionally restrained or ambiguous, and to consist largely of clichés, but the method is nevertheless convenient and inexpensive. Even the amateur photographer can buy condensed libraries of music and sound effects to dress up his home movies.

Another early use of music with film was to imitate natural sounds such as bird calls or laughter, or to represent wind, rippling water, footsteps,

---

[1] Susanne Langer, *Feeling and Form* (New York: Charles Scribner's Sons; London: Routledge & Kegan Paul, 1953), p. 27. Copyright 1953 Charles Scribner's Sons and Routledge & Kegan Paul. Used by permission.

the galloping of horses, and so forth. Conversely, literal sound effects are sometimes "orchestrated" into a kind of "noise-music." A classic example of this is the nine-minute oil-well drilling scene in *Louisiana Story* (1948), which is accompanied only by the sound of the machinery shaped into a composition perceivable as such only because it is not precisely true-to-life in every detail. In cases like this the exact correspondence of sounds and visual events is not as important as the emotional suggestiveness of the overall sonorous design.

Besides serving merely as aural drapery or sound effect, music can be used to lend continuity to a film. A traditional technique is to identify distinctive themes or motifs with specific persons, places, or ideas in the story, and to introduce them whenever their visual or literary counterparts either appear or are to be remembered. This has its historical antecedent in Richard Wagner's practice of unifying his long music dramas (see p. 61) by means of "leading motifs." In television serials so-called theme music serves to identify the series aurally and to imply continuity from week to week, although the relationship between the theme and any of the characters or actions is seldom more than circumstantial.

Music may also help to give continuity to a film by serving as a cushion between scenes containing radically different emotional implications. One procedure is to use a polyphonic texture with lines of contrasting character in such a way as to suggest the visual technique of fading from one image into another. Atonal or twelve-tone style is also well suited to this demand, for reasons that will be explained presently.

The expressive power of music is exploited most fully when it is called upon to intensify the emotional focus of a scene, or else to reveal hidden significances, perhaps producing an ironical effect. In the latter case, the music is said to be written "against the scene." In the long opening episode of *Louisiana Story,* for example, we see a boy paddling his canoe through a swamp. He is evidently somewhat afraid, and we are shown all sorts of intimations of mystery and danger. But Virgil Thomson's lyrical *score* * clearly suggests that nature here is benign, the bayou is really a peaceful place, and the boy has nothing to fear after all.

More often, perhaps, music is used to build suspense rather than dispel it. Frequently its force is even brought to bear upon brief instants in a film, to qualify isolated gestures, words or images. Consider, for instance, a

* The term *score* here refers to the music of a film as opposed to the visual or literary elements and the sound effects. It is also used to denote the music to an opera or musical comedy, as opposed to the *libretto* or *book.* In either case, it may also be applied to the notated form of the music from which the conductor works—called a *full score*—as opposed to the individual *parts* the performers play from.

typical situation in a TV western: We are looking over the shoulder of a cowboy who is scanning the distant horizon. Suddenly a lone horseman appears there, silhouetted against the rising moon. Is he friend or foe? The cowboy cannot tell for sure, but a sudden loud (*sforzando*) dissonance played by muted brasses warns us that danger is imminent. Obviously, in cases like this the musical effect must be synchronized with the other parameters of the film as precisely as possible if it is to have the maximum effect.

SYNCHRONIZATION

Music that is to be synchronized with a given scene or episode may be recorded either before, simultaneously with, or after the shooting of the picture. Singing, as well as dance music, is usually *prerecorded* and the matching of the sound with the film is a simple matter. A singer, for instance, merely listens to a playback of his own performance while he mouths or *lip-syncs* the words before the camera. Recording simultaneously, or *on the set*, eliminates all possibility of error or unnaturalness in synchronization for singers and dancers but often presents insurmountable technical problems at the same time. For one thing, the successive cuts that comprise a scene are not necessarily filmed in the same order in which they occur in the finished movie.

Although, as we have seen, prerecorded orchestral background music is sometimes used where synchronization is unnecessary, it would be both impractical and absurd to try to achieve close correspondence between musical effects and physical or verbal gestures by having the actors follow the music, whether it was prerecorded or recorded on the set. Therefore the most common procedure for achieving synchronization is to both compose and record the music after the film is almost complete in all other respects. This procedure is called *underscoring*.

There are three basic techniques for synchronizing an underscore. After all the scenes are arranged in their proper order and the film is "cut to length," its temporal dimension is permanently fixed, and the intervals among the visual or verbal events in any scene can easily be measured in terms of time, distance, or beats. Thirty-five-millimeter film moves through the camera at a standard rate of 24 pictures, or *frames*, per second, and there are 16 frames to the foot, so one foot of film lasts ⅔ of a second. Moreover, equally spaced perforations along the channel that passes over the optical playback head of a movie projector will produce an audible metronomic pulse or click; perforations spaced 16 frames apart, for example, would produce clicks at a tempo of 90 beats per minute. Thus any event with which music is to be matched (called a *cue*) can be pinpointed with absolute accuracy by composing to *timing, footage,* or *clicks.* The majority of underscoring is done to timing, but certain circumstances may require the finer precision of measurement in footage or frames. For rhythmic accuracy in extended passages, or when a number of consecutive cues must be reinforced musically, the *click-track* technique is used.

After the composer has viewed the film and, in consultations with the director, determined which scenes should be underscored, a more or less detailed *breakdown* or *timing sheet* is prepared containing the dialogue, along with a description of every cut and camera angle, and the timing of each cut, action, or bit of dialogue down to a third of a second. Next the composer decides on the general style of music to use and selects the cues that should be synchronized with specific musical effects.

In the timing sheet shown in Figure 14-a the composer, Earle Hagen, has circled three cues—the beginning of the movement or *panning* of the camera across the floor, the discovery of the microphone wire, and the appearance of the tape recorder. Observing that a tempo of 60 beats per minute will allow all three cues to fall neatly within the framework of a 4/4 metrical pattern, the composer is able to use a 24-frame click track. Next he marks on his music manuscript paper the *measures* (indicated by vertical lines), the clicks (the x's above the uppermost *staff*), and the timing of the scene in seconds (the figures in the boxes), as shown in Figure 14-b. Now he can begin to write down his musical ideas, distributing and orchestrating them to achieve the desired results.

At the recording session for such an episode a 24-frame click track is played over headphones for the conductor, and perhaps each member of the orchestra as well, assuring that the music will be performed at exactly the right tempo, and that when the recording is transferred or *dubbed* to the film the two will be perfectly matched. If the underscore has been composed to timing or footage the conductor may follow a stopwatch calibrated in seconds or feet, and may also be aided by visual signals such as "punches," "streamers," and "flutters" projected on a screen from a working copy of the film, which warn him when an important cue is approaching.

STYLES IN FILM MUSIC

The basic determinants of style in film music are implicit in the nature of the medium and the process of filmmaking. The story-telling process of the film requires that music obey the laws of language rather than its

M-25	Picture Tonia has caught herself laughing at Scott's mess with the oven. He, reflecting, observes: "JUST REMEMBER - THOSE WHO CAN LAUGH, CAN ALSO FEEL PAIN."
:00	Music Starts in the C.U. of Scott-just after his line.
:02 1/3	Cut to B.C.U. Tonia smiling (an expression she-up to now- has not often used.)
(:04)	Camera begins slowly panning down to right toward floor and base-board.
:06 2/3	Tonia, O.S. starts talking-quite pleasantly for a change: "YOU KNOW, I MUST ADMIT THAT YOU WERE RATHER IMPRESSIVE IN THE BAR TONIGHT." (Ends :12)
(:12)	The camera - still panning - reveals a microphone wire lying on floor and continues panning to follow it.
:13 2/3	Scott's voice, O.S.: "AND I MUST ADMIT I WAS TERRIBLY, TERRIBLY FRIGHTENED."
:18 1/3	She starts a small protest in his favor: "NO, YOU SHOWED COURAGE, WHAT YOU SAID HAD MERIT EVEN THOUGH I DISAGREE WITH YOUR...PHILOSOPHIA." (Ends :26 1/3)
(:26 2/3)	Cut to exterior showing the sinister looking wire leading out over window ledge. The camera still following it stealthily.
:27 1/3	Scott's voice O.S.: "YEAH, WELL I FIGURED YOU'D DO THAT." (Ends :29) Camera continues to follow wire hanging down outside wall of the tenement building.
:30 1/3	Tonia, O.S. resumes: "PERHAPS IT WOULD BE VALUABLE TO KNOW YOU BETTER-AH-IT WOULD SHARPEN MY OWN CONVICTIONS. "Scott agrees: "YEAH, I THINK SO." She continues: "THIS WOULD BE IN THE SPIRIT OF POLITICAL SCIENCE OF COURSE." Scott agrees: "OH YES, I'M IN FAVOR OF SCIENCE, I THINK IT'S A WONDERFUL THING-SCIENCE." (Ends :46 1/3)

FIGURE 14-a   A portion of a timing sheet from a television drama. "C.U." and "B.C.U." stand for "close-up" and "big close-up," respectively. "O.S." means "off-stage"—that is, not in the camera's view. Reproduced by permission of Earle Hagen.

M-25 (P. 2.)

:33 1/3   Cut to interior of C.U. window sill-showing
                 the wire coming into a room. (NOTE: The
                 previous lines of dialogue are continuous, and
                 overlap this cut as camera continues panning
                 wire.)

:44   At this point the camera reveals wire leading
                 to a tape recorder in operation on a table.

:45 1/3   Camera stops panning - centered on recorder.

:46   Start Dissolve.

:48   Music Ends as picture Full-In on high angle
                 view of broad street & large buildings.

                 (NOTE: Seques to Cue M-26/31)

                        TOTAL TIME :48

FIGURE 14-b The beginning of the underscore to the scene outlined in Figure 14-a. The first visual cue is reinforced by the entrance of the flute and "vibe" (that is, *vibraphone,* a percussion instrument consisting of metal bars to be struck with hard mallets). The line is marked *non espressivo,* meaning without dynamic nuances. The next cue circled on the timing sheet is matched by the entrance of the French horns, *con sordino* (with mutes, abbreviated *sord.*), on an accented note ($>$), followed by a decrescendo from *mezzo-forte* to *piano.* At just after 26 seconds the dramatic tension is heightened by having more instruments join the expressionless, undulating eighth-note motion of the texture. Reproduced by permission of Earle Hagen.

own; the mechanical aspect of the film which permits precise synchronization of music with the visual and literary parameters places even further restrictions on the music. Many of the structural procedures that are most natural to music are incompatible with the logic of words. An underscore based on the principle of repetition-after-contrast, for example, would be unlikely to correspond with the consecutive moods or events in an ordinary dramatic episode. Even extended or emphatic final cadences are unwelcome anywhere but at the very end of a movie, or at a commercial break in a television drama. Furthermore, now that music is no longer needed merely to mask unwanted sounds as in the days of silent movies, it is quite properly omitted from all scenes where its presence is not aesthetically necessary.

Thus although a full-length (180-minute) feature film may contain a total of forty minutes of music, and a one-hour television drama up to 30 minutes or more, an underscore normally will consist of unrelated episodes anywhere from a few seconds to no more than two or three minutes in duration. Consequently the more positive and integral an underscore is, the less capable it is of standing by itself apart from the film. Recordings of excerpts from popular films usually require extensive revision in order to sound right. Also, the composer is sometimes compelled to orchestrate his music so as to compensate for the rather limited frequency-response of the film sound-track in ways that are unnecessary in the medium of the "high-fidelity" recording.

Purely practical considerations can also affect the style of a film score. For instance, scheduling and costs are often the main determinants of how much music is written, how complicated it will be, and how many instruments can be used. In this regard the film composer is like the composer of art music who accepts a commission for a certain type of work suitable for a particular group of players on a specific occasion. On the other hand, while the artist is often obliged to write for a standard set of instruments such as a string quartet or a symphony orchestra, the film composer is at liberty to specify any instrumentation he believes will achieve the best results in a given scene or film. Such unorthodox combinations as six oboes, six French horns, two harps, and a large percussion battery are not uncommon in film music. Moreover, the film composer may consistently aim at a high level of technical difficulty, for although recording sessions are always limited in number and duration by the economic factor, Hollywood studio musicians are among the most highly skilled and versatile performers in the world—as well as the most highly paid—for all their anonymity.

Finally, a film is the product not of one but of many diverse and interrelated talents and skills. Unlike the composer of art music, who is normally free to do as—and when—he pleases, the film composer must at all times work closely with the producer and director, as well as the music editor or "cutter," one or more sound technicians and recording engineers who ultimately control the fate of the composer's own efforts, and sometimes with choreographers and lyricists, not to mention various assistants such as orchestrators, copyists, and conductors. This intricate teamwork must proceed more or less smoothly, or else scheduling may be thrown off and budgets disastrously overrun.

All these limitations notwithstanding, some of the best European and American composers have written music for the film. Until the late 1930s the majority of underscores were stylistically parallel with current conservative tastes in concert music. In fact, in a great many films excerpts from standard symphonic works by late-nineteenth-century composers like Tchaikovsky, Rachmaninoff, and Grieg were used verbatim without concern for the structural contradictions that might exist between the music and the film.

Around 1940, a few American composers began to enliven the older tradition with some of the compositional techniques of the Frenchmen with whom or under whom many of them had studied. Some assimilated the chromaticism bordering on atonality, and the innovations in orchestration, of composers like Erik Satie, Georges Auric, Darius Milhaud, and Arthur Honegger. They also laced their scores with the impressionistic sounds of Debussy (see Example V-8) and the primitivistic rhythms of Stravinsky.

American composers like Aaron Copland and Virgil Thomson frequently sought inspiration from American folk music styles. For instance, Thomson laboriously searched the folk songs of the South and the Appalachians for the melodies he used in *The River* and acquainted himself with the music of the Cajuns of the bayou country before composing the score to *Louisiana Story*. The emotional implications of folk tunes are neither wide nor subtle, but concise and elementally profound. For film and television dramas with western or rural settings they still provide the most direct and convenient means of emphasizing the atmosphere of the location and establishing the personalities of the characters.

Among the heirs of the French symphonic and American folk styles are the composers Elmer Bernstein, Jerry Goldsmith, Bernard Hermann, Sol Kaplan, André Previn, and David Raksin.

ATONALITY

The asymmetrical phrases and irregular rhythms of speech, as well as sudden visual changes, can more readily be supported by atonal music than by music that is limited strictly to the scales of the major/minor system. The major/minor system relies for extension of sound in time principally on tension and release produced through a calculated arrangement of the hierarchy of tones comprising the scale and the chords built on those tones. Atonal music, on the other hand, is generally free of these "logical" relationships among pitches and chords. Compared with tonal music, atonal music can employ a freer treatment of dissonances, heterogeneous timbres, and the irregularity or even the apparent absence of meter, which permits the creation of a wide variety of subtle and instantaneous effects. In short, the unfolding events in atonal music are interruptible and even reversible.

The basic vocabulary of atonal style in film underscoring may be found in various concert works by Arnold Schoenberg and his pupils Alban Berg and Anton Webern dating from around 1910, though it was not adopted by film composers until much later. Some of the devices that have since become clichés in the idiom appeared in Schoenberg's *Accompaniment to a Film Scene,* Op. 34, composed in 1930. The *Accompaniment* was not intended for synchronization with a specific film but was merely meant to evoke three typical moods—"Threatening Danger," "Fear," and "Catastrophe." In the three excerpts contained in Example XI-1 the following *XI-1* may be heard: a string *tremolo* (moving the bow back and forth rapidly on the string) played close to the bridge of the instrument, producing an eerie, "glassy" sound; muted brasses playing staccato notes; intricate polyrhythms against a trembling ostinato; playing on the string with the wood rather than the hair of the bow; and low, dissonant, "muddy" chords beneath a mournful, disjunct melody.

JAZZ AND ROCK IN FILM AND TV

Since the early 1950s various popular idioms have been used with increasing frequency in film and television underscores. They function effectively because, for one thing, there is such a wide variety of styles from which to draw—bebop, blues, boogie-woogie, soul, Dixieland, free jazz, folk rock, acid rock, and so on. At the same time, they are so familiar to the majority of listeners that moods can be evoked merely by hinting at them with the appropriate stylistic clichés. Moreover, the rhythms and melodic inflections of jazz and rock are more or less compatible with those of informal American speech, and this has prompted some composers to treat spoken dialogue in the film as but one of the independent lines in a contrapuntal texture. The first important underscore in jazz style was Henry Mancini's music for the TV detective serial, *Peter Gunn,* which began in 1953. Mancini demonstrated how flexible and expressive jazz could be in conjunction with the visual medium.

The most successful composers in this style so far have been those who have amalgamated jazz with some of the compatible features of the symphonic tradition. Their number is large, including Hugo Friedhofer, Dave Grusin, Neal Hefti, Earle Hagen, Quincy Jones, Michel LeGrand, Alex North, Pete Rugolo, Eddie Sauter, and Lalo Schifrin. And though none of them has yet been admitted to the roster of the academic musical establishment, there may be among them one or more who will, generations hence, be considered among the most important composers of our time.

The most significant aspect of style in film and television background music is that it is continually changing. Within a matter of weeks or months the evolution of the genre may take a new direction following the successful introduction of some new concept or device. Already the electronic *synthesizer,* with which the composer/performer himself can produce an infinite variety of sounds, has begun to revolutionize the craft, and its full potential remains to be explored.

INCIDENTAL MUSIC IN THE THEATER

In a sense, the relationship of music and drama in television and the film resembles that which prevailed centuries ago in the theater. In ancient Greece, music was more than incidental to the total effect of a drama. It was helpful in open-air performances to emphasize and unify the large bodily gestures the actors had to use, and to lend a sonorous dimension that would be commensurate with the expansiveness of a stage unconfined by a proscenium arch.

Music was also important in the medieval mystery and miracle play, but in this case it was because the religious drama developed spontaneously from the acting-out of scriptural stories which were originally sung or chanted in the context of the worship service.

During the Renaissance the art of the theater gained renewed momentum outside the church. In Italy the end products of the experimentation which the new freedom fostered were the oratorio and the opera, in which music almost completely dominated drama. In England, however, the integrity of the drama retained its force, and the play with incidental music became so important that the Italian *dramma per musica* (drama *through* music) never really took root there.

The functions of music in the modern theater became clearly defined during the Elizabethan era, and they have not changed substantially since then. First, and most importantly, music was used to introduce a play as well as to fill time between acts, in the latter instance often forming a kind of bridge that helped to sustain the general mood of the play. In these capacities music was at liberty to assume its own organically motivated shapes—to obey the structural implications of the tonal system, such as the return to a tonal center after a departure or the return of melodic material after contrast.

Beethoven's Overture to *Egmont,* one of the ten pieces of incidental music he wrote for a revival of Goethe's play in 1810, is one of the best known works in the entire repertoire of music for the theater (see Preface). The purpose of this particular overture was to point up the essential emotional structure of the play: doom faced courageously; strength gained through the faith, love, and sacrifice of others; resignation; and ultimate triumph in martyrdom. To this end the principal elements of Viennese classical style were well suited: broad contrasts of melodic type, timbre, tonality, and tempo. Knowing the play, one could easily recognize in Beethoven's overture the essential emotional structure of the drama.

Secondly, music could appear as part of the action, in songs that helped to further the plot, or in dances and other stage ceremonies. Beethoven wrote memorable settings of the two songs sung by Klärchen, Count Egmont's ill-fated sweetheart.

Finally, music could be called upon to heighten dramatic effects, with fanfares to herald the entrances of supernatural or royal personages, or to increase emotional tension in a passage of dialogue. Since the visual and literary parameters in the live theater are not absolutely immutable as they are in the film, precise synchronization can be achieved only through compromises in the inflection and timing of words and gestures. Late in the eighteenth century this procedure, known as *melodrama,* arose as an independent musico-dramatic form and was frequently thereafter incorporated in full-scale theatrical productions. Beethoven included one episode in melodrama style among his incidental pieces for *Egmont.*

The musical literature of the theater has been enriched by most of the world's greatest composers during the past several hundred years and, owing to the relative independence of the music from the drama, a great deal of it has become part of our traditional concert repertoire, by far out-living the plays it once enhanced.

The seventeenth-century French composer Jean-Baptiste Lully wrote in-cidental music for many of the plays of Molière. Felix Mendelssohn wrote some music for an 1843 revival of *A Midsummer Night's Dream,* including a wedding march that is among the most familiar compositions in the whole world. Georges Bizet, better known for his opera *Carmen,* wrote some extremely attractive music for Alphonse Daudet's play, *L'Arlésienne* (The Woman of Arles) in 1872. In 1876 the Norwegian, Edvard Grieg, com-posed at Henrik Ibsen's behest, special music for a new production of the playwright's poetic drama *Peer Gynt.* The Frenchman Gabriel Fauré and the Finnish composer Jean Sibelius both provided music for productions of Maurice Maeterlinck's Impressionist play, *Pelléas et Mélisande,* around the turn of this century. The eminent American composer Roger Sessions was commissioned in 1923 by Smith College to supply music for a produc-tion of Leonid Andreyev's play *The Black Maskers.* Finally, one of the early classics in the field of electronic music is the score to Orson Welles's New York City Center production of *King Lear* (1956), by Otto Luening and Vladimir Ussachevsky.

MUSIC IN THE BALLET THEATER

Throughout its six-century history, modern theatrical dancing has been alternately—and sometimes simultaneously—influenced by the realistic ges-tures of the drama, the expressive representations of the pantomime, and the abstract designs of the social dance. Similarly, the relationship of music to the dance has in some periods been essentially formal, and in others it has been but the obedient servant of the scenario or story-line. That is, sometimes music has been merely an accompaniment to the dance, at others it has served, somewhat like modern film music, mainly to reinforce the gestures of the dancers. Thus the amount of ballet music that can stand alone as concert repertoire is extremely small compared with the amount of it originally written for the *ballet* theater.

During the sixteenth and early seventeenth centuries the ballet was a mode of aristocratic entertainment in which members of royal courts them-selves took part. It consisted of short dances of various national origins such as the *allemande, courante, saraband, gigue, bourée, chaconne, gavotte, passepied, branle, rigaudon, polonaise,* and *minuet* (which eventually were grouped together in the *suite;* see above, p. 60).

These dances consisted chiefly of stylized patterns of correct social intercourse—promenading embellished with gestures of respect, admiration, and coquetry, interspersed with gallant poses exhibiting the dancers' poise and elegance of manner and breeding, and topped off with bits of polite conversation. The elaborate formalities in dress and conduct impeded the development of dance as a dramatic art, but it assured stability and independence in musical style.

The character of each dance was reflected in the music in terms of meter, tempo, melodic line, length or shape of phrase, structural balance, and sometimes even texture and instrumentation. A story of some kind, often an allegorical representation of the courtly participants as living counterparts of some of the more admirable heroes and heroines of Greek mythology, was occasionally superimposed on a series of such dances, but grandiosity, not storytelling, was the real point of the presentation.

The popularity of the ballet as a mode of aristocratic entertainment during the eras of the Renaissance and the baroque prompted the production of a tremendous amount of music, and if little of it has survived that is mainly because it was trivial in character. Thanks only to the few composers who were occasionally able to produce something slightly out of the ordinary, like Lully and Rameau, we are still privileged to hear a little of the music to some of those dances whose steps and social significances are now only inert historical data.

By the latter half of the eighteenth century the ballet had become an integral part of the opera as a form, but at the same time it began to assume an independent existence, combining increased dramatic motivation with a revival of the Greek concept of ballet which emphasized the display of the inherent beauty of abstract bodily poses and motions. But music remained as much the obedient handmaiden as ever.

Even when composers of towering stature—such as Mozart, Gluck, or Beethoven—wrote for the ballet, their efforts were often of only limited intrinsic value, like their incidental music for the drama. Beethoven, for instance, composed sixteen pieces for an allegorical ballet entitled *The Creatures of Prometheus* (1801), but only three of them, including the Overture, have emerged from the luminous background of his own corpus of works, not to mention the obscure shadows of the rest of the ballet repertoire of the time.

"CLASSICAL" BALLET; THE BALLET RUSSE

The few nineteenth-century ballet compositions that transcended the limitations of the dramatic dance sufficiently to become part of the standard concert repertoire nevertheless clearly reveal their origins in their very strengths. Adolphe Adam's *Giselle* (1841), Léo Delibes's *Coppelia* (1870) and *Sylvia* (1876), and Tchaikovsky's *Swan Lake* (1877), *Sleeping Beauty* (1890), and *The Nutcracker* (1892) are thoroughly enjoyable to hear because of their vitally compelling rhythmic force and their eloquent melodic lines.

Listening to any one of them, you will readily notice the suggestions of physical energy created by the sudden crescendos, especially when supported on the timpani; the sforzandos and abrupt decrescendos; the rubatos, ritardandos, and accelerandos; the staccato or pizzicato accompaniments to legato lines which suggest buoyant patterns of delicate steps executed *en pointe* (on tiptoe).

Marius Petipa, the *choreographer* (designer of dance) for whom Tchaikovsky composed the music to *Sleeping Beauty* and *The Nutcracker,* assumed the prerogative of dictating many of the details he expected in the music, in terms of melodic style, meter, tempo, rhythmic pattern, and orchestration; he even specified the exact number of measures he felt were needed to support a given mood or movement. The result was a closer correlation between music and action than had ever before been achieved. Tchaikovsky clearly understood the essence of the composer's obligation to the dancer, which is to keep in mind the potential capabilities and limitations of the human physique. The dancer cannot defy the implications of the music; musical complexity inspires a corresponding intricacy in choreographic rhythm and movement.

However, not until the establishment of the so-called *Ballet Russe* (Russian Ballet) in Paris in 1909, and for some twenty years thereafter, did a true and complete collaboration occur among all parties to the production of a dramatic ballet. Sergei Diaghilev was the director; Michel Fokine (who was influenced by the innovative ideas of the American dancer Isadora Duncan), Vaslav Nijinsky, and Leonid Massine were the principal choreographers; the most notable designer was none other than Pablo Picasso; and the composers included Igor Stravinsky *(The Firebird,* 1910; *Petrushka,* 1911; and *The Rite of Spring,* 1913), Maurice Ravel *(Daphnis and Chloé,* 1912), Claude Debussy *(Jeux,* 1913), Manuel de Falla *(The Three-cornered Hat,* 1919), and Darius Milhaud *(The Creation of the World,* 1923). The complete aesthetic integrity of the Ballet Russe was transmitted to the United States during the 1930s by the Russian choreographer George Balanchine, for whom Stravinsky wrote *The Card Party* ("a ballet in three deals") in 1937. Early in the twentieth cenutry an older choreographic genre was revived—the dance pantomime. Stravinsky's *Story of the Soldier* (1918; see Example IV-1) and Bartók's *Miraculous Mandarin* (1919) are dance-pantomimes, with the emphasis simply upon telling a story and dramatizing characters, rather than on displays of choreographic technique.

AMERICAN BALLET

A distinctively American style of ballet was established in 1938 in Chicago with *Billy the Kid,* based on the life of the notorious outlaw, William Bonney, with a libretto by Lincoln Kirstein, choreography by Eugene Loring, décor by Jared French, and music by Aaron Copland.

The music used in the recorded suite from *Billy the Kid,* arranged by Copland himself from about two-thirds of the original score, is generally self-sufficient and interesting enough by itself, though the listener may reconstruct the plot from the titles of the movements: "Introduction," "The Open Prairie," "Street in a Frontier Town," "Card Game at Night," "Gun Battle," "Celebration after Billy's Capture," and "The Open Prairie." However, the full dimensions of the music can be appreciated only if one actually can see the ballet for which it was designed.

The music of the gunfight, for example, is but a brief contrasting interlude in the suite (XI-2). The multimetric percussive reports obviously represent erratic gunfire, and melodic material is all but absent. The episode virtually demands the presence of the choreography, in which Billy executes a double turn in the air symbolizing the force of the explosion and the velocity of the flying bullet; when the victim falls Billy delivers a mighty kick to suggest the bullet's deadly impact.

XI-2

The momentum provided by *Billy the Kid* has subsequently produced a number of memorable scores composed for choreographers like Martha Graham, Agnes De Mille, Jerome Robbins, and Anthony Tudor. They include Copland's *Rodeo* and *Appalachian Spring* (see Examples V-3 and XIV-5), Morton Gould's *Fall River Legend,* Leonard Bernstein's *Fancy Free,* and William Schuman's *Undertow.*

The great expense of commissioning special music for a ballet has always prompted directors and choreographers to adapt existing compositions to their purposes. At its most sublime level this practice led to the so-called symphonic ballets of Massine and Balanchine in which the formal struc-

FIGURE 15   A scene from the American Ballet Theater production of *Billy the Kid*. The music enlarges the physical energy of the dancers' movements. Photo by Martha Swope.

ture and the emotional implications of works like Beethoven's Seventh Symphony are interpreted in the dance.

The availability of recorded music and the pliability of the medium of the tape recording, which can be cut and spliced to produce any conceivable combination of musical material, have made the practice of adapting and arranging music easier and more economical than ever before. One salutary consequence has been the stimulation of amateur and pre-professional activity in ballet at the levels of the college and university, the community, and the secondary school.

BALLET ON BROADWAY AND TELEVISION

Ballet continues to thrive in the Broadway musical theater, as it has ever since the mounting of the first extravaganza, *The Black Crook,* in New

York in 1866. Its continuing vitality is due to the presence of men and women like dancer/choreographer Peter Gennaro, whose fame rests on his contributions to musicals like *Fiorello, The Unsinkable Molly Brown,* and *West Side Story,* as well as to television programs like *The Ed Sullivan Show.* Gennaro also choreographed an award-winning television commercial for a popular cold remedy in 1969, which may serve to remind us not to ignore the musical and visual qualities of that miniscule and often-derogated idiom.

One of the most conspicuous characteristics of television as a medium is that it consumes an incredible amount of material from week to week, year to year, summer reruns notwithstanding. This might seem to be an insuperable obstacle to the achievement of superior quality in drama or dance, or in the music for either. Yet television's insatiable appetite might also be its greatest strength. Many of us have learned to think of the live media such as the concert hall, the opera house, the Broadway theater, and the ballet, as the most conducive to genuine creativity because of the relative leisure at which the artist can work. But television demands the same technical facility and lightning-bolt inspiration that seventeenth- and eighteenth-century composers of opera and oratorio—like Lully, Rameau, Alessandro Scarlatti, Vivaldi, Mozart, Handel, and Haydn—had to possess.

A Broadway musical score may represent the labor of several years; the underscore to a feature film may require from two to six months of work; an episode in a television dramatic serial may consume several weeks of a composer's undivided attention. The music for a dance routine in a TV variety show may have to be literally pasted together in a matter of a few days. Out of this kind of pressure could well appear—indeed, might already have appeared, could we but recognize him—a modern counterpart of the great Mozart, the kind of composer who is more than a match for the demands as well as the limitations of the medium.

XII

ceremonial music, public and private

In a formal ceremony such as a religious service, a civic or patriotic observance, or a fraternal rite, music may serve to focus attention on the proceedings, to accompany a ritual, or to spotlight an idea. In modern Western civilization this use of music is of decidedly minor importance compared with those we have discussed in the four preceding chapters. But it deserves our attention because so much ceremonial music of the past has since become part of our concert repertoire and because there are still many special events in which music could be used more effectively if only the persons responsible knew more about its potentials in this connection.

MUSIC IN PRIVATE CEREMONIES

During the baroque era, before the public concert became central to Western musical life, a great deal of music other than opera was more or less broadly ceremonial in purpose in that it was written either for a religious service or for a private or public secular celebration.

Owing to the pride which every powerful ruler took in displaying his armed forces in impressive reviews and pageants, the march was one of the most important musical genres of the period, and many eminent composers contributed to the repertoire, as Lully did at the behest of Louis XIV.

Even the everyday life of the upper classes was highly formalized. The most ordinary social or personal event could provide the basis for an elaborate ceremony—receptions, anniversaries of all kinds, inductions into civic or courtly offices, not to mention christenings, weddings, and funerals. And so intimate and natural was the relationship between life and music that none of these was conceivable without some kind of musical observance. In one situation the music might function merely as aural drapery, much like present-day mood music. In another it might serve a dramatic purpose; many celebrations were deliberately theatrical in character. Often the musical performance was the climax of a ceremony.

Ideally the music was commissioned expressly for a particular occasion, and if it employed a text an allusion might be made to the person or occasion being commemorated. There must have been an incalculable amount of such music written at that time, but because of its topical characteristics it was ephemeral, and that which has not been lost altogether attracts our attention now more as a kind of historical document than because it is aesthetically satisfying as art music. J. S. Bach, who composed more than three hundred cantatas for the Lutheran churches in which he worked, also wrote five cantatas for the inaugurations of councilmen in various cities, three for weddings, several for birthdays and name-days, and a dozen more for events like the appointment of a professor and the accession of a prince to the control of his hereditary estate.

Many European musicians of the eighteenth and nineteenth centuries were active in Freemasonry, and some of them composed music especially for the ceremonies of their own lodge. Mozart, one of the most notable Masons in the history of the society, wrote several works for the rituals of his lodge in Vienna, including one of his most beautiful compositions, the *Masonic Funeral Music,* K. 477. *

MUSIC IN PRIVATE CEREMONIES TODAY

In contemporary private life the potential function of music in ceremonies of the types just mentioned is virtually ignored. A more equitable distribution of wealth since the eighteenth century has impoverished many of those individuals and organizations who might formerly have commissioned music for such special occasions. There are now cheaper ways of paying obeisance to deserving persons, such as photographic portraiture. Moreover, the ideals of democracy not only discourage the conspicuous display of private wealth but also dictate that honors shall be less permanently

* *K.* stands for *Köchel-Verzeichnis,* a chronological catalog of Mozart's works compiled by Ludwig von Köchel.
Mozart's opera *The Magic Flute* also reflects his devotion to Masonry; several elements of Masonic doctrine and ritual are implied in the plot, characters, and action.

held than they once were and that privileges of position or office shall be passed around periodically and systematically.

Above all, the concept of music as essentially an *art* has inhibited serious composers and patrons from creating works of such temporary value as, say, an ode for the installation of the president-elect of an international service organization. Instead we simply make do with whatever the local high school, college, or amateur entertainment group has ready, whether it has any topical connection with the occasion or not.

Nowadays special musical productions are sometimes sponsored by large corporations at meetings of executives, salesmen, stockholders, or customers. These are often elaborate revues resembling the television variety program and consisting of skits, songs, and dances in which the virtues of the company and its products are extolled, and the competition is held up to ridicule. The writing and producing of these so-called "industrial shows" is a large and profitable part of the music entertainment industry, but it seems unlikely that a composer of the stature of a Bach or a Mozart would ever emerge from it.

MUSIC AS PROPAGANDA

Since the revolutionary era of the late eighteenth century, music has often been used by national and political powers as propaganda. Simple, memorable melodies naturally work best for such purposes, for they conveniently announce slogans and deeds, and make the propagation of ideals inspiring and pleasurable. Furthermore, when the tunes themselves become familiar they function as symbols of the doctrinal statements they first embellished. Not that every piece of patriotic music is strictly ceremonial in intent, but it can be a portable, ever-ready unifier of people in public gatherings.

Music was an important tool in the hands of Robespierre and the other mentors of the Directory after the first French Revolution. Consistent with their belief in the doctrines enunciated by Plato in his *Republic,* according to which exposure to the proper music would insure the loyalty of the citizens, they commissioned composers like Hector Berlioz to create music that would serve the state by keeping before the people the dominant precepts and goals of the new republic. In addition to operas and oratorios based on incidents in the history of the new regime, hymns were composed celebrating such epochal events as the execution of Louis XVI, or exalting the impersonal "Supreme Being." These songs were taught to mammoth choirs and performed at gigantic ceremonies in which the masses were coached to join in the refrains.

PATRIOTIC MUSIC IN THE UNITED STATES

Patriotic music was no less important in the United States during the Revolutionary and Federal periods than it was in France, but it was fundamentally of a different character. Its creators were inspired by the charisma of their leaders, Washington, Adams, Jefferson, and the rest; they were motivated by the self-evident rightness of their divinely guided cause. They had no need for official decrees or sanction, sought no commissions from a paternalistic bureaucracy, and required no grandiose ceremonial settings for their songs. They were self-taught composers—more accurately, tunesmiths—who were able to write the kind of music that would appeal directly to the common people. They were under no compulsion to be sublime, and they were incapable of it anyway. Nevertheless they managed to produce some songs and marches that remain unsurpassed in all the music of Western civilization for simplicity, fervor, and immediacy of effect.

Typical of the genre is the song illustrated in Example XII-1, which was among the best-loved of all Revolutionary hymns. Both the words and the tune, called "Chester" (it was customary to identify all such tunes by given names rather than by association with specific texts) were written by William Billings of Boston, a tanner by trade, a tunesmith by inclination, and a patriot by conviction. He scorned the rules, the subtleties, and the intricacies of the music of his more renowned European contemporaries, Gluck, Haydn, Mozart, and Beethoven, believing instead that "Nature must inspire the Thought" and that every composer must be "his own *Carver.*" *XII-1*

The bold and artless text needs no explication:

Let tyrants shake their iron rod,
And Slav'ry clank her galling chains.
We fear them not, we trust in God,
New-england's God for ever reigns.

Howe and Burgoyne and Clinton too,
With Prescot and Cornwallis join'd,
Together plot our Overthrow
In one Infernal league combin'd.

When God inspir'd us for the fight,
Their ranks were broke, their lines were forc'd.
Their Ships were Shatter'd in our sight,
Or swiftly driven from our Coast.

The Foe comes on with haughty Stride,
Our troops advance with martial noise.
Their Vet'rans flee before our Youth,
And Gen'rals yield to beardless Boys.

What grateful Off'ring shall we bring,
What shall we render to the Lord?
Loud Hallelujahs let us Sing,
And praise his name on ev'ry Chord.

The tune is heard in the tenor part. Its attractiveness and vigor result from a unique balance of unity and variety as well as tension and repose. Unity is present primarily in the rhythmic parameter. The four phrases, all equal in length, end with the same pattern, short-short-short-long. The very last phrase contains the most short notes and therefore the most motion, giving the effect of steadily increasing energy from beginning to end.

Variety is present chiefly in the melody, for no two phrases have exactly the same contour (Fig. 16). Tension is sustained throughout by the postponement of arrival at the lower tonic. The first three phrases begin on the dominant (fifth); the last begins on the upper tonic. The cadence of the first phrase is on the dominant, the second on the supertonic (second), and the third on the upper tonic; a sense of rest is achieved only at the end of the final phrase with its arch over the lower tonic.

Except for rare examples of transcendent quality like "Chester," most patriotic music is short-lived, as it should be. A national anthem like the "Star-Spangled Banner," or the "Marseillaise," and a hymn or two such as "America, the Beautiful" and "My Country, 'Tis of Thee" may remain in use along with a few marches of general utility like "Hail to the Chief," while the more specifically functional music is discarded when it has fulfilled its purpose.

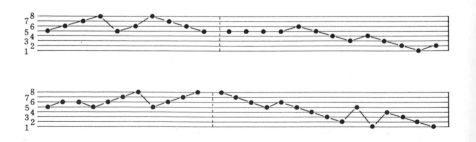

FIGURE 16   Graphic presentation of the contours of Billings's tune, "Chester." The lines merely represent the degrees of the scale.

Effective civic ceremonial music must serve an immediate end with as much force and effect as possible, and timeliness is consequently its best feature. Indeed, it might be a threat to the evolution of a political system for its music to outlast its expedient doctrines and shifting goals. Thus the songs of the American leftists and labor organizers of the thirties, forties, and fifties, which helped to inspire enthusiasm and solidarity among proselytes, had lost both their meaning and their usefulness by the end of the sixties and are now only historical curiosities.

About the only non-political, secular public events in modern life in which music serves a kind of ceremonial function are athletic contests. The half-time band shows at football games are sometimes topical in content. An athletic event of major importance such as the World Olympics often requires music to accompany processions and to highlight introductions and presentations.

MUSIC IN RELIGIOUS CEREMONIES

Throughout the history of modern Western civilization music has seldom functioned more consistently or more positively in any area of life than in the rituals of the Christian churches. As a result, religious music now comprises one of the longest and most varied musical traditions of all. Relatively little of it belongs to the repertoire of adult professional concert life, but a great deal is now available on records and, as we have already noted in Chapter VIII, some of it works quite well in the high school vocal music program.

In the more formal liturgies such as those of the Roman Catholic, Anglican, and Lutheran churches, music has at times been so completely integrated with the ceremony as to be virtually inseparable from it. In churches of evangelical persuasion, such as the Methodist, Baptist, and Presbyterian denominations, which stress salvation through personal acts of faith rather than through corporate sacraments, music has been used in a more independent and flexible manner. On the one hand we have a body of music intended for performance by trained, official musicians in a prescribed rite; on the other we have a type that will permit the layman to take part in the ceremony himself.

THE MASS

The main public rite in the Roman Catholic church, which includes the sacramental reenactment of the Last Supper or Eucharist, is called the *Mass*. There are eighteen separate textual units in the Mass, all in prose, ranging in length from a sentence or two to several paragraphs or a chapter of Scripture. Some of these are always spoken, but certain ones may optionally be sung, in which case the celebration is called a *High Mass*. The texts are also classified into those that change from day to day, called the *Mass Proper,* and those that remain the same throughout the church year, called the *Mass Ordinary*.

When set to music the texts of the Proper are usually sung in chant style, in unison (Example III-1). During the Late Middle Ages and the Renaissance, portions of various Propers were sometimes set in polyphonic style and were referred to as *motets* (Example VIII-1).

Usually only five sections of the Ordinary are set to music, either in unison or in parts, and it is to these that the musician habitually, though incorrectly, refers with the term *Mass*. The *Kyrie* consists of three phrases each repeated three times—"Lord, have mercy; Christ, have mercy; Lord, have mercy"; it is the only symmetrical text in the Ordinary. The *Gloria* is a long, unrhymed hymn of praise. The *Credo* is a statement of the essential dogmas of the church. The *Sanctus* is a short acclamation that occurs at the climax of the Mass, and the *Agnus Dei* is a penitential supplication which follows soon after, just before the sharing of the bread and wine by the celebrants and the congregation.

Between about 1400 and 1600 these items of the Ordinary were set to unaccompanied modal polyphony, and by one means or another a basic stylistic consistency was maintained among them which lent a degree of aesthetic unity to the ritual as a whole. A familiar sacred or secular tune might be used as a *cantus firmus* (fixed melody) for each movement of the Ordinary. Up to the end of the Renaissance more than thirty polyphonic Masses had been based on the popular fifteenth-century song *L'Homme armé* (The armed man). A simpler procedure was to unify the movements by means of an identical motif at the beginning of each.

A Mass in which each movement used some of the music of a pre-existent polyphonic composition, either sacred or secular, was called a *parody,* meaning "derivation" rather than "caricature." One of Palestrina's Masses is a parody, in this sense, of a popular sixteenth-century polyphonic *chanson*— the French counterpart of the Italian madrigal—entitled *Je suis desheritée* (I am desolate).

After 1600 the unaccompanied modal *antique style* of the Renaissance continued to be favored in conservative places, while new settings of the Ordinary for the more progressive churches and cathedrals showed the unmistakable influence of the pervasive secularism of the age, such as elaborate instrumental accompaniment. On festive occasions the Mass assumed a conspicuously theatrical proportion and effect. The text of each of the five movements was divided into short sections and treated according to one of the current structural or stylistic procedures such as the operatic aria or ensemble, the fugue, or the concerto.

By the middle of the eighteenth century composers began to regard the Ordinary as an independent form. They treated the poetic and dramatic implications of the text in elaborate fashion, often at great length. Thus Bach's great *Mass in B Minor* is entirely unsuitable for liturgical use because of the dimensions of its separate movements and its total duration of more than two hours and fifteen minutes. And Beethoven's titanic *Missa Solemnis,* eminently symphonic in style and spirit as well as dimension (about an hour and twenty minutes) is hardly imaginable as part of a worship service.

It is no wonder that this happened, for the Mass (in the larger, correct sense) is essentially a drama, and though all its elements are integrally related and their effects are cumulative, nevertheless even the Ordinary offers the composer a number of unique challenges. Its texts present moments of tender lyricism *(Benedictus qui venit in nomine Domini!*—Blessed is he who cometh in the name of the Lord) contrasted with dramatically potent phrases ranging from penitence *(miserere nobis*—Have mercy upon us) to exaltation *(Hosanna in excelsis!*—Hosanna in the highest!), and the whole is implicitly suffused with the profound import of the original context—the symbolic sacrifice of the Eucharist. *

A MODERN CELEBRATION

The culmination of some three centuries of development of the Ordinary as an artistic vehicle outside the context of the Roman Catholic service of worship has been achieved by Leonard Bernstein in his *Mass,* written for the dedication of the Kennedy Center for the Performing Arts in Washington, D. C. in 1971. The composer called it "A Theatre Piece ['about a Mass'] for Singers, Players and Dancers." Indeed, *Mass* might have been more appropriately discussed in Chapter XI. However, a full appreciation of the work seems to depend on an understanding of the implications of its title, as well as an awareness of the problem of ceremony and ritual in contemporary life, so it is brought up here instead.

Mass includes a part of a Eucharistic sacrifice, but it is not a functionally

---

* The *Requiem Mass,* for the burial of the dead, is basically the same as the regular mass, but musical settings of it usually include portions of the Proper as well as the Ordinary, and the emphasis is on moods of solemnity as well as triumph.

liturgical work like any of Palestrina's 105 versions of the Ordinary. And nearly every word of the *libretto,* or text, is set to music, but it is not a concert work like Bach's *Mass in B Minor.* Its text and structure are freely derived from both the Proper and the Ordinary, yet it is not even specifically Christian, much less Catholic. The central figure, the Celebrant, is not a priest, nor in fact a "character" at all, but the representation of a quality of life—"that element in every person," as the composer himself put it, "without which you cannot live, without which you cannot get from day to day, cannot put one foot in front of the other." [1] It is a pseudo-religious ritual celebration of the ideal of salvation through brotherly love, self-denial, and self-discovery. It is closer in spirit to the finale of Beethoven's Ninth Symphony (the "Ode to Joy") than to the *Missa Solemnis.*

Mass is, like the age-old rite on which it is based, both a visual and an aural experience; it is dance, music and, above all, drama. Even the purely sonorous aspect of it eludes capture in any single medium. Some parts are prerecorded and broadcast in the auditorium through four separate speakers simultaneously with the live elements from which multidimensional effects are also available. The performers include numerous soloists, two choruses, an orchestra in the pit, and a brass band plus a rock group onstage.

XII-2   "The Lord's Prayer" (XII-2) is a beautiful example of monophonic music in free rhythm. It is sung by the Celebrant alone in unison with the piano. The song is symmetrically constructed: the pitches for the words "Our Father, who art in heaven, hallowed be Thy name" are the same as those for the words "And lead us not into temptation, but deliver us from evil."

Appended to the Lord's Prayer is another song, a soliloquy, entitled "I go on." The composer has termed it a *trope,* meaning a textual and musical expansion of and commentary on the ideas and emotions contained or implied in the preceding piece. This also binds *Mass* to ancient ecclesiastical tradition, for troping was a common practice in the music of the Roman Catholic church from the ninth through the twelfth centuries. The resemblance of the first phrase of "I go on" to that of a popular American song of the 1930s, "I remember you," might be coincidental. In either case, listeners who know the latter will be reminded of it, and the ironic appropriateness of the lyric will be recognized. The rising motif at the words "Lauda, Lauda, Laudé" is an important unifying element in the work as a whole.

Immediately following the trope is the *Sanctus* (Holy). First we hear the text recited by the Celebrant in English. Immediately the boys' choir, di-

---

[1] Leonard Bernstein, quoted in "The Three Faces of Lenny," *High Fidelity,* XXII, No. 2 (February, 1972). Used by permission.

vided into two groups, sings the same text *antiphonally* (alternating from side to side) and continues in Latin: "Blessed is he who comes in the name of the Lord. Hosanna in the highest!" The rhythm is multimetric.

Next we hear one of the numerous puns the work contains. It is a play on the tone-syllables "mi, sol" and the concepts "me, soul." The first two notes of the Celebrant's song are *mi* and *sol*, the third and fifth degrees of the scale from which the melody is built:

> Mi . . . Mi . . .
> Mi alone is only mi.
> But mi with sol
> Me with soul
> Mi sol
> Means a song is beginning
> Is beginning to grow
> Take wing, and rise up singing
> From me and my soul.
> Kadosh! [Holy!] Kadosh! Kadosh! *

What makes *Mass* valid as a modern public ceremony from the musical standpoint alone is the astounding variety of styles it includes. Every note of it is unmistakably Bernstein's, yet the work purposefully draws upon a broad scope of Western musical history—the structures, textures, melodic characteristics, harmonic vocabulary, and timbres of every style-period since the early Renaissance. It contains intimations of Beethoven, Mahler, Stravinsky, Schoenberg, Copland, and Gershwin, among others. It employs original conceptions of current popular idioms such as rock, jazz, blues, and Broadway musical comedy.

The skillful combination of so many seemingly irreconcilable styles is an attribute that would be a distinct weakness in a period of stylistic unity like the Renaissance or of absolute hierarchical values like the nineteenth century. However, our present obsession with history as a source of knowledge and understanding combined with a technology which makes the continual assimilation of the present and the reassessment of the past at once easy and necessary, conspire to make eclecticism in style and taste not only inevitable but right.

CONGREGATIONAL MUSIC

One of the immediate practical results of the Protestant Reformation was the introduction of ways to involve the worshipers actively in the liturgy,

FIGURE 17   Scene from Leonard Bernstein's *Mass,* with Alan Titus as the Celebrant, members of the Alvin Ailey American Dance Theater, the Norman Scribner Choir, and the Berkshire Boys' Choir, at the John F. Kennedy Center for the Performing Arts. Photo by Fletcher Drake. Courtesy, The Kennedy Center for the Performing Arts.

where previously they had been but passive observers of the official celebrants, the priest and his retinue. The Calvinists in France and England accomplished this partly by making the singing of versified translations of the Psalms an obligatory religious exercise. The tunes of the French were rhythmically and melodically more complicated than those used by the English and ultimately by the Pilgrims and the Puritans in New England. But even the English tunes were at first livelier than are now generally to be found in a "respectable" congregational songbook. At any rate, the Calvinists eliminated all other forms of musical expression from their liturgies, including the Ordinary.

The singing of Psalms was abandoned in favor of the hymns and tunes of Isaac Watts and Charles Wesley in the eighteenth century. Thenceforth, the Calvinist churches fostered nothing of even temporary significance in the field of formal ceremonial music. Their composers produced a copious quantity of anthems often of no more specific utility than a piece of modern mood music and a sizable repertoire of oratorios and cantatas, some of which are certainly memorable but few are liturgical.

Meanwhile, for the German Protestants of the sixteenth century, Martin Luther translated some of the venerable hymns of the Roman Catholic church and set them to existing popular tunes. This procedure, then called *contrafactum,* is still employed by some denominations especially in missionary work to attract young people.

By the end of the seventeenth century in the Lutheran church the composition as well as the singing of hymns (called *chorales* to distinguish the entire tradition from that of English or American psalmody and hymnody) had lost its original vitality. The old tunes possessed a nostalgic value, but they no longer evoked the associations of the lively secular songs from which they had sprung. (Note that the effect of the musical pun in Bernstein's "I go on" is lost upon anyone who is not old enough to have known "I remember you.")

Moreover, under the inertia of disinterested congregational singing the old chorale tunes had been stripped of their rhythmic variety and melodic embellishments. In their rarefied forms, however, they at least provided a wealth of material to some of the composers who worked for the music-conscious Lutheran churches in Germany, like Johann Sebastian Bach of Leipzig.

THE LUTHERAN CHURCH CANTATA

The eighteenth-century Lutheran church cantata, a work consisting of choruses, recitatives, arias, and sometimes instrumental movements called *sinfonias,* was frequently original in its entirety, but sometimes was based on a familiar chorale. In either case the text was a poetic commentary on a passage from one of the Gospels that served as the theme of an entire Eucharistic celebration. The musical setting of each stanza constituted an embellishment of the poem and, in turn, of the Scripture. In this way the cantata was thoroughly integrated with the service; it constituted an elaborate trope on the very Word of God.

A typical example is Bach's great Cantata No. 4 for Easter Day, *Christ Lag in Todesbanden* (Christ lay by death enshrouded), which is based on a mighty tune Luther himself composed.

Throughout the history of Protestant hymnody favorite tunes have been used so often for different texts that it has been the practice in the publishing of hymnals to identify each tune by its rhythmic structure for the convenience of those who might choose to substitute a new poem for an old one. The rhythmic structure is defined in terms of the number of syllables per line. The "regular Meters" include Common (or "Ballad") Meter consisting of two alternating lines of eight and six syllables, respectively—8,6,8,6—and Short Meter—6,6,8,6. The tune of *Christ Lag in Todesbanden* is long and asymmetrical or, in the parlance of the genre, "irregular," as may be seen in the stanza of the text quoted below.

Bach's setting comprises a set of six ingenious strophic variations, followed by a simple statement of the tune in four-part, homorhythmic, homophonic texture. Each strophe is given a unique contrapuntal setting which in some way suggests the *affekt* or dominant emotional quality embodied in that stanza of the text.

XII-3 For instance, in the fourth stanza (XII-3) the soprano, tenor, and bass lines of the chorus, doubled in the orchestra, vividly express in the musical anology of a dense, chromatic contrapuntal texture the mortal struggle which is recounted in the words:

> Es war ein wunderlicher Krieg, (8 syllables)
> da Tod und Leben rungen. (7 syllables)
> Das Leben das behielt den Sieg, (8 syllables)
> es hat den Tod verschlungen. (7 syllables)
> Die Schrift hat verkündiget das (8 syllables)
> wie ein Tod den andern frass, (7 syllables)
> ein Spott aus den Tod ist worden. (8 syllables)
> Hallelujah! (4 syllables)

The English version by Henry S. Drinker is as follows:

> It was a wonderful array
> when Life and Death embattled.
> For Life is victor over Death,
> has swallowed Death in vict'ry.
> So the saying written thus will come to pass
> that Death will be swallowed up in victory.
> O Grave where is now thy victory?
> Hallelujah! [2]

---

[2] Translation by Henry S. Drinker. Reprinted by permission of the Drinker Library of Choral Music, The Free Library of Philadelphia.

There is yet another structural level that is likely to impress the listener when he first hears the entire cantata: the work is symmetrical with respect to voice groupings. Following a short orchestral introduction the voicing is Chorus-Duet-Solo-Chorus-Solo-Duet-Chorus.

The delicate balance of unity and variety within each movement, and in this cantata as a whole, and the subtlety of the treatment of the dramatic implications of the text are among the factors that make this a work which has secured, like many of the remainder of Bach's nearly 200 extant church cantatas, a permanent place in both professional and amateur concert repertoire. The church cantata was brought to the climax of its brief evolution by Bach; after that nothing more marvelous could be done with the chorale.

MUSIC IN THE REVIVAL MOVEMENT

After the Civil War the revival movement led by Dwight L. Moody and his soloist Ira D. Sankey—forerunners of Billy Graham and George Beverly Shea—gave rise to a new genre of folk song, the *gospel hymn*. It was America's first, though hopefully not its last, genuine contribution to the music of the churches.

The text of the gospel hymn expresses the religious experience as an intensely personal one, using the words and thoughts, the everyday conversational clichés of the ordinary man in the street rather than the ponderous, archaic diction of the Scriptures. "What a Friend we Have in Jesus," and "Hold the Fort, For I Am Coming" are typical opening lines.

The music of a gospel hymn is characterized by slow harmonic rhythm with sometimes less than one chord change per measure. It often features chromatic embellishments of the melody, parallel thirds and sixths between the melody and an inner part, echo effects, solo or duet passages over contrasting accompaniments, syncopations, dotted rhythms, and fairly fast ternary meter.

In contrast, a "superior" hymn uses frequent changes of harmony within the phrase, little or no chromaticism, predominantly equal note-values in duple meters at moderate tempos without quick syncopations or dotted rhythms, and intervallic as well as rhythmic independence between all voices.

To be sure, the gospel hymn was a trivial and a tawdry thing to the ears of serious music lovers for the reasons just mentioned, but its historical and religious significances far outweigh the questionable musical worth of any single instance of it. Its very obviousness is its strongest virtue.

The scope and vigor of its popularity proved at least that there was a potential urban congregation that could be reached through a certain kind of music. For those who were indifferent to the distinctions traditionally made between superior and inferior hymns, hymn-singing once again became a pleasure and an inspiration—a personal, ritualistic act rather than an obligatory exercise obediently performed or a kind of painful penance, as satirized by Mark Twain in *Letters from the Earth*. It brought up an issue which the leaders of the established churches of Christendom declined to take seriously until about a century later.

CONTEMPORARY POPULAR MUSIC
IN THE ESTABLISHED CHURCHES

At the Second Vatican Ecumenical Council in 1963 all the established denominations represented there promulgated the so-called Constitution on the Liturgy in which the desire to update public ceremonies of worship was declared. One of the most important passages in the document is the first paragraph of the section establishing "Norms for Adapting the Liturgy to the Culture and Traditions of Peoples":

In the liturgy, the Church has no wish to impose a rigid uniformity . . . ; rather does she respect and foster the genius and talents of the various races and peoples. Anything in these peoples' way of life which is not indissolubly bound up with superstition and error she studies with sympathy and, if possible, preserves intact. Sometimes in fact she admits such things into the liturgy itself, so long as they harmonize with its true and authentic spirit.[3]

This, along with the insistence that the liturgies always be conducted in the language of the people, was immediately interpreted at the parochial level to mean that a musical vernacular could be used whenever and wherever it might be deemed appropriate and necessary. Soon nearly every church took positive steps to encourage musical settings of portions of their liturgies in some locally popular idiom. An immediate result was the appearance of some interesting "ethnic" settings of the Mass, including the *Missa Luba* from the Congo, the *Misa Criolla* from Argentina, and the *Missa Japonica*. In all cultures, but especially that of the United States, there were some fundamental details that interfered with the literal adaptation of popular idioms to accomplish the ends the Ecumenical Council had in mind.

As the gospel singers of a century ago must have sensed, music that

[3] Reprinted by permsision of the National Catholic Welfare Conference.

stimulates the emotions briefly and intensely without involving the intellect can provide a welcome and harmless release from the unnatural pressures of conventional, rational codes of behavior. But those same codes which suppress the sensual instincts will cause some guardians of sectarian orthodoxy to regard popular music, associated as it often is with the unholier aspects of secular life, as a threat to the faith.

In addition, there are some strictly musical factors that make the use of popular idioms problematical. Improvisation is an essential element in jazz, but although the spontaneity of it might be just what a modern, progressive church would value most, real jazz can be performed only by musicians with special technique and experience, and that means the congregation must not interfere on its own level. Nevertheless there have been a few jazz Masses that clearly reveal the advantage of letting the professional jazzman do the whole job.

A rock performance similarly excludes congregational participation on an equal basis. Moreover, since so many of the effects we have learned to expect from a rock performance are introduced electronically in the recording studio, a live performance is apt to fall somewhat short of the standards established by the medium through which most of us hear rock. Finally, the volume level at which rock is often performed is utterly intolerable in a church, which is usually designed to be acoustically resonant.

Folk music, which is presumed to be the indigenous expression of the people, is not entirely adequate either. In the first place the cultural, social, and aesthetic diversity which we accept as a normal part of contemporary life prevents the establishment of a common, stable community repertoire. In the time it takes a community to learn enough tunes by heart to carry them through a liturgical year, a whole new fund of song can be established via the media, and the memorized tunes are then out of date. In addition, folk music, like jazz and rock, generates its own linguistic expressions, which are often inconsistent with the traditional, educated diction many churches wish to preserve.

In order for any kind of popular music to be used to achieve the aims of the Second Vatican Ecumenical Council, compromises must be made that touch upon the essence of its style. Considering the energy and determination of most contemporary Christian churches and the vitality of the popular tradition in music it is quite likely these compromises will take place, with or without the benefit of rational analysis.

music as entertainment

The kind of music on which we shall focus our attention in this chapter is that which serves the purpose of entertainment, even though we often recognize its style in music serving other functions—mood music, background music in film and television, ceremonial music, and school music. We frequently use the term *popular,* although that is not entirely appropriate either. In fact, most such vocabulary obscures rather than clarifies the fundamental differences between the music of this category and the kind usually referred to as *art* or *classical* music, for the criteria implied are largely extrinsic to real musical values. Here, our aim will be to identify some of its intrinsic features as a general category, and we shall do so partly through stylistic comparisons of the two traditions.

THE EXTRINSIC DISTINCTIONS

Entertainment, according to *Webster's,* "engages the attention agreeably" and "amuses or diverts," while *art* is a product of "the application of skill and taste according to aesthetic principles." But some art music can be entertaining to some people, and the writing of a piece of entertainment music can be considered an art in another sense—that is, a skill or craft.

In common parlance art music is often said to be "serious," implying that there is another kind with the opposite quality. But to many persons the latter, occasionally called "light" music, is by no means frivolous.

140

Most jazz musicians, for instance, insist that the term popular has connotations that do not apply to jazz, which they take very seriously.

Another distinction between the two traditions holds that art music is perpetuated by means of written documents and formal education, while popular music depends on informal transmission of its lore and techniques. However, certain genres of the popular tradition have recently found places in academic curricula, while the phonograph record has made possible the purely aural study of many aspects of classical music.

A more subjective explanation of the difference between popular and classical music appeals to the so-called "generation gap." From one side of the supposed abyss the argument goes something like this: An unwillingness to postpone satisfaction of the appetites is a mark of immaturity; popular music appeals directly and immediately to the elemental emotional sensibilities; therefore popular music is for adolescents. Yet even among the most sophisticated devotées of musical art there are few who can bear to spend their every waking moment in its rarefied atmosphere. Innumerable persons, including many otherwise mature individuals, remain unregenerate musical adolescents all their lives. Indeed, popular music is the music of the youth that is potentially in all of us when, from time to time, to paraphrase Bob Dylan's song, "My Back Pages," we are younger than we once were.

COMMERCIALISM

Of all the extrinsic distinctions between entertainment music and art music the one which we might call the economic hypothesis brings us closest to intrinsic musical issues.

The serious artist devotes himself to a kind of music that, in general, both requires and survives *extensive* exposure—that will be appreciated by an audience that enjoys being challenged to gradually, patiently discover the aesthetic satisfactions a complicated musical experience might provide and that admires the recondite more than the obvious, and the genuinely creative over the merely clever. Just like the popular musician, of course, he may seek and receive fees for his compositions through agents, publishers, and licensing organizations such as ASCAP (The American Society of Composers, Authors, and Publishers) or BMI (Broadcast Music, Inc.). He may produce works consistent with an established style, hoping to gain for himself a modicum of recognition and remuneration, but he is also at liberty to foster an idiom of his own without regard for the interests of any known audience, foregoing the probability of profit and risking permanent oblivion for himself and his creations.

On the other hand, the composer of popular music is engaged in a *commercial* enterprise. He must produce works that will sell quickly and in large quantities to audiences—rather, markets—that can be clearly identified with respect to age, social status, education, and geographical or ethnic origin. More importantly, his music must be able to survive *intensive* exposure for a relatively short period of time, perhaps a year or two. It must be interesting enough—even innovative within rather severe limitations—that a potential audience will want to hear it more than once. At the same time it must be ordinary enough that they can identify immediately with its sounds, its sentiments, or its humor, and tolerate the frequent repetitions that are assured by the mass media. In other words, it must be timely.

Paradoxically, a popular piece that survives intensive exposure over a very long period—say, a generation or more—may be recognized as a "classic" of its type. Even an entire genre that once belonged to the popular tradition may become classical when it is dispassionately reconsidered by critics better able to separate its highlights from its overall background and to discern among them the qualities that might be worth admiring.

THE CREATIVE PROCESS

In general, popular music is the product of individuals who are more or less self-educated. To be sure, there are a few academic institutions in which the elements of the tradition are taught systematically if not exclusively, but they do not supply a significant number of composers or performers to the popular-music business. A structured curriculum in music, with its orderly courses of study and its insistence upon both breadth and depth, does not always meet the needs of the commercial musician.

Actually, the composer as well as the performer of popular music need only have a thorough awareness of what is going on at the latest moment in his chosen style, and he must achieve this largely through exhaustive and attentive listening. He must develop the ability to imitate that style and perhaps make slight but noticeable changes in it. Finally, he must be able to recognize the moment when his particular talent can best be placed on the market, and A&R (artists-and-repertoire) men can even be hired to take care of this.

Since the basic material of the popular tradition is song, the composer of popular music might be described as a tunesmith. Unlike most of the tunesmiths of colonial America, however, many modern popular composers and performers cannot even read music, much less write it down, and therefore have to depend on an *arranger* to fashion their songs into real compositions. An arranger is a musically literate person capable of perceiving various possibilities for the setting of a tune. He "charts" the arrangement, using appropriate chords, countermelodies, and rhythmic patterns. He orchestrates the piece also, and writes out a separate part for each player or singer.

Rock and folk performances, however, are often merely "worked up" by trial and error from a *lead sheet* consisting of the tune and the words with some symbols indicating the chords to be used, as in Figure 19. In this event the songwriter depends on the skill and imagination of each member of the performing group. Furthermore, a recording engineer may add special electronic effects, and is ultimately responsible for presenting a performance in the most attractive manner possible as a purely auditory experience. Finally, the designer of the album cover for a recording may contribute to the total effect of a group of songs by adding a visual focus in terms of artwork and photographs.

The composer of a popular tune is often comparatively anonymous. The average listener does not usually identify popular songs by their composers' names. Many composers, especially in the field of rock, write both tunes and words *(lyrics)* and also perform them. This is not feasible in every area of entertainment music, of course, and there have been many great song writers who were not performers at all, such as Stephen Foster, Cole Porter, Frank Loesser, and Jerome Kern. On the other hand, men like George Harrison, Stephen Stills, and Paul Simon belong to a long line of song-writing showmen like America's George M. Cohan and Ireland's Thomas Moore.

A popular song as a complete composition, then, really does not exist apart from a specific performance of it. It is the more or less elaborate, cooperative, and cumulative product of one or more groups of specialists. A work of musical art, on the other hand, is created entirely by one broadly educated and highly skilled individual who can conceive every minute detail of a hypothetical performance in his own mind. The serious composer is also able to write down his conception with sufficient preci-

FIGURE 18-a The rock group, Woodstock, in the spotlights onstage. The character of their performance is partly dependent on visible and audible feedback from the large audience before them. A responsive audience is likely to stimulate a performance of superior spontaneity, imagination, and vitality, while a "dead" audience may produce the opposite result. Photo by Elliott Landy/Magnum.

sion that performers in other times and places can realize his intentions accurately, whether or not they have ever heard anything like it before. Furthermore, his music is always identified not only by its title but also by his name.

FORM: THE SONG

In serious music the structure of the composition and the structure of the performance are identical. In popular music, however, there is invariably a difference between the structure of the basic idea—the tune—and that of any single arrangement or performance of it. A popular tune is usually brief and simple, but a performance of it may be comparatively long and complex.

In Western music as a whole, the optimum length of a musical phrase

FIGURE 18-b   The James Cotton blues band in a recording session. With at least one microphone focused on each instrument, the musicians partially relinquish control over the volume and balance of their respective contributions to the total effect. Moreover, in the absence of a live audience they must rely entirely on their own self-generated emotional forces. Photo by Elliott Landy/Magnum.

seems to be about four measures, because our normal conceptual time-span—that is, the longest space of time within which consecutive events seem to belong to the "present moment"—is about twelve seconds, which is the duration of four measures of music in 4/4 meter at a moderate tempo. Composers of art music have been inclined to challenge our sense of the "psychological present" by combining motives and phrases so as to exceed that limit, whereas the majority of popular tunes are built entirely of four-measure phrases.

The 12-bar blues chorus (see p. 53), which was the structural basis of early rock, consists of a four-measure phrase which is repeated once, followed by another four-measure phrase that complements or answers the preceding one and brings the tune to a full cadence. We may graph it *a-a-b*. Another time-honored formula is that of ragtime's four 16-bar tunes or *strains* in the order *a-b-c-d*. The verse-and-chorus structure common to folk and country/western songs is often made up of two 2-line, 16-bar periods of 2/2 measures, or, more simply, two 8-bar phrases. Both, which are graphed *a-b,* are useful as vehicles for simple narrative texts, but they are too brief and simple to stand alone as interesting melodies.

A great many popular tunes consist of a single short introductory *verse* followed by a *32-bar chorus* made up of four 8-bar *periods* (consisting of two 4-bar phrases each) arranged in the order *a-a-b-a.* The opening period is called the *statement,* or *front strain.* The repetition of it may be identical, or it may differ just enough to progress smoothly into the *b* period, or *bridge,* sometimes called the *release.* The final recurrence brings the tune to a decisive conclusion. Many of the "old standard" tunes used in mood music, and in the "pops" programs by Arthur Fiedler, André Kostelanetz, and Mantovani are in this form.

It is relatively easy to write a short tune using 4-bar phrases according to one of these formulas, but it is difficult to be original. Irving Berlin met the challenge in "A Pretty Girl Is Like a Melody" by writing four 8-bar, 2-phrase periods in the order *a-b-a'-c,* as shown in Figure 19. Other song writers, especially during the late sixties and early seventies, have abandoned the conventional forms and contrived tunes in phrases of unequal length. Paul Simon's "Bridge Over Troubled Waters" is a good example.

"Bridge" was originally built of a 9-measure period (a 4-bar phrase and a 5-bar phrase), a 6-measure period (4 plus 2), and an 8-bar refrain (4 plus 4), a total of 23 measures. The phrases are dissimilar in contour as well as length, so we may say that the melody emphasizes the structural principle of superposition (meter and key are the unifiers) rather than repetition-after-contrast. Achieving a sense of balance and coherence in such a short, asymmetrical melody is difficult, and success is much easier to recognize than to accomplish.

FORM: THE PERFORMANCE

No matter how interesting a popular tune may be, however, it cannot stand alone as a composition. Sung at a moderate tempo, the tune to Paul Simon's song is less than a minute long, yet in Western urban culture we have come to expect the performance of a popular song to last approximately three to five minutes. Therefore the performer is confronted with the same basic challenge as the serious composer: to extend a sonorous design in time while maintaining a delicate balance between unity

FIGURE 19   Lead sheet for "A Pretty Girl Is Like a Melody."

and variety.

Given a song with several verses, the classical composer might consider writing a new melody for each verse, but the popular performer traditionally allows the song to extend itself in modified strophic form. If a song has only one verse and chorus, as is often the case, or if the tune is to be performed by instruments alone, the performer ignores the various options the serious composer might consider, such as rondo, minuet-and-trio, three-part, or sonata form, and instead uses theme-and-variations procedure. He may repeat the tune one or more times, introducing more or less elaborate embellishments and alterations of phrase-lengths, melodic contours, meter, tempo, tonality, chord structures (the "changes"), or even wording. Thus whether the tune itself exhibits the principle of juxtaposition or not, a performance of it will almost certainly be a continuous structure in which unity and variety are superposed.

Details of interpretations of a given tune are determined partly by the idiom of the arrangement. A "bluegrass" version would feature guitars and banjos, stressing rhythmic embellishments in each variation. A mood-music setting might be arranged for a small orchestra of strings, woodwinds, and brasses, using the tune throughout as originally conceived, but dressed up in the variety of timbres which that ensemble is capable of producing. A jazz interpretation might be performed by a small group of instruments such as piano, saxophone, trumpet, bass, and drums, with a straightforward statement of the tune followed by a series of melodic improvisations by one or more of the soloists, over the same set of changes.

Within a single idiom there are bound to be differences among interpretations by various performers. We expect all performers in the classical tradition to follow the composer's score as closely as possible, revealing their individual insights only through their handling of the most minute particulars such as nuances or shadings in timbre, the control of dynamic gradations and accents, blend, and balance. But a popular entertainer must develop his own peculiar style of interpretation and apply it to every piece he performs, whether or not it is his own song. No one expects two singers like Roberta Flack and Aretha Franklin to sing the same song in the same way, nor would we approve of a jazz trumpeter who merely imitated Louis Armstrong. (Non-professional performers of popular music, such as high school or college "swing choirs" and "stage bands" must use published, or *stock,* arrangements, since it is an infringement of copyright and licensing regulations for them to make their own without written permission from the copyright holder.)

Developing a personal style is not as easy as the successful performer makes it appear. Only a very few of the thousands of young singers and instrumentalists who set out each year to pursue popular stardom are capable of the unswerving single-mindedness, and the willingness to invest a great deal of self-confidence, youth, and energy in pursuit of a reputation that, once achieved, can be sustained only by being perpetually innovative and original.

A CLASSIC POPULAR TUNE

The extent to which individuality in idiom and personal style can affect the form and contour both of the tune and the performance may be observed in the following comparison of three versions of the tune, "Bridge Over Troubled Waters," performed by Paul Simon, Maynard Ferguson, and Roberta Flack (see Preface). You can follow the details by counting measures at the indicated tempo while you listen to the recordings. Count 1-2-3-4, 2-2-3-4, and so on, in 4/4 meter. To locate the downbeats listen for the accented notes in the bass line, especially those coinciding with accented words.

As sung by Simon, the piece begins with an 8-bar introduction at a tempo of approximately 82 beats per minute. The first verse and chorus proceed as outlined above (three periods of 9, 6, and 8 measures, respectively); they are followed by a 5-bar interlude leading to the second verse. The second verse is almost identical musically, but at the end of the second phrase of the refrain the contour is altered, and the harmonic cadence is postponed for two more measures making the refrain ten bars long. Next comes an 8-bar interlude.

The first phrase of the last verse has the same contour as in the first two, but is heard the interval of a third higher. The second phrase has a slightly different contour to accommodate the 7-syllable line of the lyric, "All your dreams are on their way." The end of the first phrase of the second period is considerably altered, and the chorus is extended to 13 bars before the final cadence on the tonic chord is reached. The entire structure is 97 measures long and lasts 4 minutes, 52 seconds.

Jazz trumpeter Maynard Ferguson's version of Simon's tune begins with a 4-measure introduction at a slightly slower tempo of approximately 72 beats per minute. The first phrase of the first verse is shortened to 8 measures, and the refrain is shortened to 7 measures. Following a 4-measure interlude the second verse begins, and proceeds through three periods of 8, 6, and 8 measures, respectively. The saxophone section plays the first period, again of 8 bars instead of the original 9, with moderately elaborate embellishment. Since several saxes are playing in unison we may safely assume that they are not improvising, but that their line has been written out.

Ferguson plays the first four bars of the second period, unembellished except for the very end of the phrase. A solo saxophone picks up the last two measures of this period and continues through the 8-bar refrain in what is apparently a spontaneous, and extremely elaborate, improvisation. The third verse begins immediately, without an interlude, but not a third higher as in Simon's performance. Ferguson plays the first 8-bar period with some embellishment. The entire trumpet section plays the first four bars of the second period, and the sax section completes it. Ferguson plays the 8-bar refrain somewhat freely, and the performance ends with a 2-bar coda. The entire performance, 75 measures long, lasts 4 minutes, 4 seconds.

Another interesting version of "Bridge" is by the singer Roberta Flack. While the Simon and Ferguson performances were in 4/4 meter at moderate tempos in the key of E-flat major, Roberta Flack's interpretation is in 6/8 meter at a tempo of about 46 dotted-quarter-note beats per minute, in the key a half-step higher, E major. Its overall length is 136 measures, lasting 7 minutes, 13 seconds. With respect to its contour, Simon's melody is altered only slightly, but radical changes are introduced in the rhythm. The beginnings and endings of melodic phrases are often delayed so that they overlap with the harmonic and rhythmic phrases of the accompaniment.

TIMBRE AND STYLE

Besides the contrasts in structure and melodic contour among the three performances just examined, differences in timbre are also conspicuous. Although various substyles in popular music do favor certain combinations of instruments over others, there is generally no fixed grouping as there is in classical music, with its comparatively few standard combinations from the string quartet to the symphony orchestra. Thus it is in timbre that one may observe the clearest distinction between popular and classical styles in general. Nowadays all sorts of orchestral and non-orchestral instruments are heard from time to time in the popular idiom, especially in recordings, most often in orchestrations that permit each to be exploited for its distinctive timbre as a solo instrument in an essentially heterogeneous sonority. However, nearly every popular ensemble includes a keyboard instrument, guitars, and stringed bass, any or all of which may be either electrical or acoustical.

Above all one expects to hear a rhythm section that is markedly different from that used in the classical tradition, both in its makeup and in its function. It may exploit the piano, guitar, banjo, and stringed bass for their percussive qualities aside from their melodic or harmonic capacities. Most importantly, the rhythm section will include a complete set of bona fide percussion instruments commonly referred to as *traps,* comprising at the very least a *bass drum, snare drum, tom-tom,* a *ride* (single) *cymbal,* and a *high hat* (two cymbals facing one another horizontally, brought together by means of a foot pedal). The trap set is played by one person, while the so-called *percussion battery* of the symphony orchestra is often manned by two or more players.

The traps may be absent altogether from a given performance, as in Roberta Flack's version of "Bridge," or they may be present only through a part of it, as in Simon's own recording, or all of it as in Ferguson's. When they are used they are normally heard throughout every measure, as an integral but variegated palette of color in the total sonority. In classical music, on the other hand, percussion instruments are used primarily to reinforce cadences, climaxes, or occasional accents. Rarely are they used only for their coloristic effects, as in the "Festival at Baghdad" from Rimsky-Korsakov's *Scheherazade* suite, or the Janizary (Turkish military) music heard near the beginning of the Finale to Beethoven's Ninth Symphony.

VOCAL STYLE

Vocal timbre is another important vehicle of idiomatic and personal stylization in popular music. In the classical tradition the emotional qualities of a song as the composer conceived them are implicit in the union of words and music. The composer assumes that all singers who perform his song will use a vocal color consistent with a single ideal: one "right" kind of sound cultivated through systematic study, and marked by fullness and evenness of timbre, a controlled *vibrato* (a continuous, even fluctuation in pitch, spanning approximately a half step six or seven times a second). The same timbre is supposed to be used at all dynamic levels and in all possible expressive contexts, whether lyrical or dramatic. On the other hand, in popular music the emotional burden of a song is illuminated principally by the singer's voice. Thus the multiplicity of styles comprising the popular tradition as a whole is reflected in an astounding variety of timbres (see also above, pp. 38-39).

Musical comedy sometimes requires voices trained according to classical precepts. However, at present this branch of the theater most often makes use of the singing actor, who uses a less self-conscious, comparatively "amateurish" type of sound with uneven vibrato, ostensibly arising out of the speech-style and the personality of the particular character he is portraying.

The *crooner* in the lineage of Bing Crosby, Perry Como, and Frank Sinatra uses a subdued, youngish, semi-trained baritone quality, with moderate, controlled vibrato, and an urbane and proper, albeit casual, pronunciation. The country/western singer favors an untrained but naturally "nice," clear, intense yet dignified vocal timbre, often somewhat nasal, with a stylized rural or western dialect. The folk singer displays either a conversational uncultivated sound like Bob Dylan's, or a light, carefully controlled and heady quality, sometimes with *falsetto* * inflections, with a narrow, rapid vibrato. Whatever their other distinctions, these singers' styles all identify them as belonging to the Caucasian race.

The blues singer most often uses a wailing or moaning type of vocal delivery sometimes without vibrato, in the dialect of the black American. The rock singer, whether black or white, uses a similarly untrained, intensely emotional sound, sometimes heightened by a strained throatiness that imparts an impression of tremendous physical energy. This is more than just loudness. It overrides, for the satisfaction of those who feel the need of it, the cold and inhuman power of the electronic medium through which most rock is experienced. Indeed, some people greatly enjoy the sheer kinetic quality of performances by groups like the Rolling Stones, apart from all other musical considerations.

With the exception of ragtime and boogie-woogie, which were originally piano idioms, instrumental styles in popular music have derived certain of their characteristics from performers' efforts to make their instruments imitate vocal techniques such as the *portamento* (a sliding into or away from the intended pitch), or the changing of timbre within one sustained pitch. Louis Armstrong, for instance, often made his trumpet sound like an extension of his own voice.

AN IMPETUS TO INNOVATION

Beginning in the 1960s the use of electronically generated or modified sounds in popular music provided a stimulus to the evolution of new instrumental styles. Rock guitarists, for example, such as Eric Clapton, Keith

---

* *Falsetto:* The timbre of the register above a singer's normal or "chest" voice. *Yodeling* is a rapid alternation between pitches in the two registers.

Richard, and Jimi Hendrix, have exploited some of the musical possibilities of *feedback, distortion,* the *fuzz box,* and the *wah-wah pedal.* The first is a sometimes shrill sound that results when a microphone or guitar pickup is placed too close to the speakers, allowing the amplified sound to be fed back into the transducer. The second is a sound of somewhat indistinct pitch produced by overdriving the amplifier on an electric guitar or PA system. A *fuzz box* is an electronic device that suppresses the fundamental frequency of a sound and exaggerates the harmonics. The *wah-wah pedal* is a foot-operated filter with which the performer can change the timbre of a sound instantly by increasing the amplitude of the midrange frequencies in a given tone.

These and the many other electronic devices, most of them difficult to describe in laymen's terms, which are now being used in popular performances, have enhanced the expressive potential of timbre as an independent parameter. Heterogeneity and variety in this respect have become salient features of the popular tradition as a whole. Consequently, now more than ever before the performer may be judged on his ability to manipulate timbre in an innovative and interesting way apart from tune and text. At the same time the listener is required to open his ears—and his mind—to an ever-expanding world of sound.

RHYTHM AND STYLE

The meter of a popular tune is nearly always explicit in that it is persistently audible at least in the bass line if not in the drums. Moreover, the variety of timbres present in the rhythm section are often used to produce an intricate polyrhythmic texture. In addition to the basic rhythm instruments already mentioned, others may be used, such as the *tambourine, wood block, cowbell, maracas,* the *guiro, claves,* and *bongo drums.* In Latin-American styles such as the samba, the bossa nova, the rhumba, and the mambo, there may be as many as a dozen different layers of timbre, each carrying a different rhythmic pattern. In addition, a solo chorus may be accompanied by other instruments playing a chordal rhythmic motif called a *riff,* adding yet another layer of rhythmic activity to the performance.

In classical music, however, meter is almost always implied in various subtle ways through melodic designs, harmonic structure, and texture. Downbeats and meter will be established in several ways: dynamic accents, agogic (durational) accents, increased densities, directional effects of rhythmic patterns in the melody (a rapid figure often culminates on an accented note), turning points in melodic direction, and strategically placed high or low melodic notes.

Since most of our popular music is traditionally associated with the comparatively restrained social dancing of American culture, isometric rhythm is decidedly favored. Multimeter occurs in some of our folk styles almost by mistake, and is occasionally introduced in rock, jazz, or blues performances for the sake of variety.

Accelerando and rallentando, which may be used in classical music to reinforce climaxes and transitions, are rarely heard in Western popular music. Typically, a steady underlying pulse is always present, except that an introductory verse to a ballad may be performed in a rubato manner. In jazz and blues the performers often create a high degree of tension by combining freedom or "looseness" in the melodic rhythm with strict regularity of pulse in the accompaniment, while country/western performers frequently observe a rigid meter in all parts. Except for some country/western and folk music in triple meter and some jazz in uneven meters and in free rhythm (see Example V-9), the bulk of American popular music is in duple or quadruple meter, either simple or compound—2/2, 4/4, 6/8, or 12/8.

Syncopation, which is the displacement of an accented beat (see p. 42), is often cited as one of the most common features of modern popular music, although it has also been an important device in classical music since at least the fourteenth century. In Simon's version of "Bridge," during the transitional measures between the first and second choruses (the so-called *turnaround),* a chain of syncopations seems suddenly to change the basic pulse from the quarter note to the eighth note, resulting in what at first seems to be a short multimetric passage only a few beats long. A similar instance is found in Ferguson's performance in the second verse, second phrase, third measure. A little later in the same piece syncopation produces an isolated proportional change in meter— three beats are heard in the space of two preceding beats. In every such case the full impact of the device lies in the tension between what is heard and what is felt—between the manifest accents and the ongoing thrust of the isometric rhythm before and after the disturbance.

Syncopation is an important element in *swing,* one of the most obvious and necessary but least understood characteristics of jazz. To begin with, *swing* is the performance of a simple meter as if it were compound. That is, a melody written in 4/4 is played or sung in 12/8. Furthermore, syncopation places accents at the end of the triplet rather than on the downbeat. Finally the pitch on the accented upbeat is *slurred* (connected) to the following downbeat. Thus a line written

would be performed

Swing is not merely a question of meter, syncopation, and articulation, however. It also requires certain inflections in pitch, timbre, and loudness that are much easier to recognize than to learn. Typical envelopes in swing style are suggested by the nonsense syllables used by *scat* singers who imitate instrumental jazz effects with their voices—*bwee, bow,* and the one that serves to identify an entire style, *bebop.*

To be sure, not all popular music is characterized by swing. Most country/western music is in "straight-eighth" style with all notes played as written, all subdivisions duple, and all accents on the beat. In Ferguson's performance of "Bridge," which otherwise "swings," the saxophone passage in the second verse is in straight-eighth style.

In the overall rhythmic life of every popular performance unity and variety are present simultaneously. The underlying isometric framework serves as one of the unifying factors; what happens within it—syncopation, swing, the various layers of timbre through which all rhythmic events are made explicit—constitute elements of variety.

TEXTURE: MELODY AND HARMONY

Usually the melodic parameter of a popular performance also embodies a simultaneous balance of unity and variety, since theme-and-variations structure is the conventional procedure. Thus in Ferguson's version of "Bridge" the highly varied saxophone improvisations in the second chorus, the saxophone line in the last two measures of the third verse, and the entire texture in the second half of the third chorus, must be heard against the imaginary background of the tune in its original form.

Popular music is essentially homophonic in conception, as is proven by the fact that every tune can be reduced to a lead sheet. The actual performance of a song, however, might include some polyphony or quasi-polyphony. Countermelodies may be added, for instance, by emphasizing single notes of consecutive chords in the accompaniment. Sometimes even a riff will take on a distinctly melodic character. Moreover, the performers accompanying a vocal or instrumental soloist may introduce complementary melodic lines in the spaces between the ends of a melodic phrase and the end of the 4-bar harmonic phrase (the *break*) in the blues (Example VI-3). Finally, a performance in Dixieland jazz style normally concludes with a chorus in which all the soloists improvise at the same time, creating an extremely intricate polyphonic texture.

No matter how much variety may be introduced in melodic embellishment, timbre, or rhythmic detail, unity will normally be maintained in meter and tempo as well as in tonality and harmonic vocabulary. A very large number of tunes, especially in country/western, folk, and rock, are in a single key throughout, and most of the remainder contain only a simple modulation in the bridge, usually to the key of the subdominant. Moreover, the harmonic vocabulary of, say, a country/western or rock tune will normally consist of but five or six different triads. Even though a jazz performance in the *progressive, cool,* or *bebop* styles will contain a comparatively large vocabulary of triads, as well as many extensions of them into seventh, ninth, and eleventh chords, variety from one chorus to another in this parameter is usually limited.

Atonality is rarely heard in popular music. Even in the *free jazz* of Eric Dolphy and Pharaoh Sanders, where conventional melodic and harmonic patterns are set aside to permit complete spontaneity of invention by every performer, a tonal center nearly always is present. It may be asserted by means of an ostinato or it may emerge by pure coincidence.

LYRICS AS CULTURAL DOCUMENTS

Just as in the art song, every popular song is characterized by a more or less intimate relationship between words and tune. The rhythmic characteristics of the tune will ordinarily be congruent with those of the text, and the melodic inflections will coincide with those of individual words or syllables. The two may also be united to the extent that the mood implied by the words is reflected in the tune. Unlike the art song, however, the fusion of the two is not necessarily permanent. A good tune may survive for generations while its lyric, ephemeral by its very nature, may soon be discarded.

A popular lyric presents a subjective, sentimental, timely point of view rather than an objective, philosophical one. For this reason lyrics can be studied as cultural documents and can provide us with valuable clues as to the ideals and attitudes of the people among whom they have been popular. In their topics, wording, grammar, and dialect they can reveal some of the moral and ethical preoccupations of other social strata, age groups, or generations, as well as our own.

Broadly speaking, popular lyrics may reflect moods of joy, sorrow, anxiety, or anger, and attitudes of optimism, pessimism, sentimentality, or realism. Most songs are clearly about romantic love, but any subject from the most trivial to the most momentous is likely to be encountered. It is often possible to interpret songs symbolically. A lyric may be about alienation, drugs, sexual exploitation or dependence, eroticism, narcissism, politics, or religion, depending on who is singing, and who is listening, and why. There may, for instance, be several possible interpretations of various lines in "Bridge Over Troubled Waters."

Finally, popular songs—the tunes and lyrics together—can serve as personal memorabilia. They can invoke our own past, providing a kind of private, informal musical tradition in our individual lives, just as the replaying of the art music of old can lend a semblance of stability to our larger cultural existence. Thus both traditions are indispensable in a society as fluid and fast-paced as ours.

CONVERGENCES

The fundamental nature of the distinctions pointed out so far prohibits a complete amalgamation of the popular and classical traditions without the utter destruction of one or the other. At the same time, numerous musicians have modified one tradition with some of the characteristics of the other. The results have represented mostly compromise rather than synthesis.

The first notable efforts in the twentieth century were made by George Gershwin, a self-taught musician whose success as a songwriter for the Broadway musical theater has not been surpassed by anyone since. Gershwin also composed several important classical works in "jazz" style, notably *Rhapsody in Blue* (1924), *An American in Paris* (1928), and the opera *Porgy and Bess* (1935). In each of these we hear informal melodies built mainly of 4-bar phrases over bouncy vamps or riffs, some syncopation and rhythmic swing, and suggestions of the blues. These conspicuous marks of popular style are counteracted by the large homogeneous string sonority and the small, comparatively colorless symphonic percussion section.

Other popular musicians, some with thorough academic backgrounds in music, have used the jazz band to exploit structural procedures indigenous to the classical tradition. These men include William Russo, Shorty Rogers, Jimmy Giuffre, and J. J. Johnson (see above, p. 59; Example VII-4).

A few composers belonging to the classical tradition have been inspired by the rhythmic and melodic characteristics of various popular idioms. Stravinsky's *L'Histoire du Soldat* (1918) contains the unmistakable rhythmic character of ragtime, which was still popular then. Darius Milhaud's music for the ballets *Le Boeuf sur le Toit* (The Bull on the Roof, 1920) and *La Création du Monde* (The Creation of the World, 1923), also reveal their composer's fascination with current popular styles.

A less subtle combination of the two traditions is sometimes heard in the playing of classical works in jazz or rock style. Duke Ellington's arrangements of Tchaikovsky's *Nutcracker Suite* and Grieg's *Peer Gynt Suite* are typical, as are the interpretations of the music of J. S. Bach by the Swingle Singers or the Jacques Loussier Trio.

Several so-called operas have been "composed" in rock style, such as *Jesus Christ, Superstar* and *Tommy*. As interesting or exciting as they may be, however, they do not belong to the same tradition as Britten's *Peter Grimes*. They consist of a series of separate lyrical episodes connected by a thin thread of a story, like the musical comedy, and they bear the unmistakable hallmarks of the popular idiom. Above all, their wide appeal rests partly on their recorded versions which in turn rely heavily on the technological resources of skillful recording engineers.

Perhaps the most successful attempts to combine the popular and classical traditions are found in works like "Little Blue Devil," from *Seven Studies on Themes of Paul Klee,* by Gunther Schuller. Schuller, the leading exponent of what is called *third stream* music, is thoroughly grounded in both the classical and jazz idioms. Less versatile men may produce extremely attractive hybrids, but the perceptive listener will usually be able to discern the composer's real musical origins. Jazzed classics are still jazz, a rock opera is still rock, and Stravinskian ragtime is still classical music. In other words, the two traditions may duly enliven one another to their exclusive benefits and our immense enjoyment, but they inevitably retain their own integrity.

art music in the united states

Each use of music discussed in the preceding chapters imposes definite limitations on the composer; there are some things he cannot do in one or more parameters and still remain within the boundaries of an appropriate style. To be sure, there are opportunities for the composer to be innovative, but in the long run it is less important to be original than it is to respect the requirements of the style, for they arise from causes extrinsic to music and beyond the composer's control. They are rooted in factors such as the skills and ages of the performers, the tastes and preoccupations of the hearers, the technological aspects of a given medium, the temporal or acoustical dimensions of a situation, and so on.

ART MEANS FREEDOM

Furthermore, we have often observed that the composer of art music is at liberty to choose from a wider variety of solutions to a particular problem than the composer of practical music. Indeed, it might be said that *art imposes freedom upon the composer*—freedom to determine for himself the limitations of the system within which he shall construct a design, along with the obligation to accept full responsibility for his choice. He need not take into consideration any extrinsic determinants that might confine his imagination, such as the size of an average pianist's hand or the technical facility a singer is "normally" expected to possess; but he must willingly risk the possibility his work will be deemed "unplayable" if he writes something out of the ordinary (a few of Beethoven's compositions were considered so by some of his contemporaries!), or that there may be no willing audience for it (Charles Ives's *Three Places in New England* was not performed in public until seventeen years after it was composed!). Of course, it is always possible that some performer or listener will eventually learn to hear things his way.

But the art composer does not have to tread unfamiliar ground. He may choose to work within a style already developed by the weight of tradition or the leadership of a specific individual into a major trend. He may emulate the impressionism of Debussy's *Afternoon of a Faun,* the post-romanticism of Richard Strauss's *Till Eulenspiegel,* the expressionism of Schoenberg's *Accompaniment to a Film Scene,* or the Americanism of Copland's ballets. His objective will be to exhibit his own creative ability within a style he presumes is comprehensible both to trained performers and to knowledgeable listeners.

Art imposes freedom upon the listener also—freedom to listen or not! Art music is just about the only kind we are not compelled to listen to against our will by virtue of its attachment or subordination to some other activity or circumstance. So much music is used for purposes outside itself that many persons find it difficult to concentrate on any piece written solely for its own sake.

Let it be understood, however, that the decision to *listen* to music as art must be complete and unequivocal. If one's attention wanders from the music to other subjects not specifically related to it—except perhaps in the case of *program music*—then the music is not functioning as art for him but as background sound for his private thoughts.

MAKING A VALUE JUDGMENT

Having committed himself to experiencing a work of art music, the listener ought to be prepared eventually to make some sort of a private judgment about it. Active listening demands an investment of time and attention. Time can only be spent, never saved; it can either be invested profitably, or wasted. We usually spend our time and our attention in practical ways, satisfying the necessities of everyday existence in the pleasantest way at our command. We also give our time to others (the participants in an athletic contest, the actors in a television drama, the author of a novel, or a composer and his performers) with no practical advantage in mind.

We know we have spent time profitably when the activity promises the possibility of pleasant recollections in the future. We are thus pleased not only with the activity but with ourselves. We sometimes know we are using time well when it seems to pass quickly. Conversely, we feel we are wasting our time when an activity or event bores us, and the minutes seem longer to us than they really are. Time "drags," as the saying goes, when we are pleased neither with ourselves nor with the people to whom we have entrusted our time.

Therefore, the simplest criterion for the evaluation of a work of musical art is, "Was it *worth* my time?" This kind of judgment is complete in itself, and no further questions need to be asked. Nearly every listener, regardless of his knowledge or experience, makes that kind of judgment a part if not all of his reaction to an unfamiliar piece of music, or to a new performance of an old one.

But the desire to understand *why* a given musical experience was or was not worthwhile impels some to listen inquisitively, which is to say, intellectually. Inquisitive listening can increase the value of the time expended on a piece of art music, whether the listener likes the work or not. As we observed in Chapter VII, the reward of inquiry is discovery of the ways in which the composer has solved the essential problem of extending a sonorous design in time, and has balanced unity with variety.

The process of discovery requires the investment of time and attention in the same composition over and over again. There is no shortcut to the understanding of any piece of music, nor is there any particular state of sublime consciousness or advanced intelligence from which one is privileged to secure instant insights. More importantly, the process is not always exhaustive or final, but may reflect gradual growth on the part of the listener. Indeed, regardless of our immediate sensory response, the worth of a composition may be measured by its capacity to tolerate repetition not only as a valuable sensory experience but as an object for inquisitive contemplation.

FOUR EXERCISES IN DISCOVERY

The inquisitive listener may direct his attention toward intrinsic sonorous details, or he may draw upon comparative criteria such as his familiarity with other works by the same composer or in a similar style. Usually he uses both kinds of knowledge. He may acquire his intellectual equipment through formal education, by reading books or record album notes, or through varied and extensive listening.

In the examples that follow we shall direct our attention first toward the music itself. Explanations of extrinsic details will be postponed until after the process of aural discovery has been at least temporarily completed. In order to facilitate analysis by permitting comparison, we shall study two short compositions by Charles Ives that exist in dual versions.

As a listener you are free to arrive at your own private understanding of the music, so proceed immediately to the listening experience. Listen to each example several times—five, six, a dozen or more—beginning with the purely sensory experience. Do not try to verbalize about your reactions too soon, but wait until the intrinsic characteristics of the music draw attention to themselves, one by one. When you begin to formulate objective explanations of what you hear, you need only call upon the concepts and terms discussed previously, especially in Chapters II through VII, as tools with which to identify whatever sonorous details you are able to recognize.

Make a list of the details you perceive under the general headings of the various musical parameters, beginning with those that draw your attention most forcibly and continuing in the order of your discovery. After you are satisfied that you have heard as many different details as you can, compare your lists with the ones below, keeping in mind that the analysis printed here is temporary and incomplete, just like yours. It is quite possible that you will have heard things in a different order or will have made other discoveries.

XIV-1   In Example XIV-1, Charles Ives's song, "The Pond" (composed in 1906), is performed by Adrienne Albert, mezzo-soprano, and the Columbia Chamber Ensemble under the direction of Gregg Smith. The words, written by the composer, are as follows:

> A sound of a distant horn.
> O'er shadow'd lake is borne
> My father's song.

The poem resembles a *haiku,* a type of Japanese lyric poem dealing with objects or experiences in nature which have moved the poet. Example *XIV-2* XIV-2 is an instrumental version of the same song conducted by Gunther Schuller. The analyses may be placed side by side to clarify their similarities and differences.

Vocal Version	*Instrumental Version*
Meter	Both versions seem to be *a*metrical (without meter or rhythmic differentiation at all) in the string chords at the beginning and the end, but quadruple isometric rhythm is established by percussive

sounds, and can be perceived in opening and closing sections after rehearing. Two main areas of metrical activity are evident: the downbeats in the accompaniment do not always coincide with the accented beats in the melody, creating a high degree of rhythmic tension which, as in jazz, helps move the piece along. Within the accompaniment alone are several other layers of metrical activity. The cello line consists mostly of long notes, and is rhythmically inert under the first two lines of the poem.

Within the accompaniment the various layers of rhythmic activity are clearly audible; the subdivision of the beat seems to be duple in the harp part, triple in the celesta (the instrument with the clear, bell-like sound). The meter could be either 4/4 or 12/8.

The polyrhythms clearly heard in the vocal version are less obvious here. The meter is decidedly 4/4.

Tempo

Presence of words possibly encouraged moderate tempo (about 66 beats per minute). Total length, 1:06.

Absence of words may have prompted slower tempo (about 36 beats per minute), but it does not seem too slow in comparison. Total length, 1:53.

Timbre

First element of variety is one clear celesta note at about the seventh beat. Moderately wide vibrato in voice.

First element of variety is a barely audible harp note at the same point. Very narrow vibrato in trumpet.

Piccolo imitates vocal melody beginning at first syllable of *distant.*

Flute in canon with trumpet. Other differences in instrumentation are evident.

Sustained sounds of trumpet, flute, piccolo, and strings contrast with percussive envelopes (instant growth/gradual decay) of celesta, harp, and bells (glockenspiel).

Texture

Fairly transparent, owing to contrasts in timbres and envelopes as well as rhythmic differentiation.

Less transparent than vocal version owing to a different sort of balance among instruments (perhaps a consequence of microphone placement?), and subtler instrumentation of inner parts.

Dynamic changes implied by changes in density of texture. Somewhat polyphonic in that the melody is imitated canonically, and other accompanying parts are rhythmically differentiated from one another, but homophonic in the sense that one melody dominates the texture by virtue of its cohesive design, distinctive timbre (including the presence of words in the vocal version), and higher dynamic level. The notes of both versions are identical, but differences in timbre, tempo, blend, and balance result in separate and unique performances.

Tonality   One tonal center, heard as the lowest note in the texture (*g*) is literally in the center of the piece. It is not present at the beginning or end, yet it is clearly the tonic pitch.

Form   Except that the principle of juxtaposition is present in the tonality (and seemingly, at first, in meter), the piece consists of a superposition of unifying and varying factors. The melody is an element of variety in that it unfolds continuously, even ending on a different pitch from that on which it began. Yet it unifies by its structural coherence and its dynamic prominence, even without words. A degree of tension between unity and variety is also present in the texture, which is both homophonic and polyphonic. The quadruple meter at a steady tempo provides unity, but the inner polyrhythms add variety. A climax in the overall design occurs at the word *lake*.

XIV-3 and 4   Examples XIV-3 and 4 are corresponding versions of the song "Like a Sick Eagle" (composed in 1909). The first is sung by Adrienne Albert, with the Columbia Chamber Ensemble conducted by Gregg Smith; the second is a wholly instrumental setting conducted by Gunther Schuller. The text is from a sonnet by John Keats, entitled "On Seeing the Elgin Marbles":

The spirit is too weak—mortality
Weighs heavily on me like unwilling sleep,
And each imagined pinnacle and steep
Of godlike hardship tells me I must die
Like a sick eagle looking at [towards] the sky.

Vocal Version

Instrumental Version

Timbre   Most conspicuous is the effect of utter desolation produced in the violin and voice by the act of sliding (*portamento*) from one note to the next (an apo-   The portamento is less pronounced in the string part, and is entirely absent from the English horn (solo) line.

theosis of the blues, perhaps? Compare Miles Davis, "Selim," Example V-9).

No vibrato in voice or violin lines.

Vibrato in English horn; slight vibrato in violin line.

Piano notes near end are somewhat subdued, and the last, especially, is blended with the string sound on the same pitch so as to give a unique quality to the latter, as if it were a "bowed piano tone" or a "violin note plucked and bowed simultaneously."

Piano sounds are prominent in both instances.

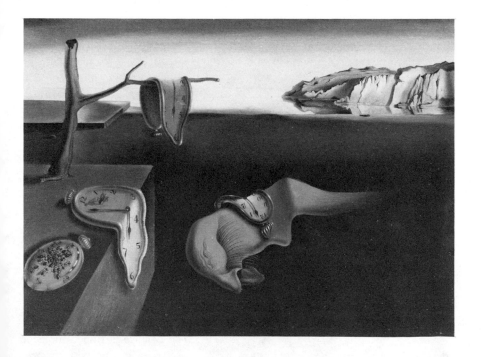

FIGURE 20   Salvador Dali, *The Persistence of Memory,* 1931. Oil on canvas, 9½ x 13". Collection, The Museum of Modern Art, New York. The distortion of recognizable objects to achieve new expressive ends, as seen in this surrealist painting, has been paralleled in the practices of certain twentieth-century composers, beginning with Charles Ives.

All lines are consistently legato and steady-state.	Gradual growth and decay (crescendo/decrescendo) envelope of opening violin notes is conspicuous.

Similarity and homogeneity of timbres in accompanying parts make lines difficult to separate aurally at times, especially in the latter part of the piece. For instance, the flute enters somewhere before or after the word "godlike," but the exact moment of its introduction is indistinguishable.

Texture Essentially homophonic, but the accompaniment is clearly polyphonic. The principal melody, like the inner lines, is mostly conjunct, chromatic, and continuously unfolding, with a climax in its arch-like contour at the word "godlike."

Meter Evidently 4/4 throughout, judging from the melodic accents which are reinforced by the locations of certain important words.

Tempo is very slow (about 40 beats per minute) and steady. Total length, 1:59.	Moderate tempo starting at about 62 beats per minute. Noticeable fluctuations in tempo—accelerando and *ritardando* (slowing down). Total length, 1:24.

Dynamics

Little change throughout, except as implied by higher notes in the voice.	Deliberate crescendo and decrescendo.

Form Built entirely on the principle of superposition. Unity is present in texture, meter, and timbre.

Portamento, stable dynamics, and steady tempo are added elements of unity. In fact, unity is emphasized in this performance.	The climax which occurs in the phrase "tells me I must die," is achieved by the combination of crescendo and accelerando; it is relieved by the ensuing decrescendo and ritardando. The balance is tipped in favor of variety in this performance.

IVES'S PHILOSOPHY: SUBSTANCE *VERSUS* MANNER

One of the more noteworthy aspects of the two preceding pairs of compositions is the flexibility of their instrumentation. Typically, Ives often failed to specify whether a song was to be sung or played. Moreover, in his strictly instrumental works he sometimes failed to indicate which instruments were to play which parts. He would write passages for a single instrument, the piano for instance, that could not possibly be played by one person, leaving it to the performer to decide how to resolve the dilemma.

Since we have already insisted that the composer of art music typically conceives his compositions in their entirety and leaves little opportunity for the performer to contribute anything, we may seem to be implying that Ives was an inferior artist. To be sure, Ives's practice was unheard of among his major contemporaries, such as Richard Strauss, Ralph Vaughan Williams, Arnold Schoenberg, and Igor Stravinsky, all of whom placed considerable emphasis upon the appropriateness of a particular timbre to a given line of music. But Ives was simply reflecting his commitment to his doctrine of the separateness of "substance" and "manner."

Ives equated substance with essential reality, quality, or spirit—we might say *idea* in the profoundest sense. Manner was to him but the outer appearance of an object or experience—we might say *style*. He himself insisted the two concepts were ultimately undefinable. Substance, he said, can only be "appreciated by the intuition, and somehow translated into expression by 'manner'—a process always less important than it seems." [1] In other words, the manner of presentation of his music is only incidental to the process of revealing the substance within it, a proposition he once put rather more succinctly in the exclamation, "My God! What has sound to do with music!"

In his separation of substance and manner in all aspects of life, Ives is clearly identified with the transcendentalist outlook of Ralph Waldo Emerson and Henry David Thoreau. One aspect of this philosophy found in his music is his dedication to the ideal of the omnipresence of cosmic unity within the infinite diversity of nature and humanity. This is reflected in his habit of building up to a tremendous climax of incredible complexity, even cacophony, only to have it cease abruptly, leaving a quiet, sustained, homogeneous chord suspended like a phantom in midair. This could be the significance of the ending of "The Pond" on the high, ethereal *harmonics* of the violins.

Still another characteristic of much of Ives's music is the "psychological structure" residing in the progression of emotions and moods aroused in

[1] Charles Ives, *Essays Before A Sonata, and Other Writings,* ed. Howard Boatwright (New York: W. W. Norton & Co., Inc., 1961), p. 75. Copyright © 1961, 1962, by W. W. Norton & Company, Inc., New York. With the permission of the publisher.

the listener. The listener and the performer are thus made partners with the composer in the creation of a work of art.

To the listener who has never heard anything like them before, Ives's four little pieces may sound extremely bizarre. However, Ives did not equate beauty with pleasantness, but with substance. "Beauty in music," he said, "is too often confused with something that lets the ears lie back in an easy chair. Many sounds that we are used to do not bother us, and for that reason we are inclined to call them beautiful. . . . A narcotic is not always unnecessary, but it is seldom a basis of progress." [2]

Frequently Ives wrote "pretty" music merely so that he could break its mood with an incongruous, humorous gesture of some sort. For instance, near the end of "Washington's Birthday," from the symphony *Holidays,* he slices off a stupendous climax to reveal the sublime aura of a fragile sonority in the strings; this evolves into a sentimental, half-recognizable tune orchestrated in modern mood-music manner. This presently is joined slyly by the entrance of "Good Night, Ladies"—in a different key! The hilarity of the entire episode could hardly be missed even by those who habitually regard all "serious" music as solemn.

Ives did not always use popular tunes just to be funny, of course. Nor was he indulging in the kind of musical chauvinism current among the nationalist composers of his time such as the American Arthur Farwell and the Bohemian Anton Dvořák. He quoted copiously from the popular tradition—love-songs, dances, patriotic songs, folk songs, Negro spirituals, hymns, circus marches, or ragtime, and he also drew ideas from the works of Beethoven, Brahms, and other classical composers. * He was fully capable of conceiving his own melodies, but he saw no reason to do so if an existing tune seemed to him to embody sufficient substance.

Whereas many composers in the romantic and post-romantic eras considered themselves alienated from the mainstream of everyday life, often widening that gap by deliberately being esoteric, Ives was always at pains to stress the positive connections between art and life. One of the more obvious examples of this illustrates his concern with the natural environment. His text to the piece for chorus and small orchestra entitled "The New River" (or "The Ruined River," 1911), reads: "Down the river comes a noise! It is not the voice of rolling waters. It's only the sounds of man, Dancing halls and tambourine, Phonographs and gasoline, Human beings

[2] Ives, *Essays Before A Sonata,* p. 97.

* Typically, Ives was not fastidious about accuracy in his quotations, whether musical or verbal. Note his use of the word "toward" in place of Keats's "at," in the text of "Like a Sick Eagle."

gone machine. Ta-ta-ra-ra boom de-ay. Killed is the blare of the hunting horn, the River Gods are gone!" [3]

His convictions regarding the relationships of art and life, integral in his music, arose from the conduct of his own life. Ives was only avocationally a composer. He made his living, and a good one at that, in the field of life insurance, so he had no need of profit from his compositions. This was fortunate, for he was ignored by musicians and listeners alike throughout his life, and he, in turn, was oblivious of them. His Third Symphony, completed in 1904, was not performed until some forty years later. It received a special citation from the New York Music Critics Circle in 1946, and the Pulitzer Prize in music in 1947, but Ives was indifferent both to the performance and to the accolades.

Ives's business career provided him with more than mere financial security; it kept before him the essential unity of art and life. As he once wrote to a friend:

The fabric of existence weaves itself whole. You cannot set an art off in the corner and hope for it to have vitality, reality, and substance. There can be nothing *"exclusive"* about a substantial art. It comes directly out of the heart of experience of life and thinking about life and living life. My work in music helped my business and my work in business helped my music.[4]

THE GIFT TO BE SIMPLE

In 1943 the eminent American composer Aaron Copland was commissioned by the noted patron of music, Elizabeth Sprague Coolidge, to write the music to a one-act ballet entitled *Appalachian Spring* to a scenario by the choreographer Martha Graham. The score received the New York Music Critics Circle Award for the 1944-45 season. In 1945 the composer arranged portions of it into an orchestral suite, which in turn won the Pulitzer Prize in music for that year.

The scenario deals with a pioneer housewarming party in the Appalachian mountains of Pennsylvania. The characters are a young farmer and his bride, an older pioneer woman, a revivalist, and four members of the revivalist preacher's flock. The suite consists of eight episodes played without pause. Example XIV-5 includes the "Solo Dance of the Bride," *XIV-5* in which her own feelings of joy and fear are suggested, followed by a

---

[3] "The New River" by Charles Ives, from *Thirty-Four Songs,* copyright 1933, Merion Music, Inc., used by permission.

[4] Quoted in Henry Bellamann, "Charles Ives: The Man and His Music," *Musical Quarterly,* XIX (January, 1933), 47.

quiet interlude, and then "Scenes of Daily Activity for the Bride and her Farmer-Husband."

The brief introductory passage to the first episode in the example consists of the exposition of a four-note pattern that might be shown graphically as \⟍⟋⟍ . This ultimately proves to be the germinal motif of the entire episode. Soon it appears as the beginning of a long melody consisting of rising and falling fragments of scales, with a smartly syncopated conclusion, which might be visualized as follows:

This theme is heard over a rapidly reiterated note *(g)* serving as the tonal center of the episode.

Beginning in a fast duple meter, the music twice shifts momentarily into triple meter, and once is interrupted by a passage apparently in free rhythm. The design consists of statements of the theme alternating with developmental treatments of the four-note motif. The forward motion of the music is halted finally by another passage consisting, like the introduction, of irregular exclamations of the motif, and the tempo broadens into that of the slow interlude. (Actually, the passages which sound as if they are in free rhythm are notated isometrically).

The slow section is built on a motif which reminds one of the popular tune, "When I fall in love," written by Victor Young in 1952; Copland's motif is thus lent an additional expressive dimension by association after the fact. The motif is explored briefly, emphasizing the rising interval of a fourth with which it begins. A fragment of the military signal "taps" is heard, suggesting repose at evening. The glowing timbre of the clarinet, signalling the dawn of another day, transforms the rising interval into the first two notes of the next episode.

"Scenes of Daily Activity" consists of five variations on a theme derived from the tune "Simple Gifts," a hymn of the Shakers, a colonial sect of religious fundamentalists. The first stanza and the refrain of the original hymn run:

> 'Tis the gift to be simple, 'tis the gift to be free,
> 'Tis the gift to come down where we ought to be,
> And when we find ourselves in the place just right,
> 'Twill be in the valley of love and delight.

When true simplicity is gain'd,
To bow and to bend we shan't be asham'd,
To turn, turn will be our delight,
Till by turning, turning we come round right.

In the opening statement of the dance-like theme a striking effect is heard in the accompanimental line to the first four bars, produced by flute and harp in unison. The two timbres blend so well we seem to be hearing a harp tone that is magically sustained instead of dying away instantly.

After a modulation to a new key, the first variation is begun by the oboe accompanied at the interval of a tenth by the bassoon. The second variation is played exactly half as fast as the preceding one, giving a more fluent, lyrical quality to the melody. The accompaniment suggests the whirr of a spinning-wheel. Beginning with the second period the theme is played as a canon between two groups of stringed instruments.

The third variation, again in a fast tempo, is begun by the trumpets and trombones accompanied by rapid scales in the high strings. An abbreviated variation—the first two periods only—is played slowly by the woodwind section. Finally, the first four bars are played by the entire orchestra at a broad tempo in a full, majestic sonority, concluding the episode in a mood of solemn, stern dignity.

The suite as a whole has the same outstanding attributes as these three sections—simplicity and unity. Simplicity is present in the brief and distinctive melodic themes. Overall unity is achieved mainly through repetition of the motif that is the subject of the quiet interlude we have just heard: it opens and closes the suite and serves as a transition among other episodes.

In addition, the contour of the opening motif of the "Solo Dance of the Bride" corresponds with that of the second episode of the suite, a portion of which was heard in Example V-3. Most important of all is the fact that, as we have seen in the present example, there is an organic relationship among melodic elements—and their rhythmic skeletons—at first present more to the listener's intuition than to his consciousness. The overall design grows and changes out of these basic ideas, not like a flower growing from a seed, but like the evolution of a crystal. The fact that the presence of that organicism has escaped neither the scrutiny of the critics nor the sensibilities of casual listeners for the past generation suggests that there might be in Copland's work a high degree of what Ives would have called substance.

Although few composers have been known for their philosophical persuasions, it so happens that the substance in Copland's music is present by virtue of his profound personal beliefs about the possible relationships between life and art, as was the case with Ives. But while the apparent complexity of Ives's music issued out of his commitment to the central doctrine of transcendentalism, the manifest simplicity of much of Copland's music is the consequence of his essentially pragmatist point of view: that the meaning of a proposition or a course of action lies in its practical consequences. In a musical context this suggests that the "meaning" of a composition is measurable in the audience's appreciation of it.

This means that the composer must recognize and respect the identity of the audience addressed through a given piece. One measure of a great composer is his ability to achieve this aim, and Copland has nearly always succeeded. Thus every one of his compositions must be regarded first of all from the perspective of the audience it was intended for. Throughout his life Copland has been non-exclusive in this regard, for he has written for many different types of audiences.

At the same time, even when he has written expressly for the least sophisticated listener or performer, stressing simplicity to the point of ordinariness, he has not compromised his artistic integrity. And when, at the other extreme, he has addressed the most elite and limited audience at a frankly esoteric level, he has not simply imitated the mannerisms of a current fashion.

Some of the characteristics of Copland's inimitable and unmistakable style are traceable to the circumstances of his background and experience. He was born of Jewish parents in Brooklyn, New York, in 1900. During the early years of his life he eagerly assimilated the elements of a wide variety of styles and idioms from the venerable masters of the past to the leading figures on the contemporary scene, especially Debussy and Stravinsky. Moreover, from the start he was sensitive to the popular tradition in American music, and recognized its potential implications for the composer of serious music.

As a young composer, the product chiefly of the tutelage of Nadia Boulanger in Paris, he belonged to a rising generation of American composers who were intensely aware of their nationality, but who considered themselves above the facile expediency of quoting homespun tunes. They sought instead, as Copland put it, to create a new musical language "on a level that left popular music far behind—music with a largeness of utterance wholly representative of the country that Whitman had envisaged." [5] Unfortunately, they had no way of knowing that Charles Ives had long since devised his own musical language to achieve that end in a most powerful and enduring way.

Copland's quest has been rigorous and unending. During the twenties he ventured to assimilate what appeared to him at that time to be the essential characteristics of jazz in works like *Music for the Theatre* (1925). Around 1930 he produced a number of so-called "abstract," or "difficult," works. There was the trio for piano, violin, and cello entitled *Vitebsk* (1928, "a study on a Jewish theme"), which employed quarter steps; there was the *Symphonic Ode* of 1929, which was deemed nearly unplayable at the time; and the *Piano Variations* (1931), a landmark in twentieth-century piano music. More recently he has employed the twelve-tone method in relatively austere works like *Connotations* (1962) and *Inscape* (1967).

From about 1934 until the end of the forties Copland tended away from purely abstract musical designs, devoting his energies to an attempt to define a more literal relationship between music and life. Specifically, the majority of works he wrote during this period in his career were intended to serve uses and functions of the kind we have been discussing in this book.

He wrote music for the secondary school, including choral songs, the play-opera *The Second Hurricane* (1936), and the orchestral *Outdoor Overture* (1937). He wrote underscores for films such as *Of Mice and Men* (1939), *Our Town* (1940), *The Red Pony* and *The Heiress* (both 1938), as well as for documentaries like *The Cummington Story* (1945). He composed incidental music for plays, and responded to commissions from the major radio networks with pieces such as *Music for Radio* (1936, subtitled "Saga of the Prairie"), and *John Henry* (1940), that were carefully planned to capture the affections of the new mass audience. Above all, he created some of the most important music of the entire twentieth century for the ballet theater in *Billy the Kid* (1930; see Example XI-2), *Rodeo* (1942), and *Appalachian Spring*.

Partly to assure the accessibility of these works to their intended audiences, Copland relied for melodic material upon whole tunes as well as aphoristic clichés gleaned from both the rural and urban popular traditions in music: cowboy songs and country dances, jazz from the big-city

[5] Aaron Copland, *Music and Imagination* (Cambridge, Mass.: Harvard University Press, 1962), p. 111.

nightclub, and even the popular music of Latin America for which he had a personal affinity, and which reflected the general interest in inter-American friendship current during the thirties and forties. He had a special way of handling such material, altering it just enough to redeem it from banality and make it his own without weakening its substantialness.

Copland has expressed the view that the essence of Americanism in music is a unique quality of rhythm found in American vernacular speech —syncopations and multimetric patterns created by successions of qualitative, strong-versus-weak accents spun out by the words we use and the inflections with which we speak them. This is in contrast to European music, which since the end of the Elizabethan era has reflected the quantitative, long-versus-short rhythmic patterns of the Romance languages. He discerned this characteristic in our popular music, especially jazz, its effect heightened by a powerful tension between the rhythmic freedom of the melodic line and the regularity of the underlying pulse.

Transmuting this substance into a personal musical style, Copland developed the attractive habit of establishing firmly in the listener's mind the regular, isometric pulse of, say, a common dance step, to the extent of almost demanding an overt physical response, and then suddenly introducing the erratic meters of an animated musical conversation, as in the first episode in Example XIV-5. Combined with this is his use of brief, disjunct, angular melodic ideas. These elements have made his style perfectly adaptable to the ballet and film.

Considered together, the two composers studied in this chapter represent in their music the principal opposing attitudes in the aesthetic dichotomy peculiar to American musical life throughout our history—the aristocratic versus the democratic. Charles Ives, who had no historical antecedents, appears to us today as a descendant of our leading cultural aristocrats—Emerson, Thoreau, and Thomas Jefferson. Aaron Copland's staunch individuality, optimism, and sincere respect for the tastes both of the common and the uncommon man, plus his irrepressibly exuberant delight in living, place him in the lineage of Benjamin Franklin and William Billings.

XV

international trends in contemporary art music

Among the recently composed art music which a listener is likely to encounter in concerts or on records, four major trends will appear to be in current usage: *neoclassicism, serialism, chance,* and *electronics*. It is safe to say that no living composer has entirely avoided the influences of all of them. Each trend originated during the first half of this century, if not earlier. Each reflects one or more dominant realities of contemporary existence in Western civilization. Finally, each has numerous ramifications of which only a few can be adequately illustrated and discussed here.

NEOCLASSICISM: THE USES OF THE PAST

Although the term *neoclassicism* literally suggests a renewal of some aspect of the Viennese classical style of the late eighteenth and early nineteenth centuries, actually it denotes a kind of contemporary music in which a few stylistic features peculiar to the twentieth century are combined with certain attributes of the baroque era.

To take a particular instance, let us consider Igor Stravinsky's Concerto for Piano and Wind Instruments (composed in 1924; revised in 1950). From it we may well learn something about the music of the past as well as that of the present. Listen to the first and second movements of the Concerto (XV-1) several times at the purely sensory level. Then, retaining your initial reaction if you can, listen several times more, perhaps at intervals of

XV-1

several days, using the following remarks to consolidate your viewpoint, either pro or con.

Stravinsky informs us by the manner in which he titles the first movement (*Largo; Allegro; Maestoso*) that it consists of three sections which are differentiated not only in tempo (slow; fast; slow) but also in mood ("broadly" or "grandly"; "cheerfully"; "majestically").

The theme of the *Largo* opens with a repeated-note figure in a dotted rhythm, quantitatively expressed as "long, longer, short, long, longer, short, long, etc." or in musical notation, ♩ ♩. ♪♪ ♩. ♪♪. . Coincidentally, the use of dotted rhythms and the repetition of the initial pitch is also to be found in the slow introduction of many baroque instrumental genres such as the *canzona* and the French *overture.* *

The theme is played by French horns and trombones, with the pitch and rhythm of the first four notes reinforced by the timpani. There is a brief upward modulation until the theme is heard again a minor third higher than the opening statement, this time in the trumpets. Presently it is heard for the third time beginning on the same note as at first, again in French horn and trombone. Thus the principle of juxtaposition—repetition-after-contrast—is present with regard to timbre and tonal center. The three consecutive repetitions of the melodic idea and its rhythmic pattern serve to favor unity over variety.

Stravinsky's *Allegro* is reminiscent in general style of a group of keyboard works by J. S. Bach called *inventions*. The term invention was used rather infrequently and loosely during the baroque era, but Bach employed it to denote some of his contrapuntal keyboard compositions employing two or three independent lines among which a single elaborate melodic idea was developed. The subject of Stravinsky's *Allegro* consists of three distinctive elements: a descending octave exclamation, ⌒ , which immediately identifies the tonal center of the entire section; a halting, gradually descending figure that reverses its direction several times, • •• •••••• ; and a short ascending scale passage, •••••• .

Except for one more complete statement of the theme, as if to reaffirm the tonal center and remind the listener what the music is all about, the entire section consists of ingenious manipulations of those three motifs in a contrapuntal texture that is intricate both melodically and rhythmically.

* David Ewen, in *The World of Twentieth Century Music* (Englewood Cliffs: Prentice-Hall, Inc., 1968), p. 796, calls this section a *toccata*. The term was used in the baroque era to denote a certain structural procedure used in keyboard music, but it was also applied around 1600 to a type of brass fanfare using timpani to double the bass line.

Nevertheless the attentive listener should be able to follow the separate lines at least intermittently, owing to the heterogeneity of the timbres.

The persistent use of syncopation gives a jazzy effect and serves to maintain the cheerful mood and the urgent rhythmic propulsion of the music. The regularity of the pulse is a powerful unifying element. Now and then, however, an isolated measure in a different meter creates a surprising, stumbling interruption of the forward motion which is all the more delightful if the listener has let himself be lured into tapping his foot to the music.

Sudden shifts from one motif or developmental device to another, as well as changes in timbre and in density of texture, are factors that help to make variety overpower unity during most of the *Allegro* section. Two abrupt changes in tempo—the first analogous in its effect to a stop-action movie—constitute even more radical elements of variety whose unpredictability is mitigated by the ultimate appearance of a majestic reminder of the opening *Largo*.

Taken as a whole, then, the first movement of Stravinsky's Piano Concerto is symmetrical with regard to tempo, melodic material, texture, timbre, and tonal center. It is a closed form—it circles back upon itself, ending approximately the way it began. In this sense it reflects a traditional value belonging to the distant past for, as we have already pointed out, contemporary composers generally have tended to avoid symmetrical structures. Moreover, the character of the respective sections with regard to texture, rhythm, and melodic phrasing is specifically reminiscent of the baroque. On the other hand, the harmonic structures that result from the congruence of the respective voices in the essentially polyphonic texture definitely belong to the twentieth century, and specifically to the music of Igor Stravinsky.

The second (*Largo*) movement embodies an even more intriguing fusion of the old and the new. The opening theme, stated by the piano, is repeated in a new and considerably altered version by the winds—or is it a new theme altogether? A cadenza follows, then an episode consisting of several vaguely similar ideas which somehow sound familiar, or at any rate consistent. The slow, regular pulse is once more interrupted by a cadenza in free rhythm, and the movement soon ends with a section that, dream-like, reminds us of the opening theme. There has really been no literal repetition whatsoever; new melodic ideas have continually unfolded. Nevertheless, the character and mood of the ending is so similar to that of the beginning that we are left with the almost subconscious conviction that the outline of the structure must be, roughly, *A-B-A*.

Stravinsky also managed to suggest a typical textural procedure of the baroque era while remaining entirely modern and individualistic in his treatment of it. Composers like Bach and Handel, Vivaldi and Corelli often contrasted movements in dense, turgid four- or five-part contrapuntal texture (review Example XII-3) with movements in which two or three independent treble voices or parts of equal interest were set off against a strong and relatively melodic foundation in the lower register called the *basso continuo* or *thorough bass*.

All performances in the baroque era were accompanied by a keyboard player, usually at a harpsichord. His main responsibility was to fill in the sonorous "space" between the bass and treble parts by playing the appropriate chords implied by the written parts, or indicated by numbers and other symbols in the so-called *figured bass* part. Most of the time his playing served to reinforce the basic flow of the rhythmic pulse, but frequently he improvised countermelodies or rhythmic motifs, and occasionally he was allowed a solo passage all his own. In other words, the keyboard musician in the baroque orchestra or chamber ensemble played from what corresponds to a lead sheet in modern popular music (see Figure 19), and he fulfilled about the same musical functions as the pianist in a jazz ensemble. The basso continuo procedure was abandoned by Haydn, Mozart, and succeeding composers, because the idea of the systematic development of themes gave greater importance to the inner parts of an instrumental texture, eliminating the necessity for filler.

Throughout the movement Stravinsky, who has of course written everything out and left nothing to the performer to improvise, maintains the spirit of the baroque in the essentially three-part texture, in the building of neat terraces of loudness rather than gradual slopes, and in the slow, flowing, lyrical type of melody commonly referred to as *cantilena*. At the same time the sound is emphatically that of the twentieth century in timbre, meter, and harmonic vocabulary.

Notice that Stravinsky deliberately contrasts and blends the timbres of the various wind instruments and that of the piano. Now he sets them against one another heterogeneously so as to make solo lines stand out. Now he juxtaposes brief passages of strikingly different hue. (When, at 1'40" into the movement a massive, brilliant chord in the full orchestra is cut off leaving the delicate sound of a flute dominating a transparent pianissimo sonority of piano, clarinet, and oboe, we cannot help but be reminded of Ives's method of showing the presence of oneness amid diversity.) Now he fuses a given piano pitch with a particular wind timbre so perfectly that, but for the presence of the percussive attack of the piano, one might not be able to tell which instrument is playing it.

Somewhat less noticeable is the fact that there are several multimetric episodes such as 2/4, 3/4, 2/4, 3/8, 2/4. Their obscurity is due to the legato character of the line and the extremely slow tempo. The time signature actually is 2/4, and the specified tempo is about 42 quarter notes per minute! (Compare this with the equally ambivalent metrical character of Beethoven's music in Example V-10. Try to conduct a few measures of

each, using the pattern 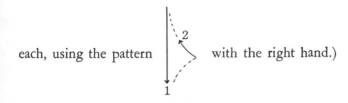 with the right hand.)

Another element of modernity that will probably escape all but the most skillful listener is the fact that the bass line does not serve a harmonic function by delineating the roots of chords, as one would find in the music of the eighteenth and nineteenth centuries. Specifically, it contains no outlines of the cadential pattern IV-V-I which is typical of music in the major/minor system. Instead it serves an independent and integral melodic role fully equivalent to that of the upper voices.

Stravinsky's Piano Concerto should not be regarded as a definitive example of neoclassicism, but as a particular instance of it. Neoclassicism is not a style but a point of view. It draws upon the present for many elements of variety, but it draws upon the past for many elements of unity. Moreover, the unity of a neoclassical composition exists not only within the music itself but also in the association which the listener may draw between what he hears and the venerable traditions in which he has been educated.

Stravinsky was notorious throughout his life for moving continually from one stylistic milieu to another, drawing successively upon sources as diverse as the fourteenth century, the baroque, the romantic era, and even jazz. He was sometimes accused of being more concerned with style than with idea, with manner more than substance. However, from the perspective of only a few years following the close of his long and tremendously fruitful career, almost any listener can easily recognize the consistency and the substantiality of his music. Regardless of which part of the past he used as a historical backdrop for a given composition, works as dissimilar in style as *Le Sacre du Printemps* (1913), *L'Histoire du Soldat* (1918; Example IV-1), the Piano Concerto, and the serial *Canticum Sacrum* (1956) and *Abraham and Isaac* (1963), all bear the unmistakable imprint of one of the most original and fascinating composers of the twentieth century to date. Above all, perhaps, that imprint consists in a clarity of detail analogous to the sharpness of outer-space photographs, which lack the delicate shading, or *chiaroscuro,* of earthly pictures.

SERIALISM: HIDDEN LOGIC

No matter how much the music of neoclassicism may differ from the styles that are the bygone sources of some of its salient characteristics, or how "difficult" it may sound, even the least sophisticated listener will concede its simplicity in comparison with most music based on the principle of *serialism.*

Serial music, by definition, contains a kind of unity and logic which sometimes can be found to permeate every possible parameter, although it is apt to strike the unprepared or unwilling listener by what seems to be the total unpredictability of it. Paradoxically, a serial composition may sound utterly disorganized even though it may really be far more unified than, say, a rock performance which is "worked up" through trial and error.

The logic in a serial composition amounts to a fixed order imposed on a series of consecutive events in one or more parameters. A serialist composer might choose a specific number and order of events in each parameter —pitch, timbre, rhythm, loudness, and envelope—and arrange them in an arbitrary order which he would consider immutable for the purpose of creating a single composition. This procedure, known as *total serialization,* has been used by many contemporary composers, including Ernst Křenek and Oliver Messiaen.

The most common type of serialism, the twelve-tone method in which the pitches of the chromatic scale are arranged in a specific series, is associated mainly with the names of Arnold Schoenberg and his most renowned pupils, Alban Berg and Anton von Webern.

The underlying premise of a twelve-tone composition is exactly opposite to that of a piece in the major/minor system. The latter may be thought of as a complicated and unique rearrangement of seven pitches belonging to a single standard consecutive sequence which we call a scale. A scale is a hypothetical, not a musical, entity, of course, for no one has ever made a satisfactory composition entirely by repeating a scale over and over. The twelve-tone composer, however, posits a unique order, or *row* of the twelve pitches available in the Western method of tuning, and treats it as a viable organism in its own right.

Expanding upon the conventional linear and spatial analogies in music (left to right and bottom to top), the twelve-tone composer regards a given series as being essentially the same in any one of four possible directions or *permutations*—forward (termed the *original* row), backward (*retro-*

grade), upside down (*inversion*), and backward-and-upside down (*retro-grade inversion*). All possible transpositions of the original and its three permutations are considered equivalent, giving a total of 144 versions of a given twelve-tone series. Finally, "octave transpositions" are disregarded; the composer chooses a particular sequence of twelve pitches without speci-fying the octave in which any one may be heard. Each of the twelve tones in a series is properly referred to not as a pitch but as a *pitch class*. Figure 21 shows the row, together with its permutations and transpositions, of which Webern's Cantata No. 1, Op. 29, is constructed.

The use of the series and any of its permutations and transpositions is extremely flexible. There are no absolute "rules." The tendency of nearly every twelve-tone composer, however, has been to set himself rather severe limitations so as to test his ingenuity to the utmost. For instance, Schoenberg and Webern normally declined to return to any one of the pitch classes in a given series until all succeeding pitches had been used once. Consecutive repetitions, of course, do not qualify as returns.

A twelve-tone row is not a melody, although it can certainly be used as one. It can also be deployed among various instruments and registers, re-sulting in what has come to be called *klangfarbenmelodie*—literally, "tone-color-melody." The row can be used in combination with other permuta-tions of itself in a contrapuntal texture, and it can be used vertically in chordal fashion.

AN ODE TO UNITY

The rational qualities of the twelve-tone system tend to invite pseudo-scientific rhetoric that would confound bona fide scientific method. Such explanations never succeed in capturing the effect of the music, because the composer's primary intention is first to conceive a row that is pregnant with possibilities, and second to construct a work the inherent orderliness of which is transcended by purely aural interest. Let us then turn to the actual sound of the third movement of Webern's Cantata No. 1 (Example XV-2). Figure 22 will show how every note is accounted for by some per- *XV-2* mutation of the row.

The performance is sung in German, so before we listen to it we should acquaint ourselves with the text in an English translation. One good reason for studying a translation is that the relation of the text to the music is bound to be significant. For instance, since the Renaissance Italian madrigal often featured "word painting," one's enjoyment will conceivably be en-hanced by an understanding of the specific meanings of the words, for he

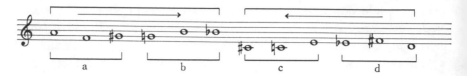

Inversion →													Retrograde ←
	1	2	3	4	5	6	7	8	9	10	11	12	
Original →1	A	F	G♯	G	B	B♭	C♯	C	E	E♭	F♯	D	
2	C♯	A	C	B	D♯	D	F	E	G♯	G	A♯	F♯	
3	B♭	G♭	A	A♭	C	B	D	D♭	F	E	G	E♭	
4	B	G	A♯	A	C♯	C	D♯	D	F♯	F	G♯	E	
5	G	E♭	F♯	F	A	A♭	B	B♭	D	D♭	E	C	
6	G♯	E	G	F♯	A♯	A	C	B	D♯	D	F	C♯	
7	F	D♭	E	E♭	G	G♭	A	A♭	C	B	D	B♭	
8	F♯	D	F	E	G♯	G	A♯	A	C♯	C	D♯	B	
9	D	A♯	C♯	C	E	D♯	F♯	F	A	G♯	B	G	
10	D♯	B	D	C♯	F	E	G	F♯	A♯	A	C	G♯	
11	C	G♯	B	A♯	D	C♯	E	D♯	G	F♯	A	F	
12	E	C	E♭	D	G♭	F	A♭	G	B	B♭	D♭	A	

↑
Retrograde Inversion

FIGURE 21   The twelve-tone row used by Webern in his Cantata No. 1, Op. 29. Notice the correspondences among its various segments: The groups marked *b* and *d* are transposed retrograde inversions of *a* and *c*, and the last retrograde inversion (no. 12) is identical with the original. This reduces the number of different permutations by half.

will then know what to listen for in the music (Example VIII-2). On the other hand, one need only catch the general mood of the text to an art song by Schumann (Example III-11), for it was the overall sentiment of a lyric rather than the concrete images in it that he sought to capture in most of his songs. Likewise, in operas such as Verdi's *La Traviata* or Gounod's *Faust*, in which the lyrical arias are both more numerous and more attractive than the other music, it is less important to understand the meaning of every word than in an opera like Alban Berg's *Wozzeck,* in which the narrative and dramatic elements outweigh the lyrical ones.

In the case of Webern's Cantata the relationship of text and music is one of mutual detachment. The music does not illustrate the text, and the text does not motivate the music. Instead the two coexist on an equal basis. Webern's music embodies his pervasive preoccupation with logic and order. His choice of text, by his friend the metaphysical Viennese painter and poet Hildegard Jone, informs us of his profound and passionate love of nature. Curiously, the one leads us to the other, for what Webern loved in nature was not the sensual beauty the romanticists had admired, but the organic, cosmic unity—the predictability—of it. Thus the Cantata is not about nature, but about unity and order. It may be regarded as an instance of the unity and predictability of nature amid apparent diversity.

> Tönen die seligen Saiten Apolls,
> wer nennt sie Chariten?
> Spielt er sein Lied durch den wachsenden Abend,
> wer denket Apollon?
> Sind doch im Klange die früheren Namen
> alle verklungen;
> sind doch im Worte die schwächeren Worte
> lange gestorben;
> und auch die blasseren Bilder
> zum Siegel des Spektrums geschmolzen.
> Charis, die Gabe des Höchsten:
> die Anmut der Gnade erglänzet!
> Schenkt sich im Dunkel dem werdenden Herzen
> als Tau der Vollendung.

> Hearing the blessed strings of the Sun god,
> who senses the Graces?
> Echoes his song in the darkening evening,
> who thinks of Apollo?
> Have not the earlier names all been gathered,
> lost in that music?
> Have not the weaker words long ago perished,
> slain by the word's might?
> Also the fainter image
> is melted as seal of the spectrum.
> Charis, the gift of the highest:
> the grace of her favor is sparkling!
> She comes in darkness, the ripening heart's gift,
> as dew of perfection.[2]

FIGURE 22   Excerpt from the third movement of Webern's Cantata No. 1, Op. 29. The symbols O-12, I-1, etc., identify permutations of the row as shown in

185

Knowing that serial music is highly organized, and having heard many of its characteristic sonorous effects in certain types of film music, one may yet wonder why the Cantata nevertheless is so difficult to comprehend. The explanation lies partly in the nature of the average person's overall background of musical experience and partly in the historical evolution of the style itself. Clearly, serial music represents a radical departure from the procedures of the major/minor system which we recognize in the music we hear daily. Furthermore, it does not rely like neoclassicism on the styles of the remote past such as we normally hear in the concert hall. Instead it has evolved out of the principle of atonality that was typical of the era of expressionism, between about 1910 and 1925. Therefore the ordinary listener has neither grown up with it nor does he encounter it often in its purest manifestations.

One way to learn to understand serial style would be to review its evolutionary process by familiarizing oneself with the music of some of the immediate precursors of the expressionists like Mahler and Wagner, and following its development through the early works of Schoenberg and his pupils. The convenience of the phonograph ought to facilitate this process, but in fact it makes it more difficult. The listener in Haydn and Mozart's time, for instance, necessarily lived through the evolution of classical styles, but because of the wide variety of styles available to us now on records we listen to music without reference to chronology. We are thus faced with the necessity of accepting or rejecting serial music simply on the bases of the interest and the persuasive power of its sound.

We might expect to be able to review the evolutionary process during our secondary-school education, as we do in most other subjects that are taught from a historical point of view, such as literature, history, and government. But we do not do that in music partly because music education emphasizes performance, and the music of the serial system, as well as its antecedents, is too difficult for young student musicians to play. It is difficult to play for the same reasons it is difficult to listen to: the lack of some of the unifying factors we have come to take for granted.

First, we are accustomed to hearing one or more distinct tonal centers in any composition, each defined for us principally by the movement of the bass line, which almost always includes one or another of the pitches of a triadic structure, inevitably culminating in strong harmonic cadences. In serial music, however, the bass does not serve a harmonic function, nor are triadic structures implicit in the scale system. There are no hierarchies. Serial music may have a tonal center, but it is likely to be established by reiteration, by rhythmic devices such as accentuation, or by timbre.

Second, the music of adult professional concert life, like that of most of the functional categories we have studied, uses timbre as an important element of unity. We are accustomed to hearing a melody played in a single timbre, or perhaps allocated phrase by phrase to two or three different but usually compatible timbres. A twelve-tone melody, which most often is deliberately designed to avoid gravitation towards the major/minor system, is hard enough to follow when it is heard in a single timbre. But when the technique of *klangfarbenmelodie* is applied the difficulty is compounded. A melody that changes both register and color every note or two, sometimes drastically, seems incomprehensible; timbre has assumed a value equal to that of pitch, and we have difficulty separating the two.

Third, we have learned to hear the rhythmic parameter in any piece of music, especially popular music, mainly as a unifying framework which not only is subordinate to melody, but usually lies beneath it, figuratively, in the texture. In serial music, however, rhythm is not subservient to any other parameter, but is equivalent to pitch and timbre as a structural element. Indeed, it often is fused with the other two to the extent that we are unaware of it as a separable factor, and tempo and meter are virtually eliminated as independent parameters qualifying rhythm.

Fourth, we are conditioned to the proposition that the individual events in a musical design tend to group themselves around climaxes within each phrase or period. Not all the notes in a given melody, for instance, are equal in importance; some serve primarily to lead up to or away from notes that thereby acquire relatively greater importance (review the analysis of "Chester" on p. 127; Example XII-1). Thus in modern popular music, just as in some classical music of the baroque era, the composer has written only the important notes, leaving to the performer the responsibility of improvising the melodic and harmonic filler. But since in serial music there are no hierarchies within any parameter, nor among them, all events are identical in value. Nothing merely "leads up to" anything else. Mere filler is omitted. Structures are so highly compressed and abbreviated that a single note can serve as a theme!

Furthermore, since every sound and every silence is crucial to the design, any extraneous sound becomes a part of the composition. Serial music must therefore be heard against a background of complete silence—not an easy requirement to satisfy in our noise-polluted world.

Finally, the equivalence among all the events in a serial composition demands that the performer as well as the listener pay full attention to every aspect of every event. Indeed, serial music requires of the performer a refinement of technique that exceeds that of almost any other kind of music. The performer must be able to maintain absolute control over every detail of every sound, and be able to place it in its proper context at precisely the right instant. The listener who has never performed music of this kind himself must try to imagine the degree of physical, mental, emotional, and aural involvement it requires of the performer, if he is to secure the fullest possible measure of appreciation.

CHANCE MUSIC: THE UNIQUE EXPERIENCE

The application of the laws of chance to music in limited ways is not new. We have encountered it in this and previous chapters under the heading of improvisation, in the realization of the thorough-bass part in baroque music, in the cadenza of the classical and romantic solo concerto and of course, to a greater or lesser extent, in current popular music of all types. In these instances, however, the operation of chance has been circumscribed by the dictates of the style in which the performer has been participating.

Only since the middle of the present century has the idea of improvisation been broadened into the principle of chance and applied systematically to all musical parameters, as well as to the very processes by which sonorous designs are conceived. In fact, the approach is so new that it is difficult for those who acquired all their basic musical preferences before chance procedures became current in art music, or whose experience has been limited to popular music, to understand and accept it. Admittedly, such revolutionary procedures as may be represented in the works of men like John Cage, whose *Imaginary Landscape* for twelve radios has already been described (see p. 51), make it all the more difficult for such persons to take the trend seriously. Ever since the mid-sixties, however, chance has been used more and more frequently, even by composers of school music. It may be employed by the composer to establish one or more details of a sonorous design, or it may be assigned to the performer so that he may choose among a number of alternatives.

To the unaware or unsuspecting listener some chance music—at least that which uses conventional musical instruments—may sound like serial music, for both require the listener to accept all consecutive and simultaneous events as having independent and equal value, with no apparent connection between what has gone before and what comes after. Fundamentally, however, the two systems are diametrically opposed. A serial relation is a fixed order, and in that sense is completely rational; a chance relation is a random order, and can be entirely irrational.

Of course, chance music cannot possibly be *all* chance. Decisions of some kind must be made, even if only to determine when the music is to begin and end. Otherwise, without the necessary framework of silence, it would be no composition at all but a part of the sonorous environment. Of course, the beginning and ending may be determined by chance, though someone must still specify the factors that shall interact to produce the chance results. In the chance system in general, anyone may make the necessary decisions—the composer, the performers, or even the audience.

Example XV-3 is a composition that was created at a public concert by   *XV-3* the entire New York Philharmonic symphony orchestra. It is entitled *Improvisation,* though it is, more accurately, indeterminate in style, for, as the conductor Leonard Bernstein explained, "Nothing has been fixed or decided upon in advance except two or three signals for starting and stopping. Otherwise, every note you hear will have been spontaneously invented by the New York Philharmonic, with its conductor serving only as a kind of general guide or policeman." [3]

The criteria upon which this piece may be evaluated reside within it and not in any extrinsic factors. Since it has no history of its own, it does not belong to any particular style; whatever resemblance it might bear to any composition that existed before or since is entirely coincidental. It cannot be repeated and thus cannot be reinterpreted; consequently there are no degrees of rightness or wrongness about it. Knowing that the performers' contributions to the work were not predetermined, we cannot presume any deliberate intention to balance unity and variety. All we can say about its form is that it shows growth in density, volume, and rhythmic excitement. It begins thin, soft, and slow, and ends thick, loud, and fast. It happens to be an instance of absolute variety, but it might just as well have turned out another way.

Moreover, the recording extends the work's indeterminacy to the ultimate by removing the visual dimension of the original performance. We are unable to see the signals given by the conductor, so for us the work is totally unpredictable. It is simply an existential phenomenon, without any meaning outside itself. It is a sonorous design that begins, exists, and ends. We may take it or leave it.

[3] Quoted with the permission of Leonard Bernstein and CBS Records.

A single experience with chance music may remind us that as listeners to most other kinds of music we have been active participants in the creative process which begins with the composer and extends through the performer to us. As listeners, we derive more or less pleasure from anticipating the possibilities of orderly progression from one sonorous event to the next. Yet we are merely passive observers of chance music.

When the composer allows chance to operate in performance, extraordinary demands are placed on the performer, who must himself be a creator of ideas rather than an interpreter of someone else's. This means he must be daring enough to make any number of decisions and then carry them out regardless of the consequences. He must have, as the saying goes, the courage of his convictions. At the same time he may be guided to some extent by what other performers in the ensemble are doing; he may play either *with* them, or *against* them. In either case he is challenged to cultivate a profound empathy with his musical companions, and perhaps even with his listeners. As the composer Roger Reynolds has put it, "no one knows, everybody listens." This is exactly what takes place in performances of free jazz by men like Pharaoh Sanders, Archie Shepp, Albert Ayler, McCoy Tyner, Elvin Jones, and John Coltrane. One must listen not so much to the music as to the musicians.

That a chance composition may contain its own unique stylistic world and that it is essentially a performer's music has recently prompted a few composers to treat music as a mode of play, admitting any sound-producing device as a musical instrument. This has prompted the development of a system of *graphic notation* which is more descriptive, more flexible, and easier to learn by inexperienced participants than conventional notation.

Figure 23, a prescription for a chance performance by the British composer Bernard Rands, is typical of the new genre. It may be "realized" by three or more persons, each individual or group reading from one of the parts of the score marked A, B, and C. The notational symbols, which are explained separately by the composer, show the performers generally what to do with the sounds, but not what specific pitches or timbres to use. There are no beats or measures to mark off a contextual "musical time." Instead Rands has made each box represent an arbitrary span of time, and the performers must learn to sense the passage of seconds and minutes more or less accurately, a feat we seldom attempt in everyday living. Moreover, synchronization among the players is not determined in advance; the performers are to practice the piece together until they dis-

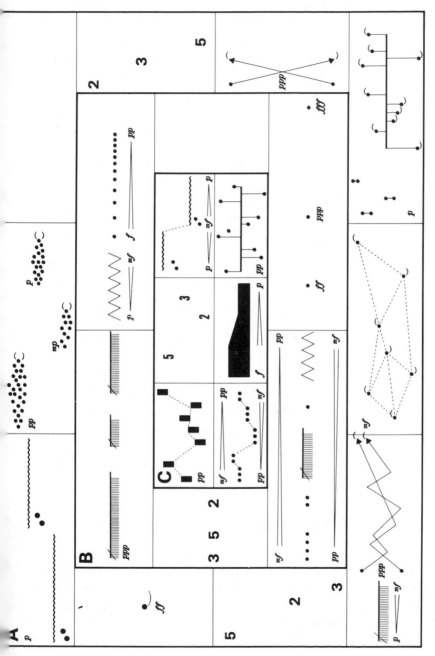

FIGURE 23 Bernard Rands, "Sound Patterns 4," for voices, percussion, piano, and melody instruments. © Copyright 1970, Universal Edition, London, Ltd. Used by permission of the publisher, Theodore Presser Company, sole representative U.S.A., Canada and Mexico.

cover some of its possibilities, and then decide among themselves how it ought to sound.

The emergence of chance music raises some issues that touch upon crucial concerns in contemporary Western culture. It reminds us that, as Leonard Meyer put it, "If we are to defend our beliefs—our faith in a world of purpose and causality, time and prediction, choice and control, communication and morality, we must ask the most fundamental questions that can be asked: questions about the nature of man, his relationships to other men, and his place in the universe." [4]

On the one hand, the validity of chance music may rest on the fact that it minimizes the composer's ego, opens the listener's ears to the vast world of sound around him, and makes a sonorous design a process rather than an object, "free of individual taste and memory," as John Cage says. On the other hand, if it is held that the artist's prime responsibility is to create order out of chaos and not succumb to irrational forces, then the philosophy embodied in chance music is invalid.

Only the future knows which of these positions will prevail (though the proponent of chance music would respond that future judgments are as irrelevant to the present as are the precedents of the past). For the time being, however, there are two more arguments in favor of experimentation in chance music, especially at the amateur and school-music level. First, anyone can now play with sound and time as he has always been encouraged to play with line, color, mass, and words, without first acquiring special skills. Second, to the extent that our astounding technology enables us to purchase an exact replica of the rarest, most priceless treasure for only a few dollars, the one-of-a-kind, never-to-be-repeated experience gains a special value and significance. The current interest in chance music may after all reflect the rise of a new humanism.

ELECTRONIC MUSIC: AN INFINITUDE OF CHOICES

Considered as a system, electronic music has two basic similarities with chance music. First, it provides the composer with the opportunity to manipulate sound and time free of the limitations of traditional musical systems. Second, it enables the composer to employ an infinite variety of pitches, timbres, rhythms, textures, and so forth. In fact, such possibilities in electronic music exceed those of chance music. For instance, not only

---

[4] Leonard B. Meyer, *Music, the Arts, and Ideas: Patterns and Predictions in Twentieth-Century Culture* (Chicago: University of Chicago Press, 1967), p. 84. © 1967 by The University of Chicago.

FIGURE 24   The late Jackson Pollock, eminent American artist, in the process of "action painting." Pollock customarily dripped paint on the canvas, or flung it on in large rhythmic sweeps, without any preconceived plan. The results are abstract designs from which the viewer may literally sense the physical gestures of the act of painting. In a similar way, the listener may infer from some chance music the spontaneous reactions of the performers to a given set of musical circumstances. Photo by Hans Namuth.

are all audible pitches available to the composer from 20 to 20,000 Hz, but voltages producing inaudible frequencies also can be used to control other voltages to produce still other sounds. In short, it is possible to create any conceivable sound, as well as an infinite number that cannot be imagined. Finally, electronic music also enables the composer to construct designs without the need of beats to hold individual musicians together.

The fundamental difference between the electronic and chance musical systems is that electronic music affords the composer absolute control over his design if he desires it. He may allow the laws of electricity to determine certain sonorous events; he may employ an arbitrary formula to control the operations of chance; he may even use a computer to produce sounds according to any logical principle whatsoever, such as Poisson's Law of Probabilities. On the other hand, he may assume personal command over every aspect of the generation, modification, and combination (synthesis) of sounds. In either case, his principal tool, or instrument, is called a *synthesizer.*

FIGURE 25   The ARP 2500 synthesizer, with inventor and namesake Alan R. Pearlman (left), and Hollywood composer/arranger Hugo Montinegro. A wide variety of synthesizers is available, ranging in price from about $1,000 to $15,000 and up. Courtesy, ARP Instruments, Inc.

It is important to understand that while we think and talk about music in terms of sounds, what the composer of electronic music actually controls with a synthesizer are voltages that are analogues of sounds. Nothing that is done with or by a synthesizer has the form of acoustical energy until the voltages have been passed through an amplifier to loudspeakers. Even sounds originating outside the synthesizer from either natural or man-made sources, can be modified and combined as pure electrical energy. (Music made entirely of such sounds is called *musique concrète.*) The core of any synthesizer consists of several *oscillators* capable of generating more or less complex patterns of alternating current called *wave forms,* in any desired frequency.

The simplest wave form is that of the pure, or *sine wave,* which consists of a frequency representing a fundamental pitch only, without harmonics. Another is the nasal-sounding *sawtooth wave,* also called a *ramp wave,* which consists of a frequency representing a fundamental pitch plus all consecutive harmonics in gradually decreasing amplitudes. Then there are the *triangle wave* and the *square wave,* both rather bright in sound, which represent a fundamental with all its odd-numbered overtones. Finally, there is an oscillator that generates a current resulting in what is called *white sound,* containing all audible frequencies at random and continually changing amplitudes.

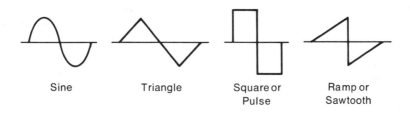

| Sine | Triangle | Square or Pulse | Ramp or Sawtooth |

FIGURE 26. Electronic wave forms.

A few of the more common kinds of modification that can be applied to electrical signals with a synthesizer are *additive synthesis, filtering, amplitude modulation, frequency modulation, envelope shaping, spatial modulation,* and *reverberation.* Some of these, along with the sounds of the basic wave forms, may be heard in Example XV-4.

XV-4

Additive synthesis is the combination of any one of the wave forms with one or more of the others, or with various other pitches and amplitudes of the same wave form.

Filtering is the elimination of some of the constituent frequencies of any sound. For instance, any complex wave form can be reduced to a single sine wave by filtering out all the overtones. (The bass and treble "tone controls" on a record player or amplifier are *high-pass* and *low-pass* filters.)

Amplitude modulation, which is the rapid periodic alternation between loud and soft of a given sound, corresponds to the effect produced on conventional instruments, especially stringed instruments, called *tremolo.* It is produced on a synthesizer by causing one voltage to act upon another so as to make the amplitude of the second vary at a rate equal to the frequency of the first. Several other kinds of amplitude modulation at rates too rapid for the human ear to detect result in sounds that include *sideband frequencies,* which blur the identity of the pitch being modified. One such device, a *ring modulator,* accepts voltages of two or more different frequencies, but emits a sound in which frequencies equal to their sums and differences are present without the original frequencies. Since the majority of sounds are actually complex wave forms, a ring-modulated sound will be proportionately more so.

In *frequency modulation* one voltage is controlled by another so as to cause the periodic fluctuation of pitch above and below a central frequency. When limited to the span of about a half step, it resembles the effect we have referred to as vibrato in conventional music.

Through the use of an *envelope shaper* the electronic composer can control the envelope, or amplitude characteristics of growth and decay of an individual sound, and can modify its wave form at any point in its duration.

Spatial modulation, sometimes called *panning,* means the routing of signals from one channel to another. Thus the composer is able to give sound a spatial dimension and make his design mobile.

One of the oldest and most familiar types of modification is *reverberation,* better known as *echo,* which sometimes gives the illusion of depth or distance to a sound.

Still another series of electronic modifications of sound can be experimented with by anyone with access to a reel-to-reel tape recorder, using *concrète* sounds. A sound can be recorded at one speed and played back at another, and then filtered by operating the treble and bass tone controls. Recorders having a "sound-on-sound" feature permit the recording and simultaneous playback of two or more different signals on the same track or channel so that they are heard together. Time-segments of sounds can easily be calculated and manipulated by measuring, cutting, and splicing the recorded tape, and rhythmic and melodic ostinatos can be produced by recording a single pattern and making a loop of that tape to pass continuously over the playback head. Other unusual effects such as feedback, echo reverberation, and canonic texture can be produced with two tape recorders and one or two tapes (see Figure 27).

The selection of sonorous events generated or modified on a synthesizer is accomplished by means of a *manual controller.* The most common type resembles a piano keyboard, an arrangement of black and white keys which actually evolved out of the need to group the mechanisms for twelve dif-

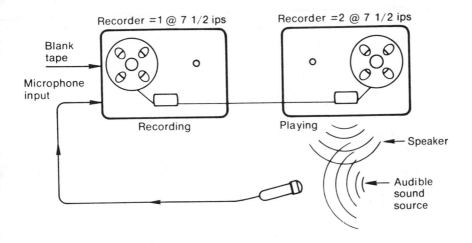

FIGURE 27 Producing echo reverberation using two tape recorders and a microphone. The volume and quality of the sound and the time between echoes are determined by the volume controls of both machines, the distance of the microphone from the speaker, and the distance between the recorders. From *Tape Control in Electronic Music,* by Anne Modugno and Charles Palmer. Reproduced with the permission of Electronic Music Laboratories, Inc. Copies of the fifteen-page booklet may be obtained at a nominal cost from Electronic Music Laboratories, Inc., P.O. Box H, Vernon, Connecticut 06066.

ferent pitches and an octave within the span of the human hand. This is not only unnecessary but impractical within the technology of electronic music, because a special manual technique is required to play it. In any case, the final combination or synthesis of sounds takes place outside the synthesizer on an elaborate tape recorder, sometimes containing as many as twenty-four parallel channels and using two-inch tape, as compared with the two-channel, four-track quarter-inch tape of an ordinary home recorder.

LIBERATION

On first thought it might appear inevitable that the flexibility and infinite potential of the synthesizer would prompt composers merely to imitate conventional instruments, eventually displacing music produced by human hands and lips. However, owing to the extreme variety and complexity of acoustical instruments, it is uneconomical in both time and money to try to make electronic music sound like any other kind. Instead, for the time being at least, most composers of electronic music view their medium as an adjunct to, or an extension of, existing traditions. They have therefore devoted themselves to the free exploration of the myriad new possibilities remaining in the universe of sound and time over which the synthesizer gives them direct control. Consequently, an electronic composition can represent a far greater involvement of the composer himself in the actual creation of a sonorous design than has ever been possible in the history of music.

The comparatively recent growth of interest in the synthesizer on the part of popular musicians, as well as the spectacular success of exercises in technological virtuosity like the well-known album, *Switched-On Bach* (1968), obscures the fact that electronic music has a fairly long history. The eventual emergence of the medium was envisioned as early as 1907 by the Italian composer Ferruccio Busoni. His prophecy was lent credibility by the invention at about that time of the first electrical instrument, the Telharmonium, by the American scientist Thaddeus Cahill. More practical instruments began to appear in the twenties and thirties, a few of which are still in common use, such as the Theremin (1924). The real beginning of an independent tradition in electronic music, however, had to await the perfection of the magnetic tape recorder during World War II. By 1952, when Leopold Stokowski included some electronic music in a concert at the Museum of Modern Art in New York, the new trend was firmly established among contemporary musical practices.

Almost from its beginning the evolution of electronic music was aided by the efforts of numerous composers to liberate music from the limitations of its traditional palette of intsrumental and vocal timbres by employing sounds previously classified as noise. The very term *noise,* which had once been used to refer to unpleasant or inexplicable sounds—even extremely dissonant music could be deprecated as "just noise"—gradually came to denote only unwanted sound. The trend toward a broader conception of musically usable sound was furthered by a few otherwise conventional works like Erik Satie's ballet, *Parade,* of 1917, which included sirens and typewriters, and culminated in 1931 with Edgard Varèse's epochal *Ionisation,* scored for forty instruments chiefly from the percussion family.

Varèse himself began to use electronically generated and modified sounds in 1954, and soon created one of the classics of the new genre in his *Poème électronique,* written for the Philips Corporation's exhibit at the 1958 World Fair in Brussels, Belgium. The eight-minute-long work was originally conceived to give a sonorous dimension to the interior of the pavilion, and to be experienced simultaneously with projections of various images

FIGURE 28   The Philips Pavilion at the 1958 World Fair in Brussels, Belgium. Varèse's *Poème électronique* originally possessed a mobile, spatial parameter corresponding to the shape of the interior of Le Corbusier's unusual edifice. Courtesy, The Museum of Modern Art, New York.

and colors selected by the building's architect, Le Corbusier. The composition—Varèse preferred simply to call his works *organized sound*—consists of both *concrète* and oscillator sounds, but a knowledge of their causes is entirely irrelevant to its appreciation. It was recorded on a three-track tape and played back through a network that moved the sound about the room among some four hundred loudspeakers in the continuous ceiling and walls.

The two-channel version of *Poème électronique* heard in Example XV-5   *XV-5* conveys an imperfect idea of the mobility of sound which reportedly was one of the most impressive features of the work in its original context. However, with playback equipment capable of reproducing a wide range of frequencies at optimum loudness, the commercial recording at least retains the other essential characteristics of the piece. The old concept of musical progression figuratively from left to right, leading up to and away from climactic points in time, is replaced by real movement from one physical location to another. We hear planes and surfaces of variegated timbres moving from side to side, advancing and receding, without reference to a metrical framework. Indeed, time and space here become one indivisible dimension.

Since many of the individual sonorous events encountered in works like *Poème* cannot be discussed in the old musical terminology, new ways of categorizing them are being used. For example, a sound may be described with respect to its timbre as more or less resembling one or another of the most distinctive wave forms, or it might be identified in terms of a natural analogy such as "chirp," "buzz," or "clang." It may be characterized as either having a definite fundamental, or a predominant pitch-area, or as being closer to white sound. It may further be said to occupy a high, middle, or low position and be of relatively wide or narrow span within the frequency spectrum. Envelope may be spoken of with regard to attack or growth (gradual, instantaneous), continuation (steady-state, crescendo, diminuendo), and decay (slow, rapid). Finally, the enhancement of a sound may be noted, such as the treatment of it by means of reverberation, amplitude modulation, frequency modulation, ring modulation, glissando, and the like.

In Varèse's work texture and timbre are fused in a way that lends the musical term texture an additional connotation somewhat closer to its literal meaning: a tactile quality. Some sound-textures are thin and willowy, others thick and fuzzy. Still others, like the sound of the "gong" at the very beginning, are almost palpable from their insides out. The persistent listener may soon discover, moreover, that many of the sounds acquire powerful emotional implications all their own. Some are soothing, others piercing or strident, a few pathetic, several even humorous. Quite a few of the effects in *Poème* seem to have come from conventional percussion instruments, but one cannot be sure. It is hard to determine which might have been made by the exertion of human muscular energy on a physical object and which are the products of the mysterious powers of electricity. Varèse himself called the *Poème* "an indictment of inquisition in all its forms," but that could have been meant as a warning against asking questions about its "meaning."

A few critics object that the rise of electronic music is a final stage in the dehumanization of the art of music. On the other hand, it might signify a new relationship between the listener and the composer and make the listener a far more active participant in the creative process than ever before. That is, his own responses become all the more important since there is often no third party, no "performer," to make an implicit prejudgment of the value of the piece merely by performing it.

SUMMARY: THE FUNCTIONS OF ART

The criteria on which one may base a judgment of school music, mood music, background, ceremonial, or entertainment music, are entirely objective. They are implicit in the relationships between the properties of the music as sonorous design and the practical use the music is supposed to serve. The criteria for the judgment of art music, on the other hand, are primarily subjective. Acts of judgment begin with sensory responses, which may be partially explained through intellectual inquiry. But extrinsic criteria may also be applied, since any art may function either as an escape from the broader realities of human existence or as a revelation of them.

Music can serve as a means of escape from reality by providing us with varieties of experience that seem to be absent from our daily lives. The music of past eras, abundantly available on records, sometimes heard in high school performances, and forming the major part of adult professional concert fare, is especially important to us in this way. A Renaissance motet may sooth us with its unity of texture, homogeneity of timbre, quiet rhythm, and subdued volume. Its sustained placidity of mood may offer a momentary respite from a world that appears to us hectic and neurotically disoriented.

When we feel that our daily lives are fraught with banality, coarseness, and uncertainty, a symphony or a chamber work by Haydn may charm us with its clarity, grace, and elegance and reassure us by the predictability of its balanced phrases and closed structures. Indeed, any composition belonging to the major/minor system may satisfy us because it constitutes a complete, self-contained experience proceeding from an auspicious beginning to one or more cumulative climaxes and culminating in a logical and consonant conclusion. It is an unrealistic but pleasing experience in that our daily lives do not usually contain such qualities of symmetry and completeness.

On the other hand we may well recognize in the music of the past some characteristics that seem to correspond with modern views of the nature of experience. The same Renaissance motet, with its interlocking melodic material that avoids the building-up of extreme tensions may remind us of equivalence of values found in certain areas of twentieth-century life. The unwavering rhythmic drive and vitality of a baroque allegro may seem to parallel the relentless pulse and pace of modern urban life. The turgid chromaticisms and extravagant dynamic contrasts of a late-romantic symphony may inspire in us recollections of the titanic international and interracial struggles of the past generation or two. In short, we often keep old music around for contemporary reasons.

But how does contemporary music reflect contemporary life? Some say the dissonance in the one reflects the anxiety in the other. Yet this is a singularly pessimistic attitude, for even if dissonance were not primarily a subjective value, it would be unreasonable to suppose that an art should embody only the negative aspects of its milieu. Thanks to our educational methods and intellectual habits we nevertheless prefer such simplified views of history. One or two Mozart symphonies, for instance, may be permitted to stand for the remainder of their type, as well as for the entire era in which their composer lived. However, even a limited acquaintance with the Western art music written since the early part of the twentieth century—the kinds we have dealt with in this and the preceding chapter, not to mention all the other musics we now use—suggests that the most significant aspect of contemporary existence which our music could reflect is its astounding variety and complexity.

The following remarks by the philosopher William Barrett support this conclusion:

I do not think we can find any . . . clear-cut image of man amid the bewildering thicket of modern art. And this is not because we are too close to the period, as yet, to stand back and make such a selection. Rather, the variety of images is too great and too contradictory to coalesce into any single shape or form. May the reason why modern art offers us no clear-cut image of man not be that it already knows—whether or not it has brought this knowledge to conceptual expression—that man is a creature who transcends any image because he has no fixed essence or nature? [5]

[5] William Barrett, *Irrational Man* (New York: Doubleday & Company, Inc., 1962), p. 61. Copyright 1958 by William Barrett.

listening guides

Each of the following Listening Guides may be used in three different ways: 1) as an aid to the private pursuit of an additional musical experience similar to one dealt with in the text; 2) as a framework for discussion between two or more individuals sharing the same experience; or 3) in a revised format, as a short-answer quiz for an elective or general classroom assignment.

Read the instructions and the questions carefully, making sure you understand all the terms and concepts used before you begin to work out a Listening Guide. If you are in doubt about any point, reread the appropriate portions of the text and review the recorded illustrations. All musical terms are printed in boldface type in the index to facilitate review.

The act of listening is a very complex process involving the interaction of factors at an unconscious as well as a conscious level, so it is impossible to exhaust the ways in which a particular musical experience could be analyzed. Consequently, although you may be asked to observe only certain details you will frequently be aware of others as well, some of which may seem even more important to you than the ones mentioned. Therefore you should feel free to add remarks or questions to any Guide, for you might thus acquire further insight into your own reactions, or raise issues that will prompt further study of a given aspect of music either as sonorous design or as a social act.

Some of the Guides are longer than others, and may be shortened or otherwise revised at will. You may also—or instead—wish to design some

Listening Guides of your own. For example, you might compare a scene from an opera with an episode from a musical comedy. You need only be able to state clearly a *subject,* a *project,* and an *objective* that are inter-related. Your Guide should require you to discuss a given musical experience in conventional musical terms. Resist the temptation to describe an experience entirely with common adjectives, for no matter how eloquent they may be, they seldom help to explain the real bases of a musical phenomenon.

Subjects of the Listening Guides

No. 1	The extra-musical aspects of a live performance.
No. 2	The concert hall versus the phonograph record.
No. 3	Criticism in musical terms.
No. 4	Some basic elements of style.
No. 5	The music of non-Western or preliterate cultures.
No. 6	Your sonorous environment.
No. 7	Mood music.
No. 8	Film music.
No. 9	Elements of popular style.
No. 10	Musical composition: the pentatonic system.
No. 11	Composing with tape recorders.
No. 12	Chance music.

LISTENING GUIDE NO. 1

Subject: The extra-musical aspects of a live performance.

Project: Attend a recital of classical music presented by a soloist, or a concert featuring a soloist, and describe your experience in terms of acoustical, psychological, physiological, and social factors.

Objective: To make a subjective evaluation of a live performance as a kind of experience, apart from the music itself.

1.   A composer must recognize the elements of monotony that are implicit in the construction of a given instrument, and balance them with variety. Considering this performance as a whole, what seemed to you to be the most conspicuous features of the sound of the solo instrument (or voice) with respect to *a)* timbre, *b)* loudness, and *c)* envelope? In each case which dominated, sameness or differentness? Overall, in which parameters were compensating factors present?

2.   Did the acoustical qualities of the auditorium have any perceptible effect on the sound of the solo instrument? If so, try to describe the effect.

3.   What appear to be the basic physiological requirements of a performer on the featured instrument?

4.   Compare the purely visual aspect of the performer with that of any performer of popular music you have seen in person, in the movies, or on television. Which of the two appeared to be the more intensely and personally involved with the music he was performing? How did each show his involvement? Would you expect both performers to act the same way? Why?

5.   Did any of the conduct of either the performer or the audience seem to be merely conventional and without practical purpose? If not, explain what functions they appeared to serve. If so, explain how you believe the people concerned might have acted, and how the conduct you recommend might alter the effect of a live performance. Have you any idea how you came to possess the attitudes you now hold regarding these matters?

6.   What aspects of this performance would you miss most in a recorded version of the same music?

LISTENING GUIDE NO. 2

Subject: The concert hall versus the phonorecord.

Project: Compare a live and a recorded version of a classical composition in the light of your own experience as well as the attitudes of one or more professional critics.

Objective: To crystallize your opinions regarding the relative merits and limitations of live and recorded performances.

It has been said that the live concert as an institution is being threatened with extinction by various circumstances, including the impact of the electronic media. Study some of the assessments of the present status of music as a performing art, as expressed by people like Dorian, Pleasants, McLuhan, Baumol and Bowen, or the Rockefeller Panel (all listed in the Bibliography for Chapter I), or any other pertinent authority you can find. You might also find the album *Glenn Gould: Concert Dropout* (Columbia BS 15) stimulating. Next, attend a concert of classical music. Finally, either purchase or borrow from a lending library a recording of any work on the program, or else a comparable work by any one of the composers represented.

1.   Considering the opinions you have read, together with the two listening experiences undergone in connection with this Listening Guide, what are the differences between them with respect to your own preparations and conduct? What do you suppose might be the differences from the performers' point of view?

2.   Describe the social and physical aspects of the environment in which each experience was undergone.

3.   In each instance, was your immediate impression of the music affected by the medium through which you gained it? How did the first (live concert) experience affect the second?

4.   Compare music with the arts of painting, literature, drama, and architecture, with respect to the materials they employ and the various media by which they can be experienced. In each instance, what factors stand between the various creative artists (and their interpreters, if any), and their audiences? In what ways do the various media affect an audience's impressions of the artist's work?

5.   Did you like the music you listened to in connection with this

Listening Guide? Did it seem to serve its intended function properly? In any case, try to describe the bases for your judgment in terms of one or more of the factors to which your attention has been drawn either in this project or elsewhere in *The Uses of Music*.

LISTENING GUIDE NO. 3

(Recommended only to the experienced listener with at least a limited ability to read music, and who has access to a fairly complete music library containing both records and scores.)

Subject: Criticism in musical terms.

Project: Compare two or more different recorded performances of a single classical work.

Objective: To focus your attention on the minute details as well as the general characteristics of a given performance.

Study two or three different recorded performances of any single classical composition for which a full score is available to you. Listen to each version carefully while following the score. Try to pinpoint the specific differences among the performances, and explain them in simple musical terms pertaining to tempo, timbre, dynamics, envelope, and so forth. Finally, try to assess the overall expressive or emotional import of the differences you have discovered, and decide which recording you prefer on that basis.

LISTENING GUIDE NO. 4

Subject: Some basic elements of style.

Project: Analyze a classical composition with regard to its scale system, texture, timbre, rhythm, and structure.

Objective: To develop the ability to recognize and describe the basic elements of design in a composition representing a given style-period.

Select from a record library, or purchase for your own collection, a recording of a work by any of the composers listed in the Chronology of Style-periods and Composers. If the work consists of several movements, choose the one that interests you most. Listen to it repeatedly and attentively in order to arrive at answers to the following questions:

1.   Does the piece seem to have a tonal center? Which scale system do you think the composer has used—major/minor, modal, pentatonic, whole tone, twelve-tone (chromatic), or none of them?

2.   Is the texture predominantly homophonic, polyphonic, monophonic, or a combination or alternation of them? Is it mostly transparent, or mostly opaque, or alternating?

3.   Are the timbres generally homogeneous, or heterogeneous, or alternating? Are they mostly bright, dark, or mixed, or do they alternate?

4.   Is the rhythm evidently isometric, multimetric, or free? If it is isometric, is the meter duple or triple? Simple or compound? Do you hear any rhythmic polyphony or is the texture homorhythmic?

5.   Are unity and variety juxtaposed within a single parameter? If so, in which parameter does the most obvious alternation or repetition-after-contrast occur? If it is evident in the melody, which of the traditional structural formulas described in Chapter VII does the piece resemble, if any? If unity and variety are superposed, which characteristic is heard in each of the basic parameters (melody, timbre, texture, and rhythm)? Are any special devices employed to provide unity such as ostinatos, pedal points, or imitative counterpoint?

6.   Music is made to move forward in time not only through the maintenance of a delicate balance between unity and variety but also through the alternation of tension and release or repose. For instance, dissonance represents tension, and we expect it to be resolved in a comparatively consonant sound. A rallentando or an accelerando may imply either

tension or repose depending on the overall tempo. Even silence within a musical design can create tension that demands to be resolved in sound. Which of these or any other means of inducing and relieving tension can you locate and describe?

7.   Did you like the music you listened to in connection with this Listening Guide? Did it seem to serve its intended function properly? In any case, try to describe the bases for your judgment in terms of one or more of the factors to which your attention has been drawn either in this project or elsewhere in *The Uses of Music*.

LISTENING GUIDE NO. 5

Subject: The music of non-Western or preliterate cultures.

Project: Compare one piece of music representing a non-Western or a preliterate culture with a style that is familiar to you.

Objective: To identify some of the differences between the music of Western civilization and that of another culture.

A.   Using the resources of a lending library or your own record collection, listen to one example of music from a non-Western or preliterate culture (Japanese, Indian, Balinese, African, American Indian, etc.). Be sure that it is genuine and not a Westernized adaptation. Let this be designated Type I, and discuss it in terms of the following questions:

1.   Does the piece seem to have a tonal center? If so, how is it established—by reiteration, harmonic cadences, or melodic cadences? Which scale system is represented—major/minor, modal, pentatonic, whole tone, twelve-tone (chromatic), or none of them?

2.   Is the texture predominantly homophonic, heterophonic, polyphonic, monophonic, or a combination or alternation of them? Is it mostly transparent, opaque, or alternating?

3.   Are the timbres generally homogeneous, or heterogeneous, or alternating? Are they mostly bright, dark, or mixed, or do they alternate?

4.   Is the rhythm evidently isometric, multimetric, or free? If it is isometric, is the meter duple or triple? Simple or compound? Do you hear any rhythmic polyphony or is the texture homorhythmic?

5.   Are unity and variety juxtaposed within a single parameter? If so, in which parameter does the most obvious alternation or repetition-after-contrast occur? If it is evident in the melody, which of the traditional structural formulas described in Chapter VII does the piece resemble, if any? If unity and variety are superposed which characteristic is heard in each of the basic parameters (melody, timbre, texture, and rhythm)? Are any special devices employed to provide unity such as ostinatos, pedal points, or imitative counterpoint?

B.   Let the kind of Western music you know and like best be designated Type II. Carefully study a specific example of it with the preceding questions in mind.

211

6. What seem to you to be the most obvious areas of contrast between Type I and Type II?

7. Did you enjoy listening to Type I? If so, can you identify the parameter(s) in which the most interest was present? If not, can you explain in musical terms what made it unlikable?

LISTENING GUIDE NO. 6

Subject: Your sonorous environment.

Project: Analysis of a segment of your sonorous environment in strictly musical terms.

Objective: To speculate on the differences between musical designs and the sonorous environment.

Study your sonorous environment as a whole from the perspective in which you normally experience it and try to locate the most interesting two- or three-minute segment of it. If you have a cassette or tape recorder, it will help to make a recording of the chosen segment in order to permit deliberate and repeated consideration of it. In any case, try to experience it as pure sonorous design, apart from any possible meanings or emotional significances it might otherwise suggest to you.

1.   Describe some of the most conspicuous sounds with respect to envelope and duration. Is the range of the overall pitch spectrum wide or narrow? Is the pitch spectrum generally high, low, or medium in register? Is there a single pitch or pitch area that seems to serve as a tonal center?

2.   Is the texture relatively transparent, or opaque? Are there any melodies present? If so, describe them with respect to contour, type of line, and phrasing. Is the texture essentially polyphonic, homophonic, monophonic, or heterophonic? Is silence an important part of the design?

3.   Are the timbres homogeneous, or heterogeneous? Are they mostly bright, dark, mixed, or alternating?

4.   Is the rhythm of the segment isometric, multimetric, or free? If it is metrical, is the meter duple or triple? Simple or compound? Is the design homorhythmic or polyrhythmic?

5.   Within the arbitrary limitations of the segment you have chosen, does the design seem to embody the principle of superposition, or juxtaposition? If the former, which parameters contain the most unity and which the most variety? If the latter, in which parameter does the most prominent alternation of unity and variety occur? Is the design monotonous from the standpoint of either unity or variety, or is there a balance between the two? Does the segment contain many points of tension and release? If so, try to explain how they are produced, using musical terms.

6. Do all the sounds issue from one general locality, or is the design stereophonic? Is the design mobile or stationary?

7. What is the effect of this particular segment of your sonorous environment upon your sense of the time it has occupied? Considered as pure sound does it seem to expand or contract clock time?

8. If you have recorded the segment in question, has the electronic medium altered the original sonorous design in any way?

9. Does the chosen segment of your sonorous environment resemble any musical composition you have ever heard? Compare it with the kinds of music you like best. Can you make any generalizations about the functions of music in your life as opposed to the functions of other sounds in your environment?

LISTENING GUIDE NO. 7

Subject: Mood music.

Project: Design a program of background music for a particular environ-
               ment.

Objective: To observe the stylistic characteristics of music that can function
               effectively as background sound in a given situation.

Explore the resources of a lending library to design a program of background music for a specific environment which you yourself regularly encounter—a social situation, a study period, an occupation, a leisure activity,
a meal, etc. The program should be at least one hour in overall duration,
including periods of silence. If possible experiment with the program in
the actual environment, and verify its effectiveness by observing the reactions of other persons who share the particular environment with you.

1.   Describe the situation. Why would background music be desirable?
What acoustical factors complicate the process of designing a program,
such as the rhythms of machines or noises extraneous to the immediate
environment?

2.   Remember that some of the sounds in a given environment may
function as important signals of danger, need, change, etc., and that they
must be clearly audible when they occur. How would you solve the problems implicit in the situation? Would merely controlling the volume of the
music be sufficient or would you use—or avoid—certain textures, timbres,
rhythms, tempos, densities, etc?

3.   Are there any special psychological problems to be dealt with, such
as unusual vigilance, fluctuations of energy, excessive monotony, sudden
distractions, or the like? What specific stylistic features would you look for
in music that would help to make it function well under the circumstances?

4.   Name one or more styles of music—or specific compositions—you
have heard that you believe would be unsuitable, and explain why, in musical terms. Can you think of any situations in which such music might function effectively as background sound?

5.   Study the background music used in a public place near you. Evaluate
it with regard to its appropriateness. In musical terminology, explain what
does or does not make it function properly.

LISTENING GUIDE NO. 8

Subject: Film music.

Project: Attend a feature film employing a substantial amount of under-scoring.

Objective: To observe ways in which music can be used to enhance a film.

This is a more difficult project than you might expect, for normally one is not consciously aware of the underscore to a film. The study of film music therefore requires careful and persistent concentration lest the literary and visual parameters of the medium absorb one's entire conscious attention. Movies about musicians and movies with sound tracks consisting mainly of dialogue and sound effects would generally be unsuitable for this project.

1.   What was the composer's name?

2.   In how many ways did music function in the film? Did it merely provide continuity irrespective of dramatic elements? Did the music ever lend dramatic color in a general way? If so, what general mood did it establish, and how did that mood compare or contrast with the mood of the literary or visual parameters of the film?

3.   Was there any thematic unity in the overall score? If so, were the themes clearly related to specific characters, objects, or situations?

4.   Was music ever used to heighten the emotional impact of a specific word, physical gesture, or other visual event? Can you explain in musical terms how some specific cues were handled?

5.   Did the music ever imitate or parody natural sounds? Were natural sounds used as a kind of music themselves or did they usually correspond literally with the visual images? Was the performance of music ever a visible part of the action?

6.   Was any one musical parameter (rhythm, melody, timbre, etc.) often more prominent than the others? If so, what dramatic or expressive purpose did this feature fulfill?

7.   Was the texture predominantly homophonic, polyphonic, or mono-phonic? Did this seem to have anything to do with the dramatic or visual content of the film at any point?

8.   Were any unusual timbres employed, such as instruments not usually found in the symphony orchestra or popular ensemble? Were the timbres

mostly homogeneous or heterogeneous? Did these features serve any particular dramatic or expressive purpose?

9. Overall, did the music function properly in this film? That is, was it carefully integrated with the visual and literary parameters, or did it sometimes distract your attention from the story? Try to explain your reaction using appropriate musical terminology.

10. Compare this movie with a specific television drama in which a considerable amount of background music is used. Do you notice any significant differences between them with regard to the relationship of music to the visual and literary parameters?

LISTENING GUIDE NO. 9

Subject: Elements of popular style.
Project: Compare examples of two different popular styles.
Objective: To focus your attention on some minute stylistic elements in popular music.

Using the resources of any record library or your own collection, compare two popular pieces representing different styles (rock/jazz, Dixieland/bebop, blues/Broadway, folk/free jazz, etc.) in terms of specific musical details.

1. What scale system is used? Is the performers' intonation (tuning) generally precise, or imprecise according to the standard of equal temperament?

2. In general are the various instruments and voices blended with one another or contrasted? Are the vocal or instrumental timbres stylized or "right"? How many different timbres do you hear in the rhythm section alone?

3. Is the texture mostly homophonic or polyphonic?

4. Is the rhythm isometric or multimetric? Is the meter duple or triple? Simple or compound? Is the texture homorhythmic or polyrhythmic?

5. Listen repeatedly until you have found the basic tune or chord scheme on which the entire performance is based. By counting measures determine the lengths of its successive phrases and periods. Using letters to identify each period, graph its structure.

6. Discuss the lyrics, if any, with regard to style and ideological content. What type of audience is the piece evidently intended for? What basic outlook or philosophy is expressed (realism, idealism, escapism, optimism, pessimism, etc.)? If the song is about love, for instance, what kind of relationship is expressed or implied?

7. Did you like the music you listened to in connection with this Listening Guide? Did it seem to serve its intended function properly? In any case, try to describe the bases for your judgment in terms of one or more of the

factors to which your attention has been drawn either in this project or elsewhere in *The Uses of Music.*

8. List the most obvious differences between the two styles, in each parameter.

LISTENING GUIDE NO. 10

Subject:	Musical composition: The pentatonic system.
Project:	Compose a short piano piece using the pentatonic scale. (You need not be able to read or write music.)
Objective:	To explore the creative processes in music through personal experience.

Using only the black keys on the piano keyboard, compose a short piece in homophonic texture. With your left hand you may play simple two-note intervals, or chords of three, four, or five pitches. With the right hand you may devise any melodic structure that pleases your imagination. The piece may be as long as you like, but probably should last at least sixty seconds. Work out your design carefully and practice it until you can play it several times through without changing it. If possible, record it on cassette or reel-to-reel tape to facilitate objective consideration.

1. Describe the melodic line in as much detail as possible, in terms of type of line (conjunct or disjunct), register, range, and phrasing.

2. Is the structure based on the principle of superposition, or juxtaposition? If unity and variety are superposed, in which parameters is unity maintained? In which parameters do you hear the most variety? If unity and variety are juxtaposed, in which parameter does the repetition-after-contrast occur? Does the structure of your composition resemble that of any of the formulas discussed in the text?

3. Is the rhythm isometric, multimetric, or free? If it is isometric is the meter duple or triple? Simple or compound? Is the piece generally homorhythmic or polyrhythmic?

4. Are the vertical structures relatively consonant or dissonant? Is the harmonic rhythm the same as the tempo of the piece, or is it faster or slower?

5. What did you discover from this experiment concerning the processes of composition? Do you think you possess an innate creative urge? Did you experience a desire to try to master the instrument to the best of your temporary technical ability? Were you frustrated by the limitations of the project or did you view them as a challenge? Did you seem to have an instinctive critical sense; that is, did you proceed by trial and error,

building new ideas out of rejected ones, or did you find that your spontaneous, intuitive efforts usually satisfied you immediately?

6. Do you like your composition as such? Try to make a value judgment of it in terms of one or more of the factors to which your attention has been drawn either in this project or elsewhere in *The Uses of Music.*

LISTENING GUIDE NO. 11

(Note: Access to two or three reel-to-reel tape recorders with microphones is essential for the completion of this Listening Guide.)

Subject: Composing with tape recorders.

Project: Compose a short piece by recording some concrète sounds and manipulating them on a reel-to-reel tape recorder. (A concise introduction to the use of the home recorder as a "synthesizer" is the article "Musique Concrète at Home," by Merrill Ellis, in the November, 1968, issue of the *Music Educators Journal,* which should be available at most libraries.)

Objective: To explore the creative processes in music through personal experience, free of conventional musical limitations.

Record some concrète sounds, either specially contrived by you or selected from your natural sonorous environment (a dripping faucet, a noisy radiator, a motor, human speech, animal sounds, etc.). Using the techniques described in the text (changes in tape speed, cutting and splicing, tape loops, spatial modulation, filtering, feedback, echo reverberation), or any others you can devise, construct a two- or three-minute composition. Remember that your fundamental task is to manipulate the forces of unity and variety, or tension and repose. When you have finished, analyze your composition according to the following points:

1. Is the structure of your composition based on the principle of superposition, or juxtaposition? If unity and variety are superposed in which parameters is unity maintained? In which parameters do you hear the most variety? If unity and variety are juxtaposed, in which parameter does the repetition-after-contrast occur? Does the structure of your composition resemble that of any of the formulas discussed in the text?

2. Are there any conspicuous points of tension? How are they created? How are they resolved?

3. Is melody an important element in the design? If so, describe it with respect to type of line (conjunct, disjunct), register, range, envelope, and phrasing.

4. Is the texture essentially homophonic, polyphonic, or heterophonic? Is it mostly opaque or transparent? Are the vertical structures relatively consonant, or dissonant?

5.   Are the timbres mainly homogeneous, or heterogeneous?

6.   Is the rhythm isometric, multimetric, or free? If it is isometric is the meter duple or triple? Simple or compound? Is the piece generally homorhythmic or polyrhythmic?

7.   Which parameter contains the most interest?

8.   What have you discovered from this exercise concerning the processes of composition? Were you frustrated or challenged by the absence of conventional musical limitations such as a traditional scale system or by the limitations inherent in the technological aspects of the undertaking? Did you proceed by trial and error, building new ideas out of rejected ones, or did you find that circumstantial or intuitive efforts usually satisfied you immediately?

9.   Do you like the composition as such? Try to make a value judgment of it in terms of one or more of the factors to which your attention has been drawn either in this project or elsewhere in *The Uses of Music.*

Note: This project might be more easily and more enjoyably carried out by a team of at least two persons, one acting as the composer and the other as the recording engineer. A third person might assume the responsibility for devising a system of graphic notation. Others could help turn it into a multimedia presentation by adding one or more visual or spatial parameters such as original slides or movie film, lights and shadows, pantomime, or dance.

LISTENING GUIDE NO. 12

Subject: Chance music.

Project: Design, notate, and perform a short chance composition.

Objective: To explore the creative processes in music through personal experience, free of conventional musical and technological limitations.

Devise a method by which specific events in the basic parameters of sound and time are arrived at by chance operations such as rolling dice, or by some sort of mathematical equation. Invent a notational system that will graphically illustrate, as clearly as possible, the details of each parameter. With the assistance of as many persons as necessary, perform your composition and record it if possible so that you can study it objectively.

1.   Did your chance method produce a balance of unity and variety, or the alternation of tension and repose? If unity and variety are superposed in which parameters is unity present? Which parameters provide the most variety? If unity and variety are juxtaposed, in which parameters does the alternation between them take place? Are there any points of extreme tension? If so, how are they created and resolved?

2.   Is melody an important element in the design? If so, describe it with respect to type of line (conjunct, disjunct), register, range, envelope, and phrasing.

3.   Is the texture essentially homophonic, polyphonic, monophonic, or heterophonic? Is it mostly opaque or transparent? Are most of the vertical structures relatively consonant or dissonant?

4.   Are the timbres mainly homogeneous or heterogeneous?

5.   Describe the rhythmic characteristics of the design. Is the piece isometric, multimetric, or free? Is it generally homorhythmic or polyrhythmic?

6.   Which parameter contains the most interest? Are any of the usual musical parameters absent altogether?

7.   What have you discovered from this exercise concerning the processes of composition? Were you frustrated or challenged by the necessity to construct an entire musical system of your own? What was the most

difficult aspect of the notational process? What was the most rewarding aspect of the undertaking?

8.   Do you like your composition as such? Try to make a value judgment of it in terms of one or more of the factors to which your attention has been drawn either in this project or elsewhere in *The Uses of Music*.

CHRONOLOGY OF STYLE-PERIODS AND COMPOSERS

| Renaissance | Baroque | Rococo | Classical | Romantic | Im-press-ionist | Post-Romantic; Express. | Neo-Class-ical | Elec-tronic |

1550 1600 1650 1700 1750 1800 1850 1900 1950

Heinrich Isaac, 1450-1517 (Netherlands)
Josquin Des Prez, 1450-1521 (Netherlands)
Cristóbal de Morales, 1500-1553 (Spain)
Jacob Arcadelt, 1505-1560 (Belgium)
Thomas Tallis, 1505-1585 (England)
Giovanni Palestrina, 1525-1594 (Italy)
Orlando di Lasso, 1532-1594 (Netherlands)
William Byrd, 1543-1623 (England)
Tomás Luis de Victoria, 1549-1611 (Spain)
Luca Marenzio, 1553-1599 (Italy)
Thomas Morley, 1557-1602 (England)
Claudio Monteverdi, 1567-1643 (Italy)
Thomas Weelkes, 1575-1623 (England)
Jean-Baptiste Lully, 1632-1687 (France)
Archangelo Corelli, 1653-1713 (Italy)
Giuseppe Torelli, 1658-1709 (Italy)
Alessandro Scarlatti, 1660-1725 (Italy)
Antonio Vivaldi, 1675-1741 (Italy)
Jean-Philippe Rameau, 1683-1764 (France)
Johann Sebastian Bach, 1685-1750 (Germany)
Georg Friedrich Handel, 1685-1759 (Germany)
Christoph Willibald Gluck, 1714-1787 (Germany)
Franz Joseph Haydn, 1732-1809 (Austria)
William Billings, 1746-1800 (America)
Wolfgang Amadeus Mozart, 1756-1791 (Austria)
Ludwig van Beethoven, 1770-1827 (Austria)
Thomas Moore, 1779-1852 (Ireland)
Niccolò Paganini, 1782-1840 (Italy)
Franz Schubert, 1797-1828 (Austria)
Adolphe Adam, 1803-1856 (France)
Hector Berlioz, 1803-1869 (France)
Felix Mendelssohn, 1809-1847 (Germany)
Frédéric Chopin, 1810-1849 (Poland)

226

CHRONOLOGY OF STYLE-PERIODS AND COMPOSERS

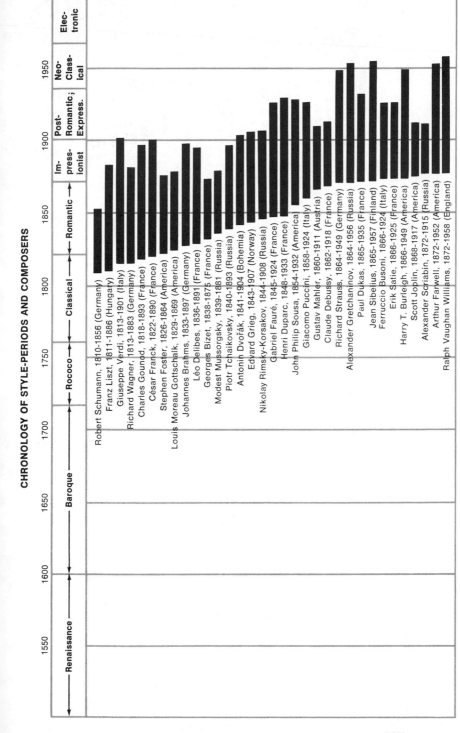

CHRONOLOGY OF STYLE-PERIODS AND COMPOSERS

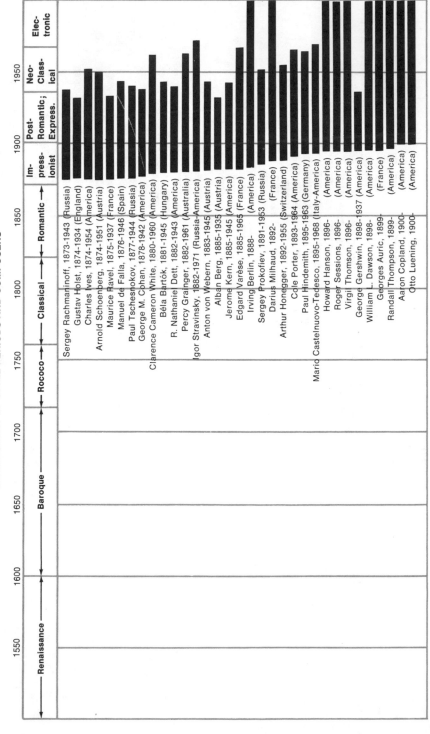

CHRONOLOGY OF STYLE-PERIODS AND COMPOSERS

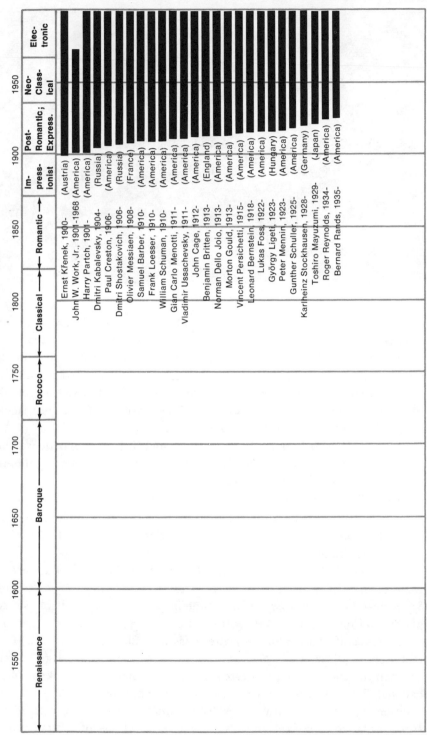

	1550	1600	1650	1700	1750	1800	1850	1900	1950	
	Renaissance	Baroque			Rococo	Classical	Romantic	Impressionist	Post-Romantic; Express.	Neo-Classical	Electronic

Ernst Křenek, 1900- (Austria)
John W. Work, Jr., 1901-1968 (America)
Harry Partch, 1901- (America)
Dmitri Kabalevsky, 1904- (Russia)
Paul Creston, 1906- (America)
Dmitri Shostakovich, 1906- (Russia)
Olivier Messiaen, 1908- (France)
Samuel Barber, 1910- (America)
Frank Loesser, 1910- (America)
William Schuman, 1910- (America)
Gian Carlo Menotti, 1911- (America)
Vladimir Ussachevsky, 1911- (America)
John Cage, 1912- (America)
Benjamin Britten, 1913- (England)
Norman Dello Joio, 1913- (America)
Morton Gould, 1913- (America)
Vincent Persichetti, 1915- (America)
Leonard Bernstein, 1918- (America)
Lukas Foss, 1922- (America)
György Ligeti, 1923- (Hungary)
Peter Mennin, 1923- (America)
Gunther Schuller, 1925- (America)
Karlheinz Stockhausen, 1928- (Germany)
Toshiro Mayuzumi, 1929- (Japan)
Roger Reynolds, 1934- (America)
Bernard Rands, 1935- (America)

bibliography of recorded examples

Following is a list of the examples contained in the records prepared to accompany *The Uses of Music,* in the order of their appearance in the text. The album from which each has been taken is identified in full, for your convenience in the event you would like to listen to the entire work. Most of the compositions are also available on various other record labels. See Preface for additional recommendations.

You may wish to systematically expand your listening experiences beyond the limits of this book by borrowing records from a lending library or purchasing some of your own. You will find the Chronology of Style-periods and Composers a good general point of departure. A more specific aid for the beginner would be the *Basic Record Library* booklet published by W. Schwann, Inc., which lists 150 basic works plus some 1,000 others classified according to style-period.

If you desire to purchase specific compositions you will find several resources helpful which are available at most record shops. The monthly *Schwann-1 Record and Tape Guide* contains all currently available stereophonic and quadraphonic LP recordings as well as 8-track cartridges and cassettes, classified according to genre (Classical, Electronic, Musicals, Current Popular, Jazz, etc.). *Schwann-2,* issued semi-annually, lists current and non-current recordings in categories such as Religious, Spoken, International Pop and Folk, and Classical works on lesser-known labels. In addition, Schwann annually publishes a *Children's Catalog* and an *Artist Issue* containing classical records cross-referenced by orchestral group, conductor, instrumental soloist, choral group, opera company, and vocalist. Popular songs are catalogued by title in *Phonolog Reports,* which may be perused at a major record dealer's.

As was pointed out in Chapter I, merely locating a composition in a catalog may only lead you to the problem of deciding whether a particular recording is musically and technically acceptable. Reviews of new popular and classical records may be found in special-interest magazines like *Stereo Review, Audio,* and *High Fidelity,* as well as some general monthlies. Popular records are discussed in *Rolling Stone* and similar periodicals. A summary of opinions concerning recent releases will be found in the monthly *American Record Guide.*

Example	*Page*	*Title*

Side I, Band 1

Example	*Page*	*Title*
II-1	18	The octave (0:10)
II-2	19	The chromatic scale (0:15)
II-3	19	Four church modes (0:50)
II-4	19	"The Foggy Dew" (excerpt), sung by Barbara Moncure. *Folksongs of the Catskills.* Folkways, FH 5311 (1:08). Courtesy of Folkways Records.

Side I, Band 2

II-5	21	The major scale (0:15)
II-6	21	The harmonic minor scale (0:15)
II-7	21	Jean Sibelius, Symphony No. 2, Finale (excerpt). Philadelphia Orchestra, Eugene Ormandy conducting. Columbia, MS 6204 (1:02)

Side I, Band 3

II-8	21	The melodic minor scale (0:15)
II-9	23	The pentatonic scale (0:10)
II-10	23	"Love Song" (excerpt). Played on the flageolet by Jerome Vanderburg. *Songs and Dances of the Flathead Indians.* Ethnic Folkways Library, FE 4445 (0:32). Courtesy of Folkways Records.

Example	*Page*	*Title*

II-11   24   Harry Partch, *Delusion of the Fury* (excerpts). Columbia, M2 30576 (1:29)

Side I, Band 4

III-1   26   Gregorian Chant, "Dignus est agnus" (Worthy is the Lamb) (excerpt). Choir of the Vienna Hofburgkapelle, Josef Schabasser conducting. *Gregorian Chants*, Vox, SDLBX 5206 (1:00). Courtesy of Vox Records.

III-2   27   "Morning Service" (excerpt). *Chinese Buddhist Music.* Lyrichord, LLST 7222 (0:45). Courtesy of Lyrichord Discs, Inc.

III-3   27   Gamelan Gong Kebyar, "Baris" (excerpt), *Music from the Morning of the World*. Nonesuch Explorer Series, H-72015 (0:35). Courtesy of Nonesuch Records.

Side I, Band 5

III-4   27   Paul Hindemith, *Mathis der Maler,* "Angelic Concert" (excerpt), Philadelphia Orchestra, Eugene Ormandy conducting. Columbia, MS 6562 (1:22)

III-5   28   African drum music (excerpts). Watutsi tribe of Ruanda. *African Drums*. Folkways, 4502 A/B (0:58). Courtesy of Folkways Records.

Side I, Band 6

III-6   28   Stephen Foster, "Ring, ring the banjo" (excerpts). Mary Jean Simpson, flute; Jerry Domer, oboe; William Manning, clarinet; Edwin Rosenkranz, bassoon (1:30)

III-7   28   Stephen Foster, "Ring, ring the banjo" (excerpt), with vamp accompaniment (0:17)

III-8   29   Triad, seventh chord (0:25)

III-9   29   Cadences: chord patterns IV-I, V-I, IV-V$_7$-I (0:40)

Side I, Band 7

III-10   30   Wolfgang Amadeus Mozart, Symphony No. 41 in C Major (the "Jupiter" symphony), first movement, *Allegro vivace* (excerpts). Columbia Symphony Orchestra, Bruno Walter conducting. Columbia, MS 6255 (1:30)

Example	Page	Title

ment, *Chaconne* (complete). High School Symphonic Band, National Music Camp, Interlochen, Michigan, Frederick Fennel conducting (4:45). Courtesy of George C. Wilson, Vice President and Director, National Music Comp.

Side IV, Band 3

IX-2   88   John Barnes Chance, *Incantation and Dance* (complete). Luther College Concert Band, Decorah, Iowa, Weston Noble conducting (6:48). Courtesy of Weston Noble.

Side IV, Band 4

XI-1   115   Arnold Schoenberg, *Accompaniment to a Film Scene,* Op. 34 (excerpts). Columbia Symphony, Robert Craft conducting. Columbia, MS 6216 (3:00)

Side IV, Band 5

XI-2   121   Aaron Copland, *Billy the Kid,* "Gun Battle" (complete). New York Philharmonic, Leonard Bernstein conducting. Columbia, MG 30071 (2:00)

Side IV, Band 6

XII-1   127   William Billings, "Chester" (complete). The Gregg Smith Singers, Gregg Smith conducting. Columbia, MS 7277 (1:27)

Side V, Band 1

XII-2   132   Leonard Bernstein, *Mass,* "The Lord's Prayer" and "Sanctus" (complete). Alan Titus, baritone, Norman Scribner Choir, Berkshire Boy Choir, Leonard Bernstein conducting. Columbia, M2 31008 (9:35)

Side V, Band 2

XII-3   136   J. S. Bach, Cantata No. 4, *Christ Lag in Todesbanden,* fourth movement, "Es war ein wunderlicher Streif" (excerpt). Vanguard 225 (2:00)

bibliography of
books and articles

The primary purpose of a bibliography in a book of this kind is to provide suggestions for the reader who wishes to expand his knowledge further according to his own interests. However, if you are uncertain where to begin, a few initial recommendations may be in order.

Articles in music dictionaries and encyclopedias are often so detailed they are confusing to the novice, or so brief as to be misleading. The paperback *New College Encyclopedia of Music* by J. A. Westrup and F. H. Harrison (Norton, 1960) is one of the best compromises. This together with two books by David Ewen would complete a basic reference library on art music for the serious music student as well as the casual record collector and concert-goer. Ewen's books are *The Complete Book of Classical Music* (1967) and *The World of Twentieth Century Music* (1968), both published by Prentice-Hall, Inc.

If you wish merely to take one small step for yourself, you might profitably read *The Art of Sound* by Jack Sacher and James Eversole (Prentice-Hall, 1971). It is excellent for the beginner as well as the experienced listener not only because it approaches the subject from an entirely different point of view than the present book, but also because it contains some extremely useful supplementary material, including a brief explanation of musical notation, a "History of Music in Chart Form," a "Basic Record Library," and short biographies of some important composers, as well as a glossary. After *The Art of Sound* you probably would want to go on to some of the more specialized books listed on the following pages.

General

Apel, Willi, ed., *Harvard Dictionary of Music* (2nd ed., rev. and enl.) Cambridge, Mass.: Harvard University Press, Belknap Press, 1969.

Blom, Eric, ed., *Grove's Dictionary of Music and Musicians* (rev. 5th ed.) New York: St. Martin's Press, Inc., 1961. 10 vols.

Ewen, David, *The Complete Book of Classical Music*. Englewood Cliffs, N.J.: Prentice-Hall, Inc., 1965.

Grout, Donald J., *A History of Western Music*. New York: W. W. Norton & Company, Inc., 1960.

Howard, John Tasker, *The World's Great Operas*. New York: Modern Library, Inc., 1959.

Idelsohn, A. Z., *Jewish Music In Its Historical Development*. New York: Tudor Publishing Co., 1948.

Kolodin, Irving, ed., *The Composer as Listener*. New York: Collier Books, 1962.

Lang, Paul Henry, *Music in Western Civilization*. New York: W. W. Norton & Company, Inc., 1941.

Langer, Susanne K., ed., *Reflections on Art: A Source Book of Writings by Artists, Critics and Philosophers*. Baltimore: Johns Hopkins Press, 1958.

————, *Feeling and Form*. New York: Charles Scribner's Sons, 1953.

Loesser, Arthur, *Men, Women and Pianos*. New York: Simon & Schuster, Inc., 1954.

Longyear, Rey M., *Nineteenth-Century Romanticism in Music* (2nd ed.) Englewood Cliffs, N.J.: Prentice-Hall, Inc., 1973.

Mueller, John Henry, *The American Symphony Orchestra: A Social History of American Taste*. Bloomington, Ind.: Indiana University Press, 1951.

Palisca, Claude V., *Baroque Music*. Englewood Cliffs, N.J.: Prentice-Hall, Inc., 1968.

Pauly, Reinhard G., *Music in the Classic Period* (2nd ed.) Englewood Cliffs, N.J.: Prentice-Hall, Inc., 1973.

Scholes, Percy A., ed., *Oxford Companion to Music* (9th ed.), rev. by Nicolas Slonimsky. New York: Oxford University Press, 1965.

Seay, Albert, *Music in the Medieval World*. Englewood Cliffs, N.J.: Prentice-Hall, Inc., 1965.

Slonimsky, Nicolas, ed., *Baker's Biographical Dictionary of Musicians* (rev. 5th ed.) New York: G. Schirmer, Inc., 1958. With supplement (1965).

Thompson, Oscar, ed., *International Cyclopedia of Music and Musicians* (9th ed.) New York: Dodd, Mead & Co., 1968.

Ulrich, Homer, *Chamber Music: The Growth and Practice of an Intimate Art*. New York: Columbia University Press, 1966.

Watson, Jack M., and Corinne Watson, *A Concise Dictionary of Music*. New York: Dodd, Mead & Co., 1967.

Westrup, J. A., and F. H. Harrison, *The New College Encyclopedia of Music*. New York: W. W. Norton & Company, Inc., 1960.

Chapter I. The Medium is the Message

Backus, John, *The Acoustical Foundations of Music*. New York: W. W. Norton & Company, Inc., 1969.

Baumol, William, and William Bowen, *The Performing Arts, The Economic Dilemma*. Cambridge, Mass.: The M.I.T. Press, 1968.

Dorian, Frederick, *Commitment to Culture*. Pittsburgh: University of Pittsburgh Press, 1964.

Farnsworth, Paul R., *The Social Psychology of Music*. New York: Dryden Press, 1958.

Gelatt, Roland, *The Fabulous Phonograph; From Edison to Stereo*. New York: Appleton-Century Press, 1965.

McLuhan, Marshall, *Understanding Media*. New York: McGraw-Hill Book Company, 1964.

Malraux, André, *Museums Without Walls,* trans. Stuart Gilbert and Francis Price. Garden City: Doubleday & Company, Inc., 1967.

Pleasants, Henry. *The Agony of Modern Music*. New York: Simon & Schuster, Inc., 1962.

Rockefeller Panel Report. *The Performing Arts: Problems and Prospects*. New York: McGraw-Hill Book Company, 1965.

Silbermann, Alphons, *The Sociology of Music,* trans. Corbet Stewart. London: Routledge & Kegan Paul Ltd., 1963.

Villchur, Edgar, *Reproduction of Sound*. New York: Dover Publications, 1965.

Chapters II-VII. Music as Sonorous Design

Brown, Calvin, *Music and Literature: A Comparison of the Arts*. Athens, Ga.: University of Georgia Press, 1948.

Cone, Edward T., *Musical Form and Musical Performance*. New York: W. W. Norton & Company, Inc., 1968.

Demuth, Norman, *Musical Forms and Textures: A Reference Guide* (2nd ed.) London: Barrie and Rockliff, 1964.

Grunfeld, Frederic V., *The Art and Times of the Guitar; An Illustrated History of Guitars and Guitarists*. New York: The Macmillan Company, 1969.

Malm, William P., *Music Cultures of the Pacific, The Near East, and Asia*. Englewood Cliffs, N.J.: Prentice-Hall, Inc., 1967.

Marcuse, Sibyl, *Musical Instruments: A Comprehensive Dictionary*. Garden City, N.Y.: Doubleday & Company, Inc., 1964.

Nettl, Bruno, *Folk and Traditional Music of the Western Continents* (2nd ed.) Englewood Cliffs, N.J.: Prentice-Hall, Inc., 1973.

————, *Music in Primitive Cultures*. Cambridge, Mass.: Harvard University Press, 1956.

————, *North American Indian Musical Styles*. Philadelphia: American Folklore Society, 1954.

Sessions, Roger, *The Musical Experience of Composer, Performer, Listener*. New York: Atheneum Publishers, 1962.

Stein, Leon, *Structure and Style: The Study and Analysis of Musical Forms*. Evanston, Ill.: Summy-Birchard Co., 1962.

Chapter VIII. Music as Accomplishment: Vocal Music in the Secondary Schools

Courlander, Harold, *Negro Folk Music, U.S.A.* New York: Columbia University Press, 1963.

Jacobs, Arthur, *Choral Music: A Symposium*. Baltimore: Penguin Books, Inc., 1963.

Johnson, H. Earle, *Hallelujah, Amen! The Story of the Handel and Haydn Society of Boston*. Boston: Bruce Humphries Publishers, 1965.

Kaplan, Max, *Foundations and Frontiers of Music Education*. New York: Holt, Rinehart and Winston, 1966.

Lovell, John, Jr., *Black Song: The Forge and the Flame*. New York: The Macmillan Company, 1972.

Odum, Howard W. and Guy B. Johnson, *The Negro and His Songs*. New York: The New American Library, Inc., 1969.

Southern, Eileen, *The Music of Black Americans: A History*. New York: W. W. Norton & Company, Inc., 1971.

Stevenson, Robert, *Protestant Church Music in America*. New York: W. W. Norton & Company, Inc., 1966.

Young, Percy Marshall, *The Choral Tradition* (1st American ed.) New York: W. W. Norton & Company, Inc., 1962.

Chapter IX. *Music as Accomplishment: Instrumental Music in the Secondary Schools*

Farmer, Henry George, *The Concert Band*. New York, Toronto: Rinehart & Co., 1946.

Goldman, Richard Franko, *The Band's Music*. New York: Pitman Publishing Corp., 1938.

———, *The Wind Band, Its Literature and Technique*. Boston: Allyn & Bacon, Inc., 1962.

Schwartz, H. W., *Bands of America*. Garden City, N.Y.: Doubleday & Company, Inc., 1957.

Swoboda, Henry, ed., *The American Symphony Orchestra*. New York: Basic Books, Inc., Publishers, 1967.

Chapter X. *Music and the Human Environment*

Allsop, Kenneth, "Music by Muzak®," *Encounter* (Feb., 1967), 58-61.

Dolan, Robert Emmett, *Music in Modern Media*. New York: G. Schirmer, Inc., 1967.

Gaston, E. Thayer, *Music in Therapy*. New York: The Macmillan Company, 1968.

O'Neill, Donald M., "Music to Enhance the Work Environment," *Management of Personnel Quarterly* (Fall, 1966), 17ff.

Wokoun, William, "Music for Working," *Science Journal* (Nov., 1969), 55-59.

Chapter XI. *Music in Film, Theater, and Ballet*

Arvey, Verna, *Choreographic Music*. New York: E. P. Dutton & Co., Inc. 1941.

Graf, Marjorie S., ed., *Stravinsky and the Dance*. New York: Dance Collection of the New York Public Library, 1962.

Hagen, Earle, *Scoring for Films: A Complete Text*. North Hollywood, Calif.: E.D.J. Music, 1971.

Kirstein, Lincoln, *Dance: A Short History of Classical Theatrical Dancing*. Brooklyn: Dance Horizons, 1969.

Krokover, Rosalyn, *The New Borzoi Book of Ballets*. New York: Alfred A. Knopf, Inc., 1956.

McCarthy, Clifford, *Film Composers in America: A Checklist of Their Work*. New York: Da Capo Press, Inc., 1972.

Rosenman, Leonard, "Notes from a Sub-culture," *Perspectives of New Music* (Fall-Winter, 1968), 122-35.

Sternfeld, Frederick W., "Music and the Cinema," *Twentieth Century Music,* Rollo H. Myers, ed. New York: Orion Press, 1968, 123-39.

Chapter XII. Ceremonial Music, Public and Private

Hitchcock, H. Wiley, *Music in the United States: A Historical Introduction*. Englewood Cliffs, N.J.: Prentice-Hall, Inc., 1969.

Nettl, Paul, *Mozart and Masonry*. New York: Da Capo Press, Inc., 1970.

Reynolds, William Jensen, *A Survey of Christian Hymnody*. New York: Holt, Rinehart and Winston, Inc., 1963.

Terry, Charles Sanford, *The Music of Bach: An Introduction*. New York: Dover Publications, 1963.

Chapter XIII. Music as Entertainment

Belz, C. I., "Popular Music and the Folk Tradition," *Journal of American Folklore* (April, 1967), 130-42.

Blesh, Rudi, *Shining Trumpets: A History of Jazz*. New York: Alfred A. Knopf, Inc., 1946.

Carey, J. T., Changing Courtship Patterns in the Popular Song," *American Journal of Sociology* (May, 1969), 720-31.

Coker, Jerry, *Improvising Jazz*. Englewood Cliffs, N.J.: Prentice-Hall, Inc., 1964.

Denisoff, R. Serge, *Great Day Coming: Folk Music and the American Left*. Urbana: University of Illinois Press, 1971.

Eisen, Jonathan, ed., *The Age of Rock: Sounds of the American Cultural Revolution*. New York: Random House, Inc., 1969.

Ewen, David, *American Popular Songs from the Revolutionary War to the Present*. New York: Random House, Inc., 1966.

————, *New Complete Book of the American Musical Theater*. New York: Holt, Rinehart and Winston, Inc., 1970.

————, *Panorama of American Popular Music*. Englewood Cliffs, N.J.: Prentice-Hall, Inc., 1957.

————, *The Story of America's Musical Theater*. Philadelphia: Chilton Book Company, 1961.

Gold, Robert S., *A Jazz Lexicon*. New York: Alfred A. Knopf, Inc., 1964.

Hodier, André, *Jazz: Its Evolution and Essence.* New York: Grove Press, Inc., 1956.

Jones, Leroi, *Blues People: Negro Music in White America.* New York: William Morrow & Co., Inc., 1963.

Malone, Bill C., *Country Music, U.S.A.: A Fifty-Year-History.* Austin and London: University of Texas Press, 1968.

Martin, Deac (C. T.), *Deac Martin's Book of Musical Americana.* Englewood Cliffs, N.J.: Prentice-Hall, Inc., 1970.

Mattfeld, Julius, *Variety Music Cavalcade, 1620-1969* (3rd ed.), Englewood Cliffs, N.J.: Prentice-Hall, Inc., 1971.

Pleasants, Henry, *Serious Music—and All That Jazz.* New York: Simon and Schuster, Inc., 1969.

Roxon, Lillian, *Lillian Roxon's Rock Encyclopedia.* New York: Grosset & Dunlap, Inc. 1970.

Schuller, Gunther, *Early Jazz.* New York: Oxford University Press, 1968.

Spaeth, Sigmund, *The Facts of Life in Popular Song.* New York: Mc-Graw-Hill Book Company, 1934.

———, *A History of Popular Music in America.* New York: Random House, Inc., 1948.

Stambler, Irwin, *Encyclopedia of Popular Music.* New York: St. Martin's Press, Inc., 1965.

——— and Grelun Landon, *Encyclopedia of Folk, Country and Western Music.* New York: St. Martin's Press, Inc., 1969.

Chapter XIV. Art Music in the United States

Chase, Gilbert, *America's Music From the Pilgrims to the Present.* New York: McGraw-Hill Book Company, 1966.

Copland, Aaron, *Copland on Music.* Garden City, N.Y.: Doubleday & Company, Inc., 1960.

———, *Music and Imagination.* Cambridge, Mass.: Harvard University Press, 1962.

———, *The New Music, 1900-1960* (rev. and enl. ed.), New York: W. W. Norton & Company, Inc., 1968.

———, *What to Listen for in Music* (rev. ed.), New York: McGraw-Hill Book Company, 1957.

Cowell, Henry, *Charles Ives and His Music.* New York: Oxford University Press, 1955.

Edwards, Arthur C. and W. Thomas Marrocco, *Music in the United States.* Dubuque, Iowa: William C. Brown Company, Publishers, 1968.

Hitchcock, H. Wiley, *Music in the United States: A Historical Introduction.* Englewood Cliffs, N.J.: Prentice-Hall, Inc., 1969.

Ives, Charles, *Essays Before a Sonata and Other Writings,* Howard Boatright, ed. New York: W. W. Norton & Company, Inc., 1962.

Schwartz, Elliott and Barney Childs, eds., *Contemporary Composers on Contemporary Music.* New York: Holt, Rinehart and Winston, Inc., 1967.

Smith, Julia Frances, *Aaron Copland, His Work and Contribution to American Music.* New York: E. P. Dutton & Co., Inc., 1955.

Chapter XV. International Trends in Contemporary Art Music

Austin, William W., *Music in the 20th Century.* New York: W. W. Norton & Company, Inc., 1966.

Barrett, William, *Irrational Man: A Study in Existential Philosophy.* New York: Doubleday & Company, Inc., 1962.

Cage, John, *Silence.* Cambridge, Mass.: The M.I.T. Press, 1961.

————, *A Year from Monday.* Middletown, Conn.: Wesleyan University Press, 1967.

Cope, David, *New Directions in Music.* Dubuque, Iowa: William C. Brown Company, Publishers, 1971.

Dorf, Richard H., *Electronic Musical Instruments* (3rd ed.), New York: Radiofile, 1968.

Fennelly, Brian, "A Descriptive Language for the Analysis of Electronic Music," *Perspectives of New Music* (Fall-Winter, 1967), 79-95.

Hansen, Peter, *An Introduction to Twentieth Century Music* (2nd ed.), Boston: Allyn & Bacon, Inc., 1967.

Judd, F. C., *Electronic Music and Musique Concrète.* London: Neville Spearman, 1961.

Kolneder, Walter, *Anton Webern: An Introduction to His Works,* trans. Humphrey Searle. Berkeley and Los Angeles: University of California Press, 1968.

Lincoln, Harry B., ed., *The Computer and Music.* Ithaca: Cornell University Press, 1970.

Mathews, Max V., *et al., The Technology of Computer Music.* Cambridge, Mass.: The M.I.T. Press, 1969.

Meyer, Leonard B., *Music, The Arts, and Ideas: Patterns and Predictions in Twentieth-Century Culture.* Chicago: University of Chicago Press, 1967.

Ouellette, Fernand, *Edgard Varèse,* trans. Derek Coltman. New York: Orion Press, 1968.

Reich, Willi, ed., *Anton Webern: The Path to the New Music.* Bryn Mawr, Pa.: Theodore Presser Company, 1963.

Salzman, Eric, *Twentieth-Century Music: An Introduction.* Englewood Cliffs, N.J.: Prentice-Hall, Inc., 1967.

Strange, Allen, *Electronic Music: Systems, Techniques, and Controls.* Dubuque, Iowa: William C. Brown Company, Publishers, 1972.

Stuckenschmidt, H. H., *Twentieth Century Music,* trans. Richard Deveson. New York: McGraw-Hill Book Company, 1969.

Varèse, Louise, *Varèse: A Looking-Glass Diary,* Vol. I. New York: W. W. Norton & Company, Inc., 1972.

Vlad, Roman, *Stravinsky,* trans. Frederick and Ann Fuller (2nd ed.), New York: Oxford University Press, 1967.

index

An italic figure indicates the page on which a term is defined. A Roman numeral refers to a recorded example.